Madrid

WHAT'S NEW | WHAT'S ON | WHAT'S BEST

www.timeout.com/madrid

Contents

Published by Time Out Guides Ltd
Universal House
251 Tottenham Court Road
London W1T 7AB
Tel: + 44 (0)20 7813 3000
Fax: + 44 (0)20 7813 6001
Email: guides@timeout.com
www.timeout.com

Managing Director Peter Fiennes
Editorial Director Ruth Jarvis
Business Manager Daniel Allen
Editorial Manager Holly Pick
Assistant Management Accountant Ija Krasnikova

Time Out Guides is a wholly owned subsidiary of Time Out Group Ltd.

This edition first published in Great Britain in 2011 by Ebury Publishing
A Random House Group Company
Company information can be found on www.randomhouse.co.uk
Random House UK Limited Reg. No. 954009
10 9 8 7 6 5 4 3 2 1

Distributed in the US and Latin America by Publishers Group West (1-510-809-3700)
Distributed in Canada by Publishers Group Canada (1-800-747-8147)

For further distribution details, see www.timeout.com

ISBN: 978-1-84670-142-9

A CIP catalogue record for this book is available from the British Library.

Printed and bound in Germany by Appl.

The Random House Group Limited supports The Forest Stewardship Council (FSC), the leading international forest certification organisation. All our titles that are printed on Greenpeace approved FSC certified paper carry the FSC logo. Our paper procurement policy can be found at www.randomhouse.co.uk/environment.

Time Out carbon-offsets all its flights with Trees for Cities (www.treesforcities.org).

While every effort has been made by the author(s) and the publisher to ensure that the information contained in this guide is accurate and up to date as at the date of publication, they accept no responsibility or liability in contract, tort, negligence, breach of statutory duty or otherwise for any inconvenience, loss, damage, costs or expenses of any nature whatsoever incurred or suffered by anyone as a result of any advice or information contained in this guide (except to the extent that such liability may not be excluded or limited as a matter of law). Before travelling, it is advisable to check all information locally, including without limitation, information on transport, accommodation, shopping and eating out. Anyone using this guide is entirely responsible for their own health, well-being and belongings and care should always be exercised while travelling.

Madrid Shortlist

The **Time Out Madrid Shortlist** is one of a series of guides that draws on Time Out's background as a magazine publisher to keep you current with what's going on in town. As well as Madrid's key sights and the best of its eating, drinking and leisure options, the guide picks out the most exciting venues to have recently opened and gives a full calendar of annual events. It also includes features on the important news, trends and openings, compiled by locally based writers and writers. Whether you're visiting for the first time, or you're a regular, you'll find the *Time Out Madrid Shortlist* contains all you need to know, in a portable and easy-to-use format.

The guide divides central Madrid into three key areas, each of which contains listings for Sights & Museums, Eating & Drinking, Shopping, Nightlife and Arts & Leisure, with maps pinpointing all their locations. At the front of the book are chapters rounding up these scenes city-wide, and giving a shortlist of our overall picks in a variety of categories. We include itineraries for days out, plus essentials such as transport information and hotels.

Our listings give phone numbers as dialled within Madrid (and also the rest of Spain). From abroad, use your country's exit code followed by 34 (the country code for Spain) and then the number given. Spanish mobile numbers have six digits and begin with a 6.

We have noted price categories by using one to four euro signs (**€-€€€€**), representing budget, moderate, expensive and luxury. Major credit cards are accepted unless otherwise stated.

All our listings are double-checked, but places do sometimes close or change their hours or prices, so it's a good idea to call a venue before visiting. While every effort has been made to ensure accuracy, the publishers cannot accept responsibility for any errors that this guide may contain.

Venues are marked on the maps using symbols numbered according to their order within the chapter and colour-coded according to the type of venue they represent:

❶ Sights & Museums
❶ Eating & Drinking
❶ Shopping
❶ Nightlife
❶ Arts & Leisure

Map key	
Major sight or landmark	
Railway station	
Park	
Hospital/university	
Pedestrian Area	
Dual carriageway	
Main road	
Airport	✈
Church	✠
Metro station	Metro
Area	CHUECA

Time Out **Madrid** Shortlist

EDITORIAL
Editor Anna Norman
Proofreader Kieron Corless

DESIGN
Art Director Scott Moore
Art Editor Pinelope Kourmouzoglou
Senior Designer Kei Ishimaru
Group Commercial Designer Jodi Sher

Picture Editor Jael Marschner
Acting Deputy Picture Editor Liz Leahy
Picture Desk Assistant/Researcher
Ben Rowe

ADVERTISING
New Business & Commercial Director
Mark Phillips
International Advertising Manager
Kasimir Berger

International Sales Executive Charlie Sokol
Advertising Sales (Madrid) Juan José
Bellod (B2B Communications)

MARKETING
**Sales & Marketing Director, North America
& Latin America** Lisa Levinson
Senior Publishing Brand Manager
Luthfa Begum
Group Commercial Art Director
Anthony Huggins
Marketing Co-ordinator Alana Benton

PRODUCTION
Group Production Manager
Brendan McKeown
Production Controller Katie Mulhern

CONTRIBUTORS
This guide was researched and written by Nick Funnell, Anna Norman and the writers
of *Time Out Madrid*. The editor would like to thank Sally Davies.

PHOTOGRAPHY

Cover Photograph: Travelpix Ltd/Getty images

Photography by pages 7, 13, 17, 23, 28, 61, 83, 99, 109, 120, 149, 164, 175 Karl
Blackwell; pages 8, 11, 20, 27, 31, 37, 38, 43, 47, 75, 80, 100, 114, 130, 140, 144
Anna Norman; page 32 Petri Virtanen/Festival Otona; pages 39, 40, 41, 44, 46, 57,
58, 63 (top), 64, 69, 70, 79, 84 (top), 89, 104, 125, 134, 143, 147, 150, 155, 160,
172 Jon Santa Cruz; page 42 Worakit Sirijinda; page 49 S Borisov; page 50 Vinicius
Tupinamba; page 63 (bottom) Photooiasson; pages 84 (bottom), 92, 133 (bottom)
Rubiphoto; page 119 Scott Chasserot; page 126 Dimitry Agafontsev; page 133 (top)
Jorgedasi.

The following photographs were provided by the featured establishments/artists:
pages 35, 55, 163, 167, 168, 169, 177.

MAPS
JS Graphics (john@jsgraphics.co.uk).

About **Time Out**

Founded in 1968, Time Out has expanded from humble London beginnings into
the leading resource for those wanting to know what's happening in the world's
greatest cities. As well as our influential what's-on weeklies in London, New York and
Chicago, we publish nearly 30 other listings magazines in cities as varied as Beijing
and Mumbai. The magazines established Time Out's trademark style: sharp writing,
informed reviewing and bang up-to-date inside knowledge of every scene.

Time Out made the natural leap into travel guides in the 1980s with the City Guide
series, which now extends to over 50 destinations around the world. Written and
researched by expert local writers and generously illustrated with original photography,
the full-size guides cover a larger area than our Shortlist guides and include many more
venue reviews, along with additional background features and a full set of maps.

Throughout this rapid growth, the company has remained proudly independent,
still owned by Tony Elliott four decades after he started Time Out London as a single
fold-out sheet of A5 paper. This independence extends to the editorial content of all
our publications, this Shortlist included. No establishment has been featured because
it has advertised, and no payment has influenced any of our reviews. And, for our critics,
there's definitely no such thing as a free lunch: all restaurants and bars are visited
and reviewed anonymously, and Time Out always picks up the bill.
For more about the company, see www.timeout.com.

Don't Miss

Museo Nacional del Prado p131

Sights & Museums

They've been busy in Madrid of late. The global economic crisis may have hit the city (with the rest of Spain) brutally hard, but it luckily arrived just as several major development projects were wrapping up. The four skyscrapers that make up the Cuatro Torres complex, completed in 2009, in the city's financial district have made a distinctive addition to the Madrid skyline. Designed by Norman Foster, the 250-metre Torre Caja Madrid is now the tallest building in Spain, while other towers contain a hotel and various embassies, including those of the UK, Australia and Canada.

The near-finished Madrid River Project, due for full completion in 2011, has seen the motorways that once ran alongside the River Manzanares pushed into underground tunnels with 3.5 kilometres of pedestrianised promenade taking their place, where *madrileños* can enjoy an afternoon stroll. The newly created esplanade next to the Puente del Rey, near Príncipe Pío, also formed the focus of the celebrations to welcome back Spain's 2010 World Cup-winning squad.

A sporting chance

Sport has played a crucial role in sprucing up Madrid, with many developments fuelled by the city's bids for the 2012 and 2016 Olympics. Though unsuccessful, they've given Madrid new sports amenities, such as the Caja Mágica tennis centre, with its quirky flip-top roof; a forthcoming Aquatic

Centre (due for completion in 2011) in the north-east of the city; and an improved transport infrastructure. Many of the city's central streets have recently been pedestrianised, including most of those fanning out from the Puerta del Sol, as well as Calle de las Huertas and the shopping street of Fuencarral.

Madrid Mayor Alberto Ruiz-Gallardón's ambitious plans to bring the city into the 21st century have certainly added to its attractions. And they are beginning to pay off in terms of increased visitor numbers, even if they have been less great for the city's coffers – Madrid has more debt than the rest of Spain put together.

The art of the matter

Madrid may still lack one defining, must-see emblem – an Eiffel Tower, Statue of Liberty, or Colosseum – but there's one tourist attraction it does have plenty of: art. The famous Museo del Prado (see p131) has recently been extended by architect Rafael Moneo, whose new subterranean construction links the main building with a new gallery space set around the nearby 17th-century cloister of the Jerónimos, a former convent. Further down the Paseo del Prado, the Reina Sofia (see p94) modern art museum's new director Manuel Borja-Villel has undertaken the most profound reorganisation of the collection in 20 years, shaking up its linear layout with an audacious personal arrangement of its pieces.

And there's a new kid on the block. Joining these two museums and the Museo Thyssen-Bornemisza (see p85) along the Paseo del Prado is the CaixaForum (see p136), opened in 2008. Identifiable by Patrick Blanc's striking vertical garden that looks over its front courtyard,

SHORTLIST

Five must-sees
- Museo Nacional Centro de Arte Reina Sofía (p94)
- Museo del Prado (p131)
- Museo Thyssen-Bornemisza (p85)
- Palacio Real (p76)
- Plaza Mayor (p65)

Best recent openings
- CaixaForum (p136)
- Matadero Madrid (p161)
- Puerta del Europa (p126)

Best art museums
- La Casa Encendida (p93)
- Ermita de San Antonio de la Florida (p149)
- Museo del Prado (p131)
- Museo Nacional Centro de Arte Reina Sofía (p94)
- Museo Thyssen-Bornemisza (p85)
- Real Academia de Bellas Artes de San Fernando (p52)

Best green spaces
- Casa de Campo (p149)
- Parque del Oeste (p149)
- Parque del Retiro (p126)

Best for kids
- Faunia Parque de Atracciones (p162)
- Parque del Retiro (p126)
- Teleférico (p152)
- Zoo Aquárium de Madrid (p152)

Best small museums
- Museo Cerralbo (p151)
- Museo de Historia (p100)
- Museo Sorolla (p154)

Best surprises
- Ermita de San Antonio de la Florida (p149)
- Museo del Traje (p151)
- Templo de Debod (p152)

www.museothyssen.org

MUSEO THYSSEN-BORNEMISZA
PASEO DEL PRADO, 8
MADRID, SPAIN

this bank-funded space is devoted to temporary exhibitions, as well as conferences, screenings, concerts and family activities. Recent exhibitions have been dedicated to Dalí and Lorca and their time at Madrid's Residencia de Estudiantes, Spanish photographer Isabel Muñoz and filmmaker Federico Fellini.

Getting your bearings

Probably the best starting-point is the heart of the city, the Puerta del Sol, where you'll find *kilómetro cero* (kilometre zero), the spot from which all distances in the country are measured and a popular meeting-point. In June 2009, a new *cercanías* (light rail) interchange was opened beneath Sol, adjoined to the existing metro station. At 207 metres long, 20 metres wide and 15 metres high, the excavated underground platform space is the largest of its kind in the world.

West of here lies historic Los Austrias. Heading along Calle de Arenal will take you to Ópera and the Palacio Real, and beyond that down to the new-look River Manzanares and the vast Casa de Campo park.

South-west, along Calle Mayor, you'll discover the impressive 17th-century Plaza Mayor (see p65), new gourmet market Mercado de San Miguel (see p73) and, beyond, the barrio of La Latina, teeming with bars and restaurants, especially around Plaza de la Paja, home to the newly reopened Capilla del Obispo (see p68).

South of Sol is multicultural Lavapiés, full of Moroccan tea houses, Bangladeshi-owned curry restaurants and a vibrant cultural scene, while south-east lie the bustling bars of Plaza de Santa Ana and Calle de las Huertas. This is also the heart of literary Madrid, former home to renowned writers such as *Don Quixote* author Miguel de Cervantes and playwright Lope

DON'T MISS

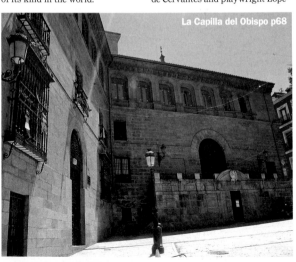

La Capilla del Obispo p68

de Vega. Further east are the art galleries of Paseo del Prado, with the main Atocha train station just below, and beyond that the Retiro park (see p126).

Head north of Sol and you'll reach Gran Vía, Madrid's main drag, lined with chain stores, theatres and lots of people. To the west, it leads down to Plaza de España, Calle de la Princesa and the neighbourhoods of Moncloa and Argüelles. North of this end of Gran Vía lies the cool, grungy barrio of Malasaña, and above that the pleasant Chamberí district (check out the terraces of the bars around Plaza de Olavide).

Above the eastern stretch of Gran Vía is Chueca, the heart of the city's gay community. At this end Gran Vía leads out into Calle de Alcalá, which stretches up east and north past the Cibeles fountain, where Real Madrid fans congregate to celebrate their sporting triumphs, and up past Las Ventas bullring (see p148). North of Calle de Alcalá is the upmarket Salamanca barrio. Dating from the 19th century, it's the place for designer shopping.

To the west, Salamanca is demarcated by Paseo de Recoletos and from Plaza del Colón by the long Paseo del Castellana, which leads up to the Santiago Bernabéu stadium (see p159) and the modern *barrios* of Tetuán and Chamartin, the latter home to the city's business district and the new Cuatro Torres development.

Moving around

Don't knock the open-top tourist bus (www.madridvision.es), which offers two different routes. Surveying Madrid from the top deck is not only a great way of getting your bearings, but also of appreciating intricate architectural details that normally pass unnoticed at street level.

The regular bus and metro system is efficient, easy-to-use and reasonably priced. A single journey costs €1, while a ten-journey Metrobus ticket is €9. You can also buy a special Tourist Travel Pass (Abono Transporte Turístico) that gives you unlimited journeys within its valid dates. A one-day pass for the centre of Madrid costs €5.20. There are also two, three, five and seven-day passes. Other modes of transport available for exploring the city include bikes (www.bikespain. info), kickbikes (www.trixi.com), Segways (www.madsegs.com) and go-karts (www.gocartours.es). A city-wide bike-hire scheme, MyBici, is due to be unveiled in spring 2011.

Truth be told though, with large swathes of the city centre pedestrianised, you're best off walking, as the main sights are all fairly close together. The city council runs walking tours in English on various themes (Essential Madrid, Chueca, Salamanca, the Changing of the Guard, and more), as well as a few on bicycles. There are also audio guides available to download direct on to your iPod from its website (www.esmadrid.com).

Tourist cards

Though not exactly cheap at €49 for 24 hours, €62 for 48 hours and €76 for 72 hours, the Madrid Card (www. madridcard.com) gives you access to pretty much everything you'd want. It includes unlimited journeys on the Madrid Vision tour bus, free entry to over 40 museums and attractions, including all major art galleries, plus the zoo and Bernabéu stadium tour, as well as discounts in certain shops, restaurants, theatres, leisure centres and on guided tours.

Estado Puro p135

Eating & Drinking

Madrid may have changed more than many cities over the last few years, but less so its restaurant scene. A firm bedrock of classic, crisis-proof venues means there's always familiar ground to be found. Indeed the world's oldest restaurant is here, Botín, opened in 1725.

But that's not to say there isn't a steady stream of openings and closures. Nor does it mean the city has been untouched by developments elsewhere in Spain. Catalonia's *nueva cocina* movement, spearheaded by the genius of experimental chef Ferran Adrià, has left its mark in the form of Adrià protégé Paco Roncero's Michelin-starred La Terraza del Casino (see p56), which in 2008 was joined by tapas bar Estado Puro (see p135) in the Hotel NH Paseo del Prado (Plaza Cánovas del Castillo 4, 91 330 24 00), where the culinarily adventurous can tackle the Madrid chef's takes on traditional tapas in more informal surroundings. Another former Adrià employee, Sergi Arola, has his own Michelin star at Gastro (Zurbano 31, 91 310 2169) and so too does David Muñoz at the hip DiverXO (Pensamiento 28, 91 570 0766), where the superstar chefs have been queueing up to sample his fusion cuisine, which mixes Chinese, Japanese, Peruvian, *madrileño* and other influences.

The international brigade

But the more fundamental change in Madrid's dining culture in the last few years has been its increasing internationalisation. As immigration has shot up in recent

JUANALALOCA
PINTXOS - BAR
PLAZA PUERTA DE MOROS, 4 - 28005 MADRID · 91 366 55 00 / 91 364 05 25

FOTO MIQUEL VEIT

decades so too have the number of high-quality foreign eateries catering to an increasingly more outward-looking populace happy to put aside their beloved *tortillas de patatas* to sample top-notch cuisine from India, Thailand, Ethiopia, Norway, Brazil and elsewhere. Unsurprisingly, cooking from the Spanish-speaking world has particularly prospered. The city is blessed with some excellent Mexican restaurants, notably the modern Tepic in Chueca (Pelayo 4, 91 522 0850) and the cosy Taquería de Alamillo in La Latina (Plaza del Alamillo 8, 913 642 088), as well as fine Peruvian establishments, such as Astrid & Gaston (Paseo de la Castellana 13, 917 026 262) and Tanta (Plaza del Perú 1, 913 502 626). Perhaps more surprisingly, sushi has been another boom area, though it makes more sense once you learn that, remarkably, landlocked Madrid boasts the biggest fish market in the world after Tokyo's, with superb produce flown in daily.

Talking tapas

Madrid is a city that revolves around eating and drinking, and heading out to share a few plates of tapas with friends is still an intrinsic part of city life. While the old favourites stand firm, smart new places are popping up all the time. One notable new addition to the tapas trail has been the Mercado de San Miguel (see p73), the new gourmet market next to Plaza Mayor modelled on Barcelona's famous La Boqueria. Not the place for a weekly shop, it is nonetheless great for picking up foodie gifts, as well as snacking on oysters or other tapas over a glass of cava or *vermút del grifo* (sweet red vermouth, served from the tap).

S H O R T L I S T

Best recent openings
- Bar Tomate (p154)
- Mercado de San Miguel (p73)
- Olé Lola (p107)
- Taberna Agrado (p118)

Best new-wave cooking
- Estado Puro (p135)
- DiverXO (p13)
- Gastro (p13)
- Juanalaloca (p81)

Best for a tipple
- Le Cabrera (p105)
- Museo Chicote (p54)
- La Palmera (p117)
- La Venencia (p90)

Madrileño institutions
- La Botillería de Maxi (p68)
- Chocolatería San Ginés (p77)
- Delic (p53)
- Freiduría de Gallinejas (p95)
- La Mallorquina (p54)
- El Sobrino de Botín (p72)

Best regional
- El Bocaíto (Andalucía) (p105)
- Casa Mingo (Asturias) (p153)
- Extremadura (Extremadura) (p106)
- Ribeira Do Miño (Galicia) (p107)

Best menús del dia
- El Bierzo (p105)
- Gastromaquia (p106)
- La Vaca Verónica (p88)

Best vegetarian
- El Estragón (p72)
- La Isla del Tesoro (p116)
- Viva La Vida! (p73)

Best rooftop drinking
- Casa de Granada (p95)
- Gaudeamus Café (p95)
- Hotel de las Letras (p165)
- El Viajero (p81)

Get the local experience

Over 50 of the world's top destinations available.

TIME OUT GUIDES
WRITTEN BY
LOCAL EXPERTS
visit timeout.com/shop

There are no hard and fast rules for tapas bar crawling. The bars around the Rastro flea market in La Latina are well worth visiting around Sunday lunchtime for atmosphere, but otherwise we recommend simply picking an area and working through the suggestions, nibbling as you go and not worrying about getting distracted by any new discoveries you make along the way. Alternatively, you can do as many *madrileños* do and pause for longer in a particular place to get a table and fuel up on a few larger *raciones* before continuing drinking elsewhere. A few recommendations to help you on your way: the gooey *tortilla* (potato omelette) in Juanalaloca (see p81), the *salmorejo* (thick gazpacho) in Taberna Según Emma (C/Conde de Miranda 4), the homemade *croquetas* (croquettes) in La Tabernilla del Gato Amadeus (see p121), the *huevos fritos con gulas al ajillo* (fried eggs with eels in garlic) at La Musa Latina (see p72) and the *tajada de bacalao* (slice of cod) at Taberna Agrado (see p118).

One word of warning: don't expect too much in the way of free stuff. You might get some olives, nuts or crisps to munch on with your drink – if you're lucky, a basic canapé – but most places won't give you anything as substantial as they do in some other Spanish cities, such as Granada. To get good grub, you have to spend some euros.

On the *menú*

In general, eating out is not so cheap any more. Since the big hike following the peseta-to-euro change, it seems restaurant and bar owners have gone on steadily increasing prices. One of the most economical ways of enjoying the city's eateries, however, is the *menú del día*. By law, all except the fanciest restaurants are obliged to offer a low-cost, multi-course meal at lunchtime, which means, for not much more than €10 to €12, you get a starter, main course, dessert or coffee, drink and bread all thrown in. It's rarely anything amazingly elaborate, but there are plenty of good offers around.

Olé Lola p107

World Class

Perfect places to stay, eat and explore.

If you've no time for a lingering lunch, most bakeries and bars will be able to serve you a basic sandwich (*boccadillo*) or salad (*ensalada*), while more and more branches of dedicated snack chains, such as Delina's, Faborit, Le Pain Quotidien and Rodilla are cropping up all the time. Also, look out for cafés offering breakfast deals, where you can get, say, a croissant or toast plus coffee for little more than a couple of euros.

In the drink

Where once rum and coke ruled the roost, Madrid is currently going mad for G&T, with many bars incorporating extensive gin menus, including the British-themed Bristol Bar (Almirante 20, 91 522 4568); the Gin Club, adjoined to the Mercado de la Reina restaurant (Gran Via 12, 91 521 3198); and the more functional Casa del Pez (Jesús del Valle 1, 91 521 31 41). Another landmark new addition to the Madrid bar scene is Diego Cabrera's cocktail venture Le Cabrera (see p105), which features a tapas menu by Sergi Arola.

For a regular beer, ask for a *caña*, though be warned that this could come in any size from a teeny-tiny 180ml *caña* glass to something double that size. If you want to guarantee a bigger beer, specify a *doble* (double) or a *jarra* (something more akin to a pint). Pints (*pintas*) are usually only served in Irish bars.

Most bars will stock a decent Rioja and Ribera del Duero red wine. Other regions to look out for include Valdepeñas, Somontano, and even local stuff from Madrid. For white wine, go for a Rueda made from the fruity *verdejo* grape, a white Rioja, or, especially in Galician bars, a Ribeiro or an *albariño*. For sherry, head to the charmingly dusty La Venencia bar (see p90), which serves nothing else.

For a small black espresso-style coffee ask for a *café solo*; for a longer black coffee ask for a café americano. A *café cortado* is a small black coffee with a splash of milk, while a milky coffee is a *café con leche*. You may also be asked if you prefer your milk hot (*caliente*) or warm (*templada*).

Times and money

As a general rule, most eating is done that bit later than you might expect in other countries. Lunch, for most *madrileños* the main meal of the day, is served from around 2pm to 4pm; dinner from 9pm to 11.30pm. Be aware that many restaurants will close for up to several weeks in July or August; we've tried to indicate where possible in the listings. It's always worth making a reservation for dinner if you have your heart set on somewhere, especially on Friday and Saturday nights and Saturday and Sunday lunchtimes.

Many places do accept credit and debit cards, though it's always worth checking before you sit down, particularly if it's a smaller place. By law, restaurants are obliged to you let you know if IVA (VAT) is included in the prices and whether there is a cover charge (normally disguised as a charge for bread), though many don't.

Tipping is something of a grey area. People tend to leave less in Spain than in many other countries – around five per cent is a reasonable rule of thumb. In a bar you'd just leave the small change given back to you, while in restaurants, a couple of euros will suffice – though don't be shy about tipping more if you're impressed.

Peseta

Shopping

The high streets of Madrid have taken on the identikit look of most European capitals, albeit with a sprinkling of Spanish chains. But off the main thoroughfares you'll find a curious mix of the traditional and the new, with international franchises rubbing shoulders with museum-piece, family-run businesses and old shops dedicated to just one product.

Where to shop

Madrid isn't large, and its main shopping areas are all within walking distance – or a short metro ride – of each other. Between Sol and Gran Vía, bustling C/Preciados and C/Carmen mix chains and smaller stores that sell cheap and mid-price clothes, shoes and accessories. El Corte Inglés (p59) and FNAC (p59) are both here, and Gran Vía is given over to flagship shops including H&M, Zara and the like.

After battling crowds of dawdling shoppers, tranquil Los Austrias is welcome respite, with its musical instrument stores, bohemian gift shops, decorative items and new foodie emporium El Mercado de San Miguel (see p73 and box p61) – for upmarket tapas and edible gifts.

For designer fashion, Salamanca has a terrific boutiques – on a single block of C/Serrano, there are Loewe, Yves St Laurent and La Perla – while Chueca's packed with hip independents: try Bunkha (p121) and vintage store Lotta (p110). Youth-oriented stores populate C/Fuencarral (for MAC, Diesel, Puma, Fornarina and Spanish brands Hoss Intropia and Hakei). Here you'll also find the El Mercado de Fuencarral mall, popular with fashionable teens and twenties for its streetwear shops (Alternativa, Cannibal), tattooists and trendy hairdressers. North up

C/Barquillo there's more refined fashion, especially between C/Argensola and Plaza Santa Barbara. To the west, trendy, newly named TriBall ('triangle of Ballesta', thus named after one of the area's best streets) and the streets around C/Conde Duque are home to some of Madrid's most interesting boutiques.

On Sunday, visiting the Rastro – the city flea market in Lavapiés – is obligatory, but for the atmosphere more than for what's on sale.

The artisan way

In medieval times, small artisans' shops clustered in specific quarters of Madrid. Many of the higgledy-piggledy streets around Plaza Mayor are still named after the guilds, *gremios*, that were there: Plaza de Herredores, 'Blacksmiths' Square', is just north of the square, while Calle Arenal runs to Calle de las Hileras, 'Spinners' Street'.

This tradition has dwindled, but some key artisans remain: check out espadrilles specialist Antigua Casa Crespo (p121), run by the Malasaña family since 1863, and the long-established Antigua Casa Talavera (p56) in Sol, selling hand-painted Spanish ceramics. A new wave of artisans includes Taller Puntera (p73), for good-quality, reasonably priced leather bags, purses and bound notebooks (its new branch in lovely Plaza Conde de Barajas is also its workshop), and the retro-style Peseta shop-atelier (p122) in Conde Duque, selling bags, laptop and passport cases, and handkerchiefs crafted from a patchwork of patterned materials; a vintage bike shop, AA Ciclos, sits above it.

Recently, the tradition of street specialisation has been partly revived: Chueca's C/Barquillo is nicknamed Calle del Sonido ('Sound Street') due to its many hi-fi shops.

S H O R T L I S T

Best recent openings
- Bunkha (p121)
- El Mercado de San Miguel (p73)
- Madrid al Cubo (p59)
- Peseta (p122)
- Taller Puntera (p73)

Best for bookworms
- La Casa del Libro (p56)
- Cuesta de Moyano book fair (p22)
- J&J Books & Coffee (p121)
- Librería San Ginés (p59)
- Panta Rhei (p110)

Best malls
- ABC Serrano (p142)
- El Jardín de Serrano (p146)

Best gourmet gifts
- La Mallorquina (p54)
- El Mercado de San Miguel (p73)
- Museo del Jamón (p90)
- Patrimonio Comunal Olivarero (p110)

Best artisan shops
- Antigua Casa Crespo (p121)
- Antigua Casa Talavera (p56)
- Taller Puntera (p73)

Best wine shops
- Bodegas Santa Cecilia (p101)
- Lavinia (p145)
- Reserva y Cata (p110)

Best local fashion
- Antigua Casa Crespo (p121)
- Farrutx (p145)
- Hakei (p110)
- Sybilla (p146)
- Vialis (p122)

Books and music

One street that's focused on a single product for decades is the newly pedestrianised Cuesta de Moyano, off the Paseo del Prado. Second-hand booksellers operate from lovely, permanent wooden stalls on the left-hand side; they're at their liveliest on Sunday mornings. C/Huertas and Calle de los Libreros ('Booksellers' Street') also have lots of rare, antique and specialist bookshops, but the most comprehensive bookshop is La Casa del Libro (p56), with a good range of English-language books.

Madrid is strong on art and design books. Try the great range at Chueca's Panta Rhei (p110), many of them in English, or explore the shops in Malasaña. Revered film bookshop, Ocho y Medio (see box p125), is handily close to many of the best cinemas and has lots of English-language material.

Don't neglect the museum shops of 'Paseo del Arte'. The Reina Sofía (p93) has a particularly wide selection, and the Prado's (p131) main shop is supplemented by a mobile shop near the ticket office.

For wannabe DJs, the plethora of record shops in Calle de la Palma and the surrounding streets stock all genres of dance and rock music. Otherwise, head to C/San Bernardo for Radio City (p122). For the broadest range, try FNAC (p59).

Fashion forward

Followers of cutting-edge fashion might be disappointed by Madrid's shops, but hip openings around Malasaña (Calle del Pez, TriBall, Calle Santa Bárbara), Conde Duque (especially around Plaza Guardias de Corps) and Alonso Martínez (just north of Chueca) have heightened consumer expectations. Vintage shops have gained popularity too, with stalwarts like Lotta (p110)

spawning competitors across Chueca and Malasaña. But Madrid really comes into its own for the shoe addict. C/Augusto Figueroa, in the heart of Chueca, is packed with factory *muestrarios*, selling samples from Spanish brands.

Opening hours

Opening times are changing, as is the traditional August break. Smaller stores still close for two or three hours at lunch and stay shut on Saturday afternoons, but some mid-size and nearly all large outlets remain open all day. If you're not yet used to two o'clock lunches and can face the summer heat, head to the bigger stores in the afternoon and you will miss the crowds.

Pressure from large retailers brought about a relaxation of laws on Sunday opening, despite the grumbling from small businesses. As a result, large retailers can – and do – open the first Sunday of each month, when Gran Vía is closed to private transport. Tourist revenue is becoming so vital to shopkeepers that Madrid no longer completely closes down in August – although some smaller shops do still take two-or three-week holidays at this time.

For after-hours shopping, OpenCor and Vip's branches open late (8am-2am and 9am-3am) and sell produce, CDs, DVDs, books, magazine and gifts. After-hours shops are not allowed to sell alcohol after 10pm (9pm on Sundays).

Taxing matters

The rate of IVA, or VAT, currently stands at 18 per cent. Non-EU residents can claim refund cheques for purchases over €90.15. You can then reclaim the VAT at the Global Refund Office in Barajas airport. Look out for the Tax Free sticker in the window of participating outlets.

69 Petalos p158

Nightlife

Sleep is almost a dirty word to this most fun-loving of people: Macbeth didn't murder sleep, Madrid did. The Spanish love to party, and they have always partied harder and later than any other nationality.

In recent years, however, it seems as if things have changed somewhat. The hedonistic days of La Movida – the libertine backlash against the repression of the Franco era – are gone. Instead, the scene is facing its own backlash, as the local government, and in turn the police, crack down on the giant night-time playground that is Madrid. This is mainly due to the unwanted by-products of excess: the noise and mess left by the party people, and the political pressure brought on by consistent complaints from the city's residents.

What happens when

Nightlife here has distinct stages. In the early evening, from 6pm until midnight, teenagers take to the streets. Most congregate in parks and squares and engage in what is known as the *botellón* – basically a pre-club piss up. Thousands of litres of red wine are mixed with Coke, to make a sticky mix known as *calimocho*, the drink that launched a million teen-hangovers. Despite an attempted crackdown by local authorities, the *botellón* is still a phenomenon in Madrid's public spaces; the focal point of a stand-off between the police and revellers is Malasaña's Plaza Dos de Mayo. But 15 squad cars can't be there every night, nor can they cover the hundreds of other squares, ensuring that it still goes on every weekend.

1000s of things to do…

1000 Great Holiday Ideas

1000 things to do in London

1000 things to do in New York

1000 things to do in London for under £10

1000 things for kids to do in the holidays

1000 things to do in Britain

**TIME OUT GUIDES
WRITTEN BY
LOCAL EXPERTS**
visit timeout.com/shop

Time Out Guides

At around 11pm a more mature crowd starts to spill out of the restaurants and hits the bars. Generally, bars break down into several distinct categories. *Bares de copas* sell spirit-based drinks with or without a DJ in the corner. Then come the *discobares*, which may require a cover charge and bang out international and Spanish pop, perfect for their alcohol-fuelled clientele. Then there are the funkier pre-club bars, often with a house DJ warming you up for a night on the town. Thanks to recent legislation, bars must close at around 3am: precisely the moment when the clubs or *discotecas* fill. (*Discoteca* carries no cheesy connotations in Spanish; in fact be careful what you ask for when talking to locals – 'club' in Spanish often means brothel.)

Time was when the party kept on going through the morning and into the afternoon, as numerous dodgy after-hours places would fling open their doors at a truly ungodly hour to welcome in revellers for whom sleep was not an option. But the police crackdown has put paid to that, and now there are only a few places to go should you want to dance *from* dawn.

To finish off a night on the tiles, be sure to engage in the *madrileño* chocolate and churros tradition, which comes into its own in the early hours. Old-school fave Chocolatería San Ginés (see p77) is open until 7am daily, and is a hive of activity once the clubs shut.

Behind the scenes

Madrid's nightlife scenes are characterised by the individual flavours of each neighbourhood. Malasaña, Chueca and Lavapiés are key nightlife areas, and many of the bars and clubs in each are very much of their *barrio*. Malasaña has a propensity for grungy rock, indie

DON'T MISS

and electronica bars, such as indie spot Sideral (C/San Joaquín 9, www.myspace.com/sideralmadrid); the gay barrio of Chueca is more about clean-lined aesthetics and house music; while Lavapiés has a more grassroots, multicultural feel, along with some great flamenco bars. La Latina, Sol and Santa Ana are also good for one-off late-night haunts, such as legendary after-hours club El Sol (in, surprise, surprise, Sol) and Marula (see p74) in La Latina, famous for its mid-week late-night jams. The latter's terrace is always packed in the wee hours.

One of Malasaña's staple night spots is indie-pop bar Tupperware (see p124), a funky perennial fave where kitsch reigns supreme. Other good bets in the area are Oui (see p123), a unique bar that's hard to find, but worth the search for its eclectic music policy; the basement club Sala de Nombre Público (see p60), good for experimental electronica; and the equally grimey Nasti (see p123), attracting an indie crowd and guest DJs.

Although just a few minutes walk from Malasaña, Chueca's nightlife scene is an entirely different ball game. Although it's the city's gay neighbourhood, many of its bars are mixed affairs, whose body-conscious customers wouldn't be seen dead in some of Malasaña's more grimey bars. For a quick initiation, head to Liquid (see p111). The bar beneath Room Mate Oscar (see p173) is another buzzing spot.

Lavapiés is different once again. To get to the heart of the scene, visit El Juglar (see p97); the DJs at this bohemian, laidback hangout on C/Lavapiés spin a mix of soul, Latin and funk tunes, and Sunday nights see flamenco performed by students from the nearby Amor de Dios school. Flamenco bar Candela (see p97) is another don't-miss in the neighbourhood.

Many of Madrid's big nightclubs are located some way out of the centre, such as relative newcomer 69 Pétalos (see p158), located near the Bernabéu stadium. Its pop art decor, stage performers and Latin jazz, indie-pop and house nights attract a mixed crowd. Macumba, meanwhile, is right by Chamartín station, and known for its Sunday Space of Sound event, the city's biggest all-day party, with an unrivalled sound system and progressive house DJs. Another out-of-centre club with a strong Sunday programme is Fabrik, whose well-established Goa session is run by the Trip Family (www.tripfamily.com), one of Madrid's biggest promoters, who also run DJ sessions in Ohm and Museo Chicote. Housed in an old warehouse south of the centre, Fabrik has an outdoor terrace complete with a fake river.

Survival tips

Having changed your body clock around to suit your schedule in Madrid, there are just a few more things you need to bear in mind before you go out seeking *la marcha*, or a good time.

Firstly, don't get too dolled up; Madrid is not generally a town where people dress to impress. Secondly, be careful with the drinks; measures poured here are such that you may, for once, actually ask the bartender to put a little less in – which is just as well, considering that some of the swankier clubs now charge as much as €12 for a long drink and €10 for a beer. Another point to note is that the ticket you are given on the door of a club is almost always valid for a drink, so keep hold of it. Lastly, be aware that there is a specific window of time for every venue in Madrid, so if you turn up to a club or bar and it's empty, it doesn't necessarily mean it isn't popular – you might just have arrived at the wrong hour.

Art in the Jardín Botanico

Arts & Leisure

As well as the multidisciplinary CaixaForum, key arts venues that have opened in the last few years include the Matadero Madrid (see p161) cultural centre and the Teatro Circo Price performance space (both 2007), the CA2M Centro de Arte Dos de Mayo arts centre in the suburb of Móstoles (2008), and the Teatros del Canal theatre complex (2009; see p157). And from 2011, the city will have another new venue in the form of the transformed Palacio de Cibeles. Formerly the city's post office, this grand landmark by the Cibeles fountain now houses a smaller post office, the mayor's headquarters and, once works are complete, a multi-purpose cultural space, including an impressive glass-roofed gallery, exhibition halls, a cinema and, from one of its towers,

views over the whole city. Plans are also afoot to convert the old tobacco factory in Lavapiés into a National Centre for Visual Arts. The labyrinthine space has been temporarily given over to a local collective for social and cultural uses while work is waiting to start.

Begun in 2006, Madrid's annual Noche en Blanco (White Night; see p37) event drew over half a million people on to the streets in 2010 to see the city transformed into an open-air art gallery, and museums stay open until the small hours. The same year also saw the city's Festival de Otoño (Autumn Festival) arts extravaganza move to a new springtime slot and confusingly redubbed the Festival de Otoño en Primavera (the Autumn Festival in Spring). The city's other major arts events, such as the enormous Arco international art fair, the PhotoEspaña (see p34) photography festival and the Veranos de la Villa (see p36) music, theatre and dance programme, have also continued to impress with their extensive offerings.

Film

Centred on Madrid, the Spanish film industry's reputation continues to grow internationally with the global success of talents such as golden couple Penélope Cruz and Javier Bardem and directors Pedro Almodóvar and Alejandro Amenábar, as well as hit genre films such as *The Orphanage* (2007) and *Timecrimes* (2007).

Unfortunately, most of the city's cinemas still insist on screening dubbed versions of non-Spanish films, though the four venues around Plaza de los Cubos, next to Plaza de España, all show movies in *versión original* (VO) – that's to say, in the original language with Spanish subtitles. Other VO cinemas dotted around the city include the Yelmo Cines Ideal between Sol and Tirso de Molina, and the Filmoteca Española (Cine Doré; see p98), Spain's national film theatre, where you can still enjoy world cinema classics for just €2.50. Opened in 2010, the smart new Sala Berlanga (see p154) in the Moncloa barrio aims to promote Spanish, Latin American and independent European film, while May's extensive Documenta Madrid (see p34) documentary festival is well worth checking out.

Opera & classical

It was all change at the Teatro Real (see p74), Madrid's principal opera venue, in January 2010 as it unveiled former Paris Opera head Gérard Mortier as its new director. Home to the Madrid Symphony Orchestra (OSM), the theatre also offers ballets, concerts, recitals and more. Elsewhere, the Teatro de la Zarzuela specialises in *zarzuelas*, Spanish light operas, and also puts on the odd recital and dance performance.

The Auditorio Nacional de Música (see p159) remains the city's most important classical venue. Home to Spain's National Orchestra (OCNE), it also puts up visiting orchestras when they're in town. Other classical venues include the Teatro Monumental (see p98), headquarters of the RTVE Orchestra and Choir, and the Fundación Juan

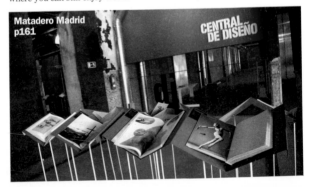

Matadero Madrid
p161

CENTRAL
DE DISEÑO

March (see p148), which hosts regular free concerts. Meanwhile, the Caja Madrid bank has plans to restore the stately Palacio de la Música on Gran Vía to its original use as a concert hall. For contemporary classical sounds, the Centro para la Difusión de la Música Contemporánea (CDMC) presents its works at the Museo Reina Sofía's Auditorio 400. Also look out for the large annual Clásicos en Verano classical music festival in July and August.

Theatre

If you speak Spanish, there's plenty of theatre to choose from in Madrid, from classic plays performed by the Compañía Nacional de Teatro Clásico in Teatro Pavón to avant-garde fringe productions in places like Sala TIS, Cuarta Pared, Teatro Pradillo and Sala Triángulo, which organises the annual La Alternativa festival. And even if you don't speak the lingo, you might enjoy one of the big musical shows along Gran Vía, or one of the award-winning Yllana comedy troupe's hilarious non-dialogue productions at the Teatro Alfil.

As for English-language shows, the Festival de Otoño en Primavera (see p34) normally wheels a smattering of English productions into town in May, while director Sam Mendes recently brought over Ethan Hawke and Simon Russell Beale to the Teatro Español for his star-studded *Bridge Project*. Also look out for kids-oriented English shows from the likes of the Face 2 Face Theatre Company, as well as the monthly Giggling Guiri event, which features top English-speaking comedians from around the world (www.comedy inspain.com).

SHORTLIST

Best new
- CaixaForum (p136)
- Teatros del Canal (p157)
- Matadero Madrid (p161)

Best cultural festivals
- Documenta Madrid (p34)
- Festival de Otoño en Primavera (p34)
- La Noche en Blanco (p37)
- PHotoEspaña (p34)
- Suma Flamenca (p34)
- Veranos de la Villa (p36)

Best flamenco
- El Aljaraque (p30)
- Casa Patas (p98)
- La Soleá (p30)
- Las Tablas (p30)

Best fringe theatre
- Sala TIS (left)
- Sala Triángulo (left)
- Teatro Pradillo (left)

Best bargains
- €2.50 film tickets at the Filmoteca Española (p98)
- Free classical concerts at Fundación Juan March (p148)
- Free PHotoEspaña festival photography exhibitions (p34)
- Free entry after 6pm to the Prado (p131) and after 7pm to the Reina Sofía (p94)
- Noche en Blanco (p37)

Best classical music venues
- Auditorio Nacional de Música (p159)
- Fundación Juan March (p148)

Flamenco & dance

Flamenco is easy to find in Madrid, though the quality varies. La Soleá, El Aljaraque, Casa Patas and Las Tablas are the best spots to experience the real deal, while festivals such as Suma Flamenca (see p34) in June, the Festival Flamenco Caja Madrid (see p31) in February and Veranos de la Villa (see p36) in July/August are good for big names. For real spectacle, try one of the Ballet Flamenco de Madrid's extravanganzas.

Now home to the Víctor Ullate Ballet – Comunidad de Madrid company, the multi-purpose Teatros del Canal (see p157) has provided a much-welcome new space for dance, complementing the dance-dedicated Teatro de Madrid, and shows at a hodge-podge of other venues. Meanwhile, it was all change at the Compañia Nacional de Danza (CND) in 2010, as director of 20 years Nacho Duato bade farewell over the government's demand for more classical ballet in the company's mostly contemporary repertoire. Also in Madrid, the state-run Ballet Nacional de España showcases the gamut of Spanish dance. The Madrid en Danza festival moved from spring to November in 2010, and events for the Veranos de la Villa, Festival de Otoño en Primavera and Escena Contemporánea festivals add to the city's dance offering.

Bullfighting

Though the Catalonia region decided to ban it in 2010, bullfighting retains a proud following in Madrid. The city's Las Ventas (see p148) bullring is the most important in the world, hosting *corridas* every Sunday from March to October and every day from mid-May to early June during the city's San Isidro festival (see p35). Unless you're looking to see a superstar such as José Tomas, tickets are usually easy enough to come by, with prices varying from a few euros for seats up in the gods to over €100 for ringside seats. Visit www.las-ventas.com to book in advance, or buy your tickets from the ticket offices (*taquillas*) outside the ring on the day.

Sport

With the national football team bringing back the World Cup, Rafa Nadal completing his career slam, Alberto Contador winning his third Tour de France and Atlético de Madrid winning the Europa League, Spanish sporting success went stratospheric in 2010. And with manager José Mourinho now installed at Real Madrid and hungry for silverware, there's even more reason to head over to the Bernabéu stadium to catch stars such as Cristiano Ronaldo, Iker Casillas, Xabi Alonso, Gonzalo Higuaín and Mesut Özil in action. Atlético – who are looking to move from their present home at the Estadio Vicente Calderón to what would have been Madrid's Olympic stadium, La Peineta, in 2013 – are also worth catching, with Uruguayan Diego Forlán and Argentinian Kun Agüero in their line-up. Die-hard football fans may also want to check out suburban side Getafe or second-division Rayo Vallecano – the latter's supporters are known as some of the most passionate in the Spanish league.

Away from football, the new Caja Mágica tennis stadium hosts the Madrid Masters tournament in May, as well as the games of the Real Madrid basketball team. The city's other basketball side, CB Estudiantes, play at the Palacio de Deportes.

Calendar

PHotoEspaña p34

Practically all year round, apart from perhaps during the late winter lull (when everybody is worn out and broke from Christmas, New Year and Reyes) and the end of the summer, anyone coming to Madrid is likely to encounter an arts festival, a music fest, a fiesta or a themed film season.

Dates highlighted in **bold** are public holidays.

January

6 Reyes (Three Kings)
All over Madrid

On the evening of 5 January, Noche de Reyes, thousands of children and their parents line up along C/Alcalá to watch the *cabalgata* (parade). Dozens of elaborate floats pass by and riders hurl sweets to the children. Later, most families have a big dinner, and the following day presents await those who have been good. Those who haven't get a piece of coal.

Late Jan-early Feb **Festival de Flamenco Caja Madrid**
Casa Encendida (p93)
www.cultyart.com

Two weeks of flamenco's top names for sessions of *cante jondo*, foot-stomping and guitar playing.

February

Ongoing **Festival de Flamenco Caja Madrid** (see Jan)

Wk of Shrove Tuesday **Carnaval**
Various venues

Carnival is a good excuse for dressing up and partying, either in the street or in Madrid's many bars and clubs. It opens in the Plaza Mayor, followed by a parade around old Madrid. On Ash Wednesday, the last day, there is a ribald ceremony during which a fish is bizarrely carted around town to the strains of a marching band, before being interred. It's known as the 'Burial of the Sardine',

Festival de Otoño p34

and was famously depicted by Goya in his painting of the same name.

March

8 Día de la Mujer/ Semana de la Mujer
Various venues
International Women's Day is celebrated in Madrid with a march, usually from Plaza Jacinto Benavente to the bottom of C/Atocha. Some of the other related events include short film seasons and concerts.

Late Mar Festival de Arte Sacro
Various venues
www.madrid.org
This three-week festival of music, dance, theatre, poetry, movies and conferences focuses on the role of religion in art over the centuries.

Late Mar Teatralia
Various venues
www.madrid.org
A regional jamboree of performing arts, including theatre, puppet shows, circus and cinema as well as workshops and other activities aimed at children and young people.

April

Easter week Semana Santa (Holy Week)
All over Madrid
www.esmadrid.com
Easter is usually a good time to be in Madrid, as many madrileños get out of town for the long weekend, and the weather is usually good. In Madrid and nearby towns, there are parish processions in which hooded *penitentes* schlep figures of Christ and the Virgin around. Regarded as the most impressive is that of Jesús Nazareño el Pobre from San Pedro El Viejo and around La Latina.

Mid April Klubbers' Day
Madrid Arena (p153)
www.klubbers.com

This dance festival sets out to be a Madrid equivalent to Andalucia's Creamfields. Despite its name, it's actually a two-day event in Madrid Arena, which, when not being used for sporting events, converts nicely into a giant club. Local and international talent steps up to the decks or does live sets, with names such as Sven Väth, Ellen Allien, DJ Hell, Slam and Cycle on the bill.

Apr-May Feria del Libro Antiguo y de Ocasión
Paseo de Recoletos, Salamanca
This two-week old and second-hand book fair, spanning a week either side of the San Isidro weekend, has been held annually for more than 30 years. Here you may stumble across rare treasures, out-of-print editions or recent remainders. Don't expect much in English.

Late Apr/early May Festimad Sur
Estadio Butarque, Leganés
www.festimad.es
Despite problems with funding and various other ups and downs in recent years, including changes of venue, Festimad, Madrid's biggest rock festival, is certainly still alive and kicking, featuring a line-up of national bands as well as some, often fairly obscure, international names.

May

Ongoing Feria del Libro Antiguo y de Ocasión (see Apr)

1 Fiesta del Trabajo (May Day)
City centre & Casa de Campo
The largest May Day march, attracting upwards of 60,000 people, is called jointly by the communist-led CCOO and the socialist UGT unions, which converge on Sol. Smaller in scale but quite animated is the anarcho-syndicalist CGT's march from Atocha to Plaza Jacinto Benavente. The anarchist purists CNT/AIT, meanwhile, march

up C/Bravo Murillo from Cuatro Caminos. Many of the participants then head to the Casa de Campo where the UGT organises a lively party.

2 Dos de Mayo
Malasaña

Commemorating the fateful day in 1808 when the people of Madrid rose up against Napoleon's occupying troops and paid for their audacity by being massacred, 2 May is now the region's official holiday and kick-starts a nearly continuous series of fiestas that go on throughout the rest of the spring and summer. Things get going in the Malasaña neighbourhood – named after the uprising's teenage heroine, Manuela Malasaña – in the Plaza Dos de Mayo.

Early May **Documenta Madrid**
Various venues
91 517 98 17,
www.documentamadrid.com
This popular international documentary film festival, organised by the Ayuntamiento de Madrid, is now in its seventh year. It consists of one week of screenings, workshops and related activities, in high-profile venues such as Matadero Madrid (also the festival's main office; see p161), Cine Doré (the Filmoteca; see p98) and Casa de América (see p146).

Mid May-early June **Festival de Otoño (en primavera)**
Various venues
91 720 81 94/3 & 012,
www.madrid.org/fo
The impressive and always enjoyable 'Autumn Festival'– now held in spring – offers somewhere in the region of 60 theatre, dance and music spectacles over four weeks, and remains one of the city's major performing arts events. The range throughout the festival is quite wide. Acts as diverse as the Brodsky Quartet, Ballets Trockadero de Monaco, musical groups from Rajasthan, La Comédie Française,

Eddie Palmieri and the Spanish Orquesta Nacional de Jazz have all popped up in recent years, with *Tartuffe* and *Romeo and Juliet* big theatrical draws in previous years. Events take place both in the capital and surrounding towns.

15 San Isidro
Plaza Mayor, Los Austrias,
& all over Madrid
www.madrid.es
See box right.

June

Ongoing **Festival de Otoño (en primavera)** (see May)

Eary June **La Feria del Libro**
Parque del Retiro
91 533 51 84
First celebrated in 1933, the Book Fair is now a major international two-week event. Hundreds of publishers are present and well-known writers show up to sign copies of their works.

June-July **PHotoEspaña**
Various venues
91 360 13 20, www.phedigital.com
Every summer since 1998, PHotoEspaña has swept through Madrid's major museums and galleries, redefining the city as an international photography epicentre. Each year has a different theme. Many of the photographic stars give workshops and lectures throughout the festival. PHotoEspaña also transforms C/Huertas into an active outdoor exhibition space and puts on slide projections in Plaza Santa Ana and Centro Cultural Conde Duque.

June **Suma Flamenca**
Various venues
www.madrid.org/sumaflamenca
The month-long Suma Flamenca is Madrid's high-profile flamenco festival, a feast of music, dance and intense emotion. The 15 different concert venues

The streets are alive…

San Isidro brings out madrileños in full force.

The six days either side of 15 May is the time to see madrileños doing what they do best: taking to the streets and having a rollicking good knees-up. The fiestas celebrate San Isidro (see left), Madrid's patron saint, a humble 12th-century labourer and well-digger to whom all manner of miracles are attributed and whose wife, María de la Cabeza, was also canonised, making them the only sainted couple in history.

The action centres on the Plaza Mayor, where the fiestas are officially declared open and nightly gigs are held (with the odd classical performance thrown in). There is more music in Las Vistillas park; music, theatre, painting workshops and more are put on for kids in the Retiro; classic zarzuela arias get an airing in the Conde Duque Cultural Centre; the Auditorium in the Museo de la Ciudad programmes classical music; in the Planetarium there are performances of early, medieval and baroque music,

and lovers of Spanish Golden Age theatre are catered for in the Plaza de San Andrés. An associated event is the Feria de la Cacharrería, a ceramics market, held in the Plaza de las Comendadoras, close to Conde Duque. Recent additions to the programming are Documenta, a short season of international documentary films; + Arte, a mixed bag of installations, performances, electronic music and sanctioned graffiti, and Universimad, a rock festival at the Complutense.

Throughout the week there are also numerous religious ceremonies in various churches. The 15th itself sees a procession of vintage cars in the Castellana. Possibly most fun of all is the traditional *romería* (pilgrimage) at and around the Ermita de San Isidro, in the park of the same name; families in traditional castizo garb drink from wine skins and stuff themselves with traditional madrileño delicacies such as morcilla.

include Teatros del Canal and the Centro Cultural Pilar Miró in Plaza Antonio María Segovia.

13 **San Antonio de la Florida**
Ermita de San Antonio de la Florida (p149)
91 547 07 22
One of the first of the summer's biggest street parties, the San Antonio celebrations can trace their history back a very long way. June 13 is the feast day of San Antonio, the patron saint of seamstresses. Single girls used to place 13 pins in the baptismal font of the hermitage. If one stuck to her finger she would marry within a year. The main party, including events for kids, takes place across the Paseo de la Florida, in the Parque de la Bombilla.

Late June **Orgullo Gay**
Around Chueca (p100)
www.cogam.org, www.orgullolgtb.org
See box p38.

July

Ongoing **PHotoEspaña**
(see June)

July-Aug **Veranos de la Villa**
Various venues
91 758 92 70, www.esmadrid.com
As part of the 'Summers in the City' festival, a good selection of top names have appeared at the patio of the Centro Cultural Conde Duque, which acts as the festival's main stage. Among them are Brazilian Caetano Veloso, many top flamenco artists, Femi Kuti, Ibrahim Ferrer and some gnarled old rockers. Elsewhere, *zarzuelas* are programmed in both the Centro Cultural de la Villa and in the Sabatini Gardens, the 'Titirilandia' puppet season for kids takes place in the Retiro, while theatre productions may be seen outdoors beside the Muralla Árabe and in the Centro Cultural Galileo.

August

Ongoing **Veranos de la Villa**
(see July)

6-15 **Verbenas de San Cayetano, San Lorenzo & La Paloma**
La Latina & Lavapiés
www.madrid.es
Madrid popular culture at its best – the streets and squares of the Lavapiés, Rastro and La Latina neighbourhoods are dolled up with flowers and bunting and the locals don their castizo gear for some serious street partying. San Cayetano is first, on 7 August, followed by San Lorenzo on the 10th and La Paloma on the 15th. Daytime sees parades and events for kids; by night there are organ grinders, traditional chotis dancing, the aroma of grilled chorizo and churros, sangria by the bucketful and a lot of good clean fun.

September

Mid Sept **Metrorock**
Campus de la Universidad Complutense de Madrid, Avda de Séneca 2, Moncloa
www.metrorock.net
As the name may suggest, this festival started its life as a series of free concerts taking place in Madrid's underground stations. In recent years though, it has grown into a full-sized even. The line-up includes a good mix of international and Spanish acts – Beck, Franz Ferdinand, Paul Weller and the Red Hot Chilli Peppers have all paid a visit.

Mid Sept **Fiestas del Partido Comunista**
Recinto Ferial de la Casa de Campo
91 300 49 69, www.lafiestadelpce.es
Now in the political minority, the Spanish Communist Party still has enough clout, however, to stage a three-day fiesta. There are performances by flamenco and rock bands,

theatre shows, stalls run by political groups, debates on many political and social issues and lots of regional cuisine in the casas regionales.

Mid Sept **La Noche en Blanco**
Various venues
www.esmadrid.com/lanocheenblanco
To have 'una noche en blanco' means to spend a sleepless night, and this is insomniac heaven. In Madrid, as in Paris, Rome and Riga, for one night only you can wander from exhibition centre to museum, from fashion show to concert all night long and all for free.

October

The **Festival de Otoño**, previously held in October, is now an important springtime fixture; see p34.

November

Late Nov-Dec **Estampa**
Palacio de Cristal, Avda de Portugal s/n, Casa de Campo. Metro Lago
91 544 77 27, www.estampa.org
A firm fixture on the arts calendar, Estampa is a well-attended show that brings together galleries and collectors from around the world to exhibit prints and contemporary art editions.

December

Mid Dec-5 Jan **Feria de Artesanía**
Plaza de España. Metro Plaza de España, Sol & Gran Via
www.agrupacionartesanosmadrid.org
This large and crowded crafts fair is an ideal place to look for original presents and coincides with Christmas, New Year and Reyes.

24-**25 Navidad (Christmas)**
All over Madrid
Christmas in Spain is less important than Epiphany (Reyes; see p31), so you are not reminded of the number of shopping days left until Christmas at every turn. However, Father Christmas, tinsel and baubles are more evident than a few decades ago. The big family blow-out is usually on Noche Buena (Christmas Eve) with shrimps, red cabbage and either roast lamb, sea bream or both.

31 **Noche Vieja (New Year's Eve)**
Puerta del Sol, Sol & Gran Vía
New Year's Eve is celebrated with gusto, usually *en familia*, and involves another blow-out meal, litres of cava and the curious tradition of eating 12 grapes as the clock chimes midnight. The Puerta del Sol is where thousands throng.

PHotoEspaña p34

Pride and Joy

Madrid's Gay Pride is one of the world's wildest.

On seizing power in 2004, Spain's Socialist government wasted no time in addressing gay rights, legalising gay marriage and allowing transsexuals to choose whichever gender they wished on their identity cards – milestone achievements that were celebrated with leather, rubber, tanned toned flesh and non-stop hedonism in the 2004 Gay Pride (Orgullo Gay) parade.

Orgullo Gay (see p36) has continued to grow since then, despite continued threats to the event by some Chueca residents, who want the week-long June party to be moved to the outskirts of the city. From 2006, the parade was extended, running from the Puerta de Alcalá to Plaza España. It attracts some 1.5 million people. For an entire week, the city is invaded by visitors from all over the world, partying hard at night, and engaging in poolside lounging by day, with the rooftop terrace of the Room Mate Oscar hotel a popular hotspot.

As well as the parties and the parades, the week boasts some 300 cultural, artistic and sporting events – kicking off with the Carrera en Tacones (a running race where contestants run in stilettos) – as well as off-site parties at the end of the week.

Despite such leaps, bounds and high-heeled trotting towards an equal Spain, there is much still to be done, according to Madrid's numerous gay-rights associations. As a reaction to the passing of the same-sex marriage legislation, thousands of protestors took to the streets to voice their deep disapproval of same-sex marriage. The protesters, who were made up mostly of right-wing families and their children, members of the clergy and politicians from the opposition Popular Party (PP), carried slogans that claimed that the traditional family unit was at stake, and demanded the resignation of Zapatero. The PP hasn't stopped there, going so far as to bring the legislation before the constitutional courts to contest its legitimacy. Throw in the occasional news story of continuing homophobia, such as the refusal of a popular Madrid restaurant to host a reception for a gay wedding, and it's clear that while, in the words of the major gay associations, Madrid is 'one of the most tolerant cities in the world', there is still plenty to march for.

Itineraries

Parque del Retiro p127

City of Grandeur

Madrid has many guises, but one of the things that differentiates it out from Barcelona is its distinct air of grandeur and strong adherence to tradition. Its wide streets, opulent buildings and impressive art collections are part of the draw for many visitors. This itinerary features several well-known institutions and is best suited to a weekday, when the crowds are thinner on the ground.

Start the day in the **Plaza Mayor** (see p65), Madrid's grandest square, which started life in the 15th century. It's best to get here early to enjoy it in the lovely morning light, and with fewer people and less heat. Enjoy a pre-breakfast stroll around the square, taking in, in the centre, the 17th-century equestrian statue of Felipe III by Giambologna and Pietro Tacca (which originally stood in the Casa de Campo) and the frescoed **Casa de la Panadería**

('Bakery House'), the square's most striking building. The latter was completed in 1590 and is typical of the Herreran style, with slate roofs, spiky pinnacles and two towers that dominate the square; however, the colourful murals on its façade were surprisingly not added until the early 1990s. Bullfights, carnivals and all the great ceremonies of imperial Madrid were held in the plaza, which is still an important hub and the focus of city-wide celebrations such as the **Veranos de la Villa** (see p36) and **San Isidro** festivals (see box p35). It's also the site of the main tourist office.

You'll probably be after a morning coffee by now, so head to the north-east corner of the square, on to C/Mayor and east to the **Plaza Puerta del Sol** (see p50), Madrid's official centre, where you'll find *kilómetro cero* (the mark

ITINERARIES

from which distances from the city are measured). Here you can enjoy a decent coffee and an *ensaïmada* pastry (a Mallorcan speciality) in **La Mallorquina** (see p54) – something of a Madrid institution. The square's most important building is the **Casa de Correos**, built in 1766 as a post office for Charles III. Today it houses the regional government, the Comunidad de Madrid, but in the Franco era it had much grimmer connotations, as the Interior Ministry and police headquarters. It was altered significantly in 1866, when the large clock tower, which is now the building's best-known feature, was added. Building works that dominated the Puerta del Sol for several years were finally completed in 2010.

Once you're done in La Mallorquina, walk to the south-eastern corner of the Puerta del Sol, and head down **Carrera San Jerónimo**. Once part of the Ceremonial Route of the Habsburg and Bourbon monarchs, today the street is one of the centres of official Madrid. One of the first places you pass, on the right-hand side is **Lhardy** at No.8 (see p87). This landmark Franco-Spanish restaurant was founded in 1839, and is credited with having introduced French haute cuisine into the culinary wilderness of Madrid. Continue down the street, past the **Congreso** on your left and the elegant **Westin Palace** hotel (see p171) on your right, until you reach the **Paseo del Prado** (see p126). Madrid's three world-famous art museums – the Thyssen, the Prado and the Reina Sofía – are all in the vicinity, but we don't suggest you try to tackle them all in one day. The **Museo del Prado** (see p131), based on Spain's royal collections, is the absolute don't-miss, and the most relevant to this itinerary. Cross over the Paseo del Prado, buy a ticket from the new machines outside to skip the queues, and head to the Goya rooms. Other highlights include Bosch's *Garden of Earthly Delights* and Velázquez's *Las Meninas*.

Lunch in Madrid is taken from 2pm, when many restaurants offer a well-priced *menú del día*. This will probably be much needed after a morning in the Prado, which, although very stimulating, can be draining. Newcomer **Estado Puro** (see p135), not far from the Prado on Plaza Cánovas del Castillo, is a good bet if you're looking for local yet modern cuisine in a chic space; for cheaper fare, head to the Huertas branch of **Viva La Vida** (see p73) for a takeaway box, to be eaten on one of the Paseo del Prado's shaded benches. Then enjoy a post-meal stroll south down the Paseo, taking in the striking **CaixaForum** (see p136), one of Madrid's latest landmarks, on your right. Its vertical garden is now one of the most photographed spots in town.

After a morning of culture and grandeur, you might like to enjoy some of Madrid's green highlights, which are equally impressive affairs. The restful **Royal Jardín Botánico** (see p135) lies just off the Paseo del Prado, and was created for Charles III by Juan de Villanueva and the botanist Gómez Ortega in 1781.

Beyond this is the **Retiro** park (see p127), which has several entrances. One of the nicest is via the recently pedestrianised **Cuesta de Moyano**, lined with upmarket second-hand book stalls, which leads to the entrance on C/Alfonso XII. The park once formed the royal gardens and palaces that were completed for Felipe IV in 1632. Gardeners were recruited from across Europe to create a park that would impress the world. It was finally opened to the general public in 1868, and is now the city's most popular spot for strolling, running, bench-sitting and general relaxing. It still has a stately air, however, with its boating lake, shady avenues and monuments to famous Spaniards.

After a few hours relaxing in the park, head back to the historic barrio of **Los Austrias** (see p65) where, just below the Plaza Mayor, you'll find the **Mercado de San Miguel** (see box p61) – a great spot for some quality tapas.

Plaza Mayor p65

Cine Doré p45

Almodóvar's Madrid

More than any other filmmaker associated with a particular city – Woody Allen and New York, Mike Leigh and London, Godard and Paris – Pedro Almodóvar and Madrid are bound together. The Oscar-winning director has lived in the city for over 40 years and all 17 of his features, from 1980 debut *Pepi, Luci, Bom* to 2009's *Broken Embraces*, have at least been partly shot here, as will his next feature, *El piel que habito* (*The Skin I Live In*), due out in 2011. As Madrid has expanded, modernised and internationalised in the years since Franco's dictatorship, the director has not only captured its transformations in his movies, but evolved alongside it, rising out of the underground and refining his style to emerge as a globally renowned auteur. 'I grew up, had fun, suffered, put on weight and matured in Madrid. Many of those things I did at the same rate as the city itself,' he has said. Perhaps nobody has done more than Almodóvar to put Madrid

on the map in recent years, his exuberant, colourful portraits of drug-taking nuns, transvestite judges and murderous housewives ironically serving as better adverts for the place than any tourist promo.

This tour takes you around some of the most recognisable locations used in Almodóvar's films. For practical reasons, it focuses on the more central spots; though, if you have time, other sites further out to discover include the blocks of flats on the M-30 near Las Ventas bullring from *What Have I Done to Deserve This?*; the Vallecas and Tetuán neighbourhoods from *Volver*; as well as the Rock-Ola nightclub (Padre Xifré, 5), a landmark of the Movida Madrileña – the city's post-Franco explosion of fun and creativity from which Almodóvar emerged – now sadly a supermarket. The tour should take a long morning or afternoon to complete.

Let's start at the beginning. The **Golem cinema** at C/Martín de los Heros, just off Plaza de España, is in many ways where it all started for Almodóvar. This was once the Alphaville cinema, which in October 1980 hosted the première of his first feature, *Pepi, Luci, Bom*, an outrageous, no-budget tale of the adventures of three girls around Madrid. Such was its success, the cinema itself decided to produce Almodóvar's second movie, 1982's *Labyrinth of Passion*, with both films playing there in packed late-night sessions for years after. The cinema now specialises in independent movies from around the world.

From here, duck into the arcade next to Golem and head up the stairs at the back into Plaza de los Cubos. Continue straight ahead across busy C/Princesa and up the stone steps into Plaza de Cristina Martos and then along C/Conde Duque to No.11. There you'll find the door of the **Cuartel del Conde Duque**, where in a famous scene from *Law of Desire* (1987), transsexual Tina (Carmen Maura) realises the urge of many a sweaty *madrileño* by getting a street cleaner to hose her down on a sweltering summer night.

Go back the way you came to Plaza de España and head along C/Bailén past the Palacio Real and over the viaduct. On the other side of the viaduct, go down to your left along C/Moreria and then left again down the steps of **Cuesta Bailén**. Here you're walking in the click-clacking footsteps of Penélope Cruz in Almodóvar's most recent effort, *Broken Embraces*. The bar on the corner, Rayuela, also features in the film and is well worth a stop-off, while the building that houses it is the location of blind filmmaker Harry Caine's (Lluís Homar) apartment in the same movie.

Halfway down Cuesta Bailén, turn right into C/Caños Viejos, then left into C/Moreria and into **Plaza del Alamillo**, where Marisa Paredes'

Museo Chicote

character steps out of a limousine on to a dog turd on the way into her basement flat in *High Heels* (1991). From here, head along C/Alfonso VI, straight over into Costanilla de San Andrés and left into Plaza de Puerta Moros where in *The Flower of My Secret* (1995) the same actress begs passers-by to help her take off her agonisingly tight shoes.

Continue left along Plaza de la Cebada, past the theatre to your left and over the roundabout by La Latina metro into C/San Millan. On the right, at No.3, you'll see a bar called **Wooster**, which may not look like much now but used to be **La Bobia**, the bar where the director and his buddies could be found hanging out every Sunday morning next to the Rastro flea market back in the days of La Movida. La Bobia forms a key location in *Labyrinth of Passion*, featuring in the opening scene and as the site where the two main characters, played by Imanol Arias and Cecilia Roth, meet. The **Rastro** (see p97) also features in one of the funniest scenes in 1983's *Dark*

Habits, in which acid-dropping nun Marisa Paredes skewers her own cheek to help drum up some custom.

Keep moving along C/San Millan into C/Duque de Alba, then C/Soler y González through Plaza de Tirso de Molina and into C/Magdalena, before turning right into C/Torrecilla del Leal and immediately left into C/Santa Isabel. At No. 3 you'll see the ornate art nouveau façade of the **Cine Doré** (see p98) aka the **Filmoteca Española**, which features in *Talk to Her* (2002). Spain's National Film Theatre, it screens classic films at bargain rates.

A cut-through alongside the Doré leads on to C/Atocha. Turn left and then, a few minutes up, go right on to C/San Sebastián and into Plaza de Santa Ana where, at No.15, on the western side, you'll come across **Villa-Rosa**. Opened in 1919, this flamenco bar, with its tiled façade depicting scenes of Andalucía, is where Judge Domínguez (Miguel Bosé, still one of the biggest singers in the Spanish-speaking world and son of renowned bullfighter Luis Miguel Dominguín) struts his stuff as female impersonator Femme Letal in *High Heels*.

Diagonally across Plaza de Santa Ana from Villa-Rosa, at C/Prado No.2 on the corner, is the **Room Mate Alicia hotel** (see p173) which takes its name from Leonor Watling's character in *Talk to Her*. Before being converted into a branch of this trendy chain, the building was the location for Geraldine Chaplin's ballet school in the film, where from his apartment across the way, obsessive male nurse Javier Cámara spied on Alicia practising.

Continue all the way along C/Prado into Carrera de San Jerónimo and left into the Paseo del Prado. Walk up past the Museo Naval, then turn right into **C/Montalbán**. No.7 is the location of the penthouse apartment where

Carmen Maura kept a rooftop menagerie of chickens and ducks, as well as a fridge of barbiturate-laced gazpacho, in *Women on the Verge of a Nervous Breakdown* (1988).

At the other end of Montalbán, turn left on to C/Alfonso XII and head up to the roundabout that houses the **Puerta de Alcalá**, the first glimpse of Madrid that baby Victor sees after mum Penélope Cruz gives birth to him inside a city bus at the beginning of *Live Flesh* (1997).

Turn left along C/Salustiano Olozaga across the busy Paseo de Recoletos and into C/Almirante and take the first right, C/Tamayo y Baus. On the right is **Teatro María Guerrero**, inside which Marisa Paredes mimes the song 'Piensa en mi' by Luz Casal in *High Heels*.

At the end of C/Tamayo y Baus, take a left into C/Fernando VI and walk up to **C/Hortaleza**, where you should turn left and walk down to find No.88. Now an HQ of Spain's UGT trade union, this former 17th-century convent was the home of the heroin-taking, tiger-owning, sex-book-writing nuns in *Dark Habits*.

Continue down Hortaleza and just before the end turn left into C/Reina. At No.16 is **Bar Cock** (see p101), where DJ Tamar Navas plays in *Broken Embraces*. Nearby, the famous **Museo Chicote** (see p56), where many a star from Frank Sinatra to Ava Gardner has sipped a cocktail, features in the same film in a scene where Blanca Portillo reveals the big secret she's been keeping for years, while across the way, the café in the **Círculo de Bellas Artes** (Alcalá, 42) is where Victoria Abril and Peter Coyote meet to discuss a script in *Kika*. Close by on C/Gravina is Taberna Ángel Sierra (No. 11), which appears in *The Flower of My Secret*. Any of these makes a great place to have a drink and imagine yourself as an extra in the maestro's next great scene.

El Rastro

Easy Like Sunday Morning

If you want to see a cross-section of all kinds of Madrid society, crammed into little more than a square kilometre, then the neighbourhood of **La Latina** (see p78) on a Sunday is a must. There's a bit of everything in this vibrant barrio, whether it's tourists and bargain-hunters heading for the Rastro fleamarket, the Lacoste-shirted crowd headed out to splash some cash on freshly pounded mojitos, or all-day revellers out to socialise in the lively tapas bars. The La Latina Sunday bar-hopping tradition is now the dominant Sunday ritual, much as going to church was some 40 years ago (but a lot more fun).

La Latina is located in the centre of Madrid, and is not to be confused with Latina, which is a district further south. The area doesn't have clearly demarcated borders,

but is, like many other places in the city, known by its metro stop. It falls within the Palacio and Embajadores neighbourhoods, and is roughly enclosed by Calle Segovia to the north, Calle Embajadores to the east, Ronda and Puerta de Toledo to the south, and Calle Bailén to the west.

Early birds stream in to the area from around 7am every Sunday to peruse the famous **Rastro** (see p96) fleamarket, which runs down Calle Ribera de Curtidores, on the western edge of **Lavapiés**, and spills out onto the adjoining streets, with everything from army surplus and kitchen goods, to antiques and picture frames on sale. If you weren't tempted by Madrid's legendary nightlife to stay out into Saturday's *madrugada* (early hours) – or if you were, and haven't gone to bed yet – then try for an early(ish) start to get

Plaza de la Paja

first market pickings. However, the Rastro is really best for browsers rather than the serious bargain-hunter, given that the goods on offer are something of a mixed bag, so it's best to think of the experience as more of a time-honoured cultural phenomenon than a shopping trip.

Start at the **Plaza de Cascorro**, and have a stroll around (while keeping an eye on your wallet/handbag – the Rastro is a notorious pickpocketing spot). Then head down **Calle Ribera de Curtidores** or have a wander eastwards down **Calle Embajadores** to see some of Lavapiés proper.

Once you're done with the market, you'll probably be in need of a coffee, a sit-down and perhaps a little sustenance (although remember you have a whole day of tapas munching ahead of you). From the Plaza de Cascorro, head west down C/Maldonadas, past La Latina metro station on your left, and on westwards towards the cluster of five tiny squares made up of **Plaza de la Cebada** (where there's a bustling food market on weekdays and Saturdays), **Plaza Puerta Moros**, **Plaza Humilladeros**, **Plaza Carros** and **Plaza San Andrés**. Here you have a multitude of cafés to choose from; however, if you've made it out good and early then not all of them will be open yet, so carry on round the corner of Plaza Puerta Moros, past the side of the Church of San Andrés to your right, to reach the sloping **Plaza de la Paja** ('Straw Square'; see p78) and **Delic** (see p71) – one of the city's most popular cafés. Grab a table outside if you can to soak up the vibe, and cast your eyes around the square from the vantage of this great people-watching spot. (The beautiful **Capilla del Obispo** in the top left corner of the square reopened in late 2010 after a 44-year restoration – much to the delight of locals, many of who had never seen inside the building.)

As one of the area's best-known institutions, Delic gets more and more packed-out as the day goes on and the punters continue to stream in. For a lesser-known diversion once you've had your refreshments, head down to the bottom of the square to a spot that few visitors know: the secluded **Príncipe Anglona gardens**, one of the few areas of greenery in La Latina. The gardens, which are accessed through an easily missed gate at the bottom of Plaza de la Paja, used to belong to the Anglona Palace, which is now home to a restaurant on adjoining Calle Segovia. With its secluded atmosphere and alluring shade, they're the perfect place to take a five-minute recovery from a La Latina Sunday.

After a short respite, you'll hopefully be ready to face the tapas ritual in its full glory. So, from the gardens, either head back the way you came through the square, which should by now be starting to fill up with people (especially if it's a sunny day) or, for a more comprehensive tour of the area, head left down **C/Príncipe de Anglona** – a tranquil cut-through that leads to **C/Humilladero**. Turn right and follow the street up the hill. Once you near the top of the street, you have three key tapas streets branching off to the left: **C/Almendro**, **C/Cava Baja** and **C/Cava Alta** – the perfect *calles* to start your tapas bar crawl.

It's probably early afternoon by now, the time when an altogether thirstier crowd arrives in the area, keen to carry on an all-nighter that has seeped past daybreak, or to start supping the first frothy *cañas* or chilled vermouths of the day. That kind of hedonism is by now evident in every nook and plaza of the 'hood, with the pierced and tattooed crowd opting to bring their own bottles to enjoy in the sunny squares you passed before at the top of C/Humilladero (as long as the police aren't around to ward them off), while the celebs and the wannabes pack out the smarter venues. Bars around here on a Sunday afternoon often resemble scenes normally associated with late-night antics

elsewhere. And if there's one word that's sure to pass every visitor's lips, it's 'mojito', the Cuban thirst-slaker being an integral part of the La Latina experience (although gin & tonic is fast catching up as the most popular tipple).

Some of the recommended spots are **El Almendro 13** (see p68), **El Tempranillo** (see p81), **Txirimiri** (see p81) and **El Viajero** (see p81). The first three all serve up top-notch tapas, (don't miss Txirimiri's *croquetas*) while the latter is one of the neighbourhood's all-time favourite locales. Punters fight tooth and nail to get a seat on the bar's top-floor terrace, given the views it affords of the bustling neighbourhood, as well as the fact that it's a great suntrap. Among the many famous faces that are in attendance on a regular basis are World Cup hero Iker Casillas and TV-presenter girlfriend Sara Carbonero – although they tend to spend most of their time dealing with autograph hunters rather than enjoying the cocktails.

You'll likely be having such a good time hopping from one bar to the next that it'll be dusk again before you know it. But before you pass out under a haze of sunshine and rum, be sure to head back up to Plaza Puerta Moros to sample the tapas at **Juanalaloca** (see p81). You can get a slice of *tortilla de patata* in any corner bar in Madrid, but at Juanalaloca they have turned the humble Spanish omelette into something of an art form. This long-standing tapas bar is famed for its tasty *pinchos*, which are all piled high on the bar for you to choose from. But the jewel in their culinary crown is the tortilla, which is made with caramelised onion and fabulously gooey in the middle. Enjoy it among a convivial crowd – the perfect end to a quintessentially Madrileño day.

Madrid by Area

Plaza Mayor p65

Old City: South of Gran Via

MADRID BY AREA

Sol & Gran Vía

The **Puerta del Sol** represents the very heart of Madrid, with a time-honoured role as the city's chief meeting place. The square's most important building is the **Casa de Correos**, built in 1766 as a post office for Charles III. Today it houses the regional government, but in the Fraco era it had a grimmer function as the Interior Ministry and police headquarters.

The **Plaza de España**, at the western end of the Gran Vía, is dominated by Franco's bombastic architecture. It is flanked by two classic buildings of the type sponsored by the regime when out to impress: the '50s-modern **Torre Madrid** (1957) and the enormous **Edificio España** of 1948-53.

The **Gran Vía** was created in 1910 by slicing through the Old City. The area's other great avenue is **C/Alcalá**, which follows the centuries-old main route into Madrid from the east. Once lined by aristocratic palaces, it is still pretty impressive today, with a wonderful variety of 19th- to early 20th-century buildings.

Running almost alongside **C/Preciados** up to Gran Vía is the pedestrianised but still shabby **C/Montera**, the main area for street prostitution in the city centre.

Sights & museums

Círculo de Bellas Artes

C/Alcalá 42 & C/Marqués de Casa Riera 2 (91 360 54 00, www.circulo bellasartes.com). Metro Banco de España. **Open** *Café 9am- 1am Mon-Thur; 9am-3am Fri, Sat. Exhibitions 11am-2pm, 5-9pm Tue-Sat; 11am-2pm Sun.* **Admission** *(excluding exhibitions) €1. Free 2-4pm Mon-Sat.* **Map** *p51 E3* ●

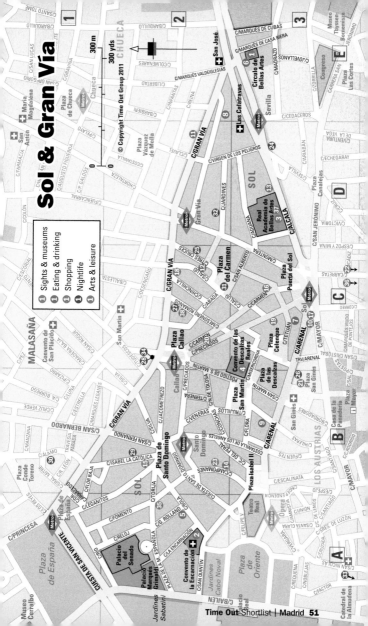

Sol & Gran Vía

Legend:
- Sights & museums
- Eating & drinking
- Shopping
- Nightlife
- Arts & leisure

300 m
300 yds

© Copyright Time Out Group 2011

Box clever

A tale of two time capsules.

On 15 December 2009, the exciting discovery of a lead box was made under the feet of the statue of Miguel de Cervantes in Plaza de las Cortes. The box had been purposefully hidden there in December 1834 to form a 'time capsule', and contained four 1819 editions of the famous author's *Don Quixote* novel and 41 other documents, newspapers and objects relating to the daily and political life of the time.

Whoever hid the box there had gone to meticulous lengths to ensure that its contents were kept in excellent condition; the box was wrapped in paper sprayed with insecticide and encased in glass. It was found by workmen remodelling the square, which lies to the south-east of the Puerta del Sol, near the Congreso.

An exhibition in honour of the box, entitled 'The Time Capsule: From Absolutism to Liberalism in the base of Cervantes', was held in the Real Casa de Correos in summer 2010. And in autumn 2010, 176 years after the original time capsule was hidden, the Madrid city council declared that it will be planting a new time capsule in the same spot that the Cervantes one was found, which will contain objects associated with present-day Madrid, including maps, newspapers, music in MP3 format, testimonies and a copy of the Spanish Constitution.

The Círculo de Bellas Artes occupies a superb building, designed by Antonio Palacios and completed in 1926. It is a key player in every aspect of the Madrid arts scene: as well as a beautifully airy main floor café, with a pavement terrace, the Círculo offers a plethora of classes, exhibitions, lectures and concerts in its theatre and concert hall, as well as an annual masked ball for carnival.

Convento de la Encarnación

Plaza de la Encarnación 1 (91 547 05 10, information 91 454 88 00). Metro *Ópera or Santo Domingo.* **Open** *Guided tours only* 10.30am-12.45pm, 4-5.45pm Tue-Thur, Sat; 10.30am-12.45pm Fri; 11am-1.45pm Sun. **Admission** €3.60; €2 concessions. Free to EU citizens Wed. **Map** p51 A2 **②**

Inaugurated as a monastery by Philip III in 1611, much of the original building, including the church, was damaged by fire in 1734 and rebuilt in a classical-baroque style in the 1760s by Ventura Rodríguez. It still contains a community of around 20 nuns, but most of the building is open to the public. It contains a great many pieces of 17th-century religious art, the most impressive of which is Jusepe Ribera's shimmering chiaroscuro portrait of John the Baptist. The Encarnación's most famous room, however, is the *reliquiario* (relics room). In its glass casements are displayed some 1,500 remains and former possessions of saints and martyrs. Its prize possession is what purports to be the solidified blood of San Pantaleón, inside a glass orb. Visits are by guided tour only, and tours leave 30 minutes after the first person signs up; so there's little point turning up as it opens.

Museo de la Real Academia de Bellas Artes de San Fernando

C/Alcalá 13 (91 524 08 64, Calcografía Nacional 91 524 08 83). Metro *Sevilla or Sol.* **Open** *Oct-May* 9am-5pm

Tue-Sat; 9am-2.30pm Sun. *June, July, Sept* 9am-5pm Tue-Fri; 9am-3pm Sat. *Aug* 10am-3pm Tue-Sun. *Calcografía Nacional* 9am-2.30pm Mon-Fri. *Temporary exhibitions* 10am-2pm, 5-8pm Tue-Fri; 10am-2pm Sat, Sun. **Admission** (excluding exhibitions) €5; €2.50 concessions; free under-18s, over-65s. Free to all Wed. *Calcografía Nacional* free. **No credit cards.** Map p51 D3 ❸

The museum's greatest possessions are its 13 works by Goya, an important figure in the early years of the Academia. They include two major self-portraits; a portrait of his friend, the playwright Moratín; a portrait of Charles IV's hated minister Godoy; and the *Burial of the Sardine*, a carnival scene that foreshadows his later, darker works. Also here is the Italian mannerist Giuseppe Arcimboldo's *Spring*, a playful, surrealistic portrait of a man made up entirely of flowers. It was one of a series on the four seasons painted for Ferdinand I of Austria in 1563. There are also important portraits by Velázquez and Rubens, and several paintings by Zurbarán. Among the later works, the best known are some Picasso engravings and a Juan Gris. Look out too for Leandro Bassano's superb *La Riva degli Schiavoni*.

The academy also has a valuable collection of books, plans and drawings, including those of Prado architect Juan de Villanueva. In the same building is the Museo de Calcografía Nacional, a similarly priceless collection and archive of engraving and fine printing, which has many of the original plates for the great etching series of Goya.

Real Monasterio de las Descalzas Reales

Plaza de las Descalzas 3 (information 91 454 88 00). Metro Callao or Sol. **Open** 10.30am-12.45pm, 4-5.45pm Tue-Thur, Sat; 10.30am-12.45pm Fri; 11am-1.45pm Sun. **Admission** €5; €2.50 concessions. Free to EU citizens Wed. **Map** p51 C3 ❹

The convent of the Descalzas Reales ('Royal Barefoot Nuns') is the most complete 16th-century building in Madrid and still houses a cloistered community. It was converted into a convent in 1556-64 after Philip II's widowed sister Joanna of Austria decided to become a nun. The Descalzas became the preferred destination of the many women of the royal family and high aristocracy who entered religious orders. Hence it also acquired an extraordinary collection of works of art, given as bequests by the novices' families. Equally lavish is the baroque decoration of the building itself, belying its sternly austere façade, with a grand painted staircase, frescoed ceilings and 32 chapels, only some of which can be visited.

The largest non-Spanish contingents in its art collection are Italian, with Titian, Bernardino Luini, Angelo Nardi and Sebastiano del Piombo, and Flemish, with Breughel (an *Adoration of the Magi*), Joos Van Cleve and Rubens. The Descalzas is also an exceptional showcase of Spanish baroque religious art, with works by Gaspar Becerra and Zurbarán and even a tiny painting attributed to Goya.

The monastery was seen by very few until the 1980s, when it was restored and partially opened as a museum. It can be visited only with official tours, which leave every 20 minutes and last around 50 minutes. Frustratingly, the guides rarely speak English, there is no printed information about the convent, and the paintings are not labelled.

Eating & drinking

La Bola Taberna

C/Bola 5 (91 547 69 30, www.labola.es). Metro Ópera or Santo Domingo. **Open** 1-4pm, 8.30-11pm Mon-Sat; 1-4pm Sun. Closed Aug. **€€**. **Castilian. Map** p51 A2 ❺

Holding court on a quiet backstreet, this dignified, classic Madrid restaurant is considered by many to be the home of *cocido*, the huge and hearty stew beloved of *madrileños*. La Bola is still run by the same family that founded it in the 19th century, and the *cocido* (which is only served at lunchtime) is still cooked traditionally in earthenware pots on a wood fire.

Café del Círculo de Bellas Artes

C/Alcalá 42 (91 521 69 42). Metro Banco de España. **Open** 9am-1am Mon-Thur; 9am-3am Fri, Sat; noon-1am Sun. **Admission** €1; free 2-4pm. **Café**. **Map** p51 E3 ⑥

A quintessential point of reference in the city's café society, the Bellas Artes is utterly elegant. It's now free to come in at lunchtime for the *menú del día*. Otherwise take a seat amid the columns and female nudes and frown over *El País* with coffee and a croissant to fit right in.

Casa Labra

C/Tetuán 12 (91 531 00 81). Metro Sol. **Open** Taberna 9.30am-3.30pm, 5.30-11pm daily. Restaurant 1.15-3.30pm, 8.15-10pm daily. **Tapas**. **Map** p51 C3 ⑦

Famously the birthplace of the Spanish Socialist Party back in 1879, this legendary bar, with its brown 1950s paintwork and luggage racks, is worth a visit for its history alone. The house speciality is the cod *croquetas* served up by dour whitejacketed waiters.

Don Paco

C/Caballero de Gracia 36 (91 531 44 80). Metro Gran Vía. **Open** 1.30-4pm, 8-11pm Mon-Fri; 1.30-4pm Sat. Closed Aug. **€**. **Andalucían**. **Map** p51 E2 ⑧

Don Paco, now in his 80s, is a former bullfighter from Jérez, and the Andalucían matador in him is charmingly apparent in his 45-year-old restaurant. With photos of famous visitors (the King and his parents were regulars) and Andalucían memorabilia, it oozes southern style. With *Tinto de verano* ('summer wine' cut with lemonade) on tap, ample sherry

options and menu options such as *tortillitas de camarones* (shrimp fritters), who needs Seville?

El Escarpín

C/Hileras 17 (91 559 99 57). Metro Ópera or Sol. **Open** 9am-4.30pm, 8pm-midnight daily. **Tapas**. **Map** p51 B3 ⑨

So vast that you'll always find a seat, this Asturian cider bar has the look – bare bricks and long wooden tables – to go with the regional tapas. Natural cider (*sidra*) should be followed by *lacón* (gammon), *fabada asturiana* (bean and pork stew) or chorizo.

La Mallorquina

Puerta del Sol 8 (91 521 12 01). Metro Sol. **Open** 9am-9.15pm daily. Closed mid July-Aug. **No credit cards**. **Café**. **Map** p51 C3 ⑩

While the atmospheric bakery downstairs supplies box after ribbon-tied box of flaky *ensaïmada* pastries, croissants and *napolitanas* to what seems like half of Madrid, the upstairs *salón* crackles with the animated chat of *madrileña* blue-rinses and savvier tourists. Windows overlooking the Puerta del Sol make this an unbeatable central spot for breakfast. The coffee is cheap and very good.

Museo Chicote

Gran Vía 12 (91 532 67 37, www.museo-chicote.com). Metro Gran Vía. **Open** 5pm-2am Mon-Sat. **Bar**. **Map** p51 D2 ⑪

Its art deco interior is starting to look a bit shabby, but Chicote is still the doyen of Madrid cocktail bars. This is where Hemingway and other international press hacks would spend their days sheltering from artillery shells during the Civil War. These days, the place is run by Trip Family, one of the biggest promoters on the Madrid nightlife scene. On a Thursday night you can catch Spain's answer to Gilles Peterson, DJ Sandro Bianchi, playing electro-soul, funk and hip hop.

A clean break

Madrid now has two stress-relieving hammams.

As traffic, work hours and the cost of living grows and the siesta diminishes, Madrid is turning to spas and alternative therapies with increasing frequency.

The shining star of Madrid's current health and relaxation infatuation is the **Medina Mayrit** hammam (see p62). An instant hit with *madrileños* from the minute they opened, the baths are still so popular you sometimes need to call weeks in advance for a weekend booking. They are an oasis of calm, located just minutes from the bustling Puerta del Sol. A series of pools span out beneath arched ceilings, half lit by flickering lamps. A shallow pool of warm water abuts another of hot water, with a deeper pool of cold water nearby for a chilly plunge.

The company behind the hammam, El Grupo Al Andalus, prioritises historic authenticity. Masons from Andalucía were hired to lay the stone floors, which replicate the streets of Granada's Albaicín (Moorish quarter). The mosaic walls at the entrance are designed in the red, blue and green tiles found in the Alhambra. The Colina de Almanzora café/restaurant specialises in historic Arabic food.

Enthusiasts claim the hammam provides relief for almost any ailment, from the common cold to arthritis and hangovers. The heat improves circulation, eliminates toxins and keeps the skin clean and supple. After a visit most people feel energised, though if it's some deep relaxation you're after, book a 15-minute massage (for an extra fee).

In spring 2010, no doubt inspired by the success of the Medina Mayrit, Madrid's second authentic hammam opened, in the upmarket Salamanca neighbourhood. The **Hammam Ayala** (pictured; see p148) claims to be a totally authentic hammam, with steam baths pumping out eucalyptus and mint infusions, said to open the pores to release toxins, and with the use of traditional 'black soap' to exfoliate the skin.

MADRID BY AREA

19 Sushi Bar

Salud 19 (91 524 05 71, www.19 sushibar.com). Metro Gran Vía. **Open** 1.30-4pm, 8-11.30pm Mon-Thur; 1.30-4pm, 8.30pm-midnight Fri; 8.30pm-midnight Sat. Closed 2 wks Aug. €€.
Japanese. Map p51 C2 ⑫
Going strong since 2005, 19 Sushi Bar is a favourite among aficionados of Japanese cuisine. The Kobe beef sashimi, tuna fillet with wasabi and the king prawn tempura roll are just three of the star dishes. Just off the Gran Vía, the decor is typically cool and minimalist, but at least there's nothing on display to distract you from the food.

La Terraza del Casino

C/Alcalá 15 (91 532 12 75, www.casinodemadrid.es). Metro Sevilla. **Open** 1.30-4pm, 9-11.45pm Mon-Fri; 9-11.45pm Sat. Closed Aug. €€€€.
Nueva cocina. Map p51 D3 ⑬
The sumptuous environs of this gentlemen's club provide the setting for a restaurant inspired and partly overseen by gourmet god Ferran Adrià. Paco Roncero, a former disciple, is at the helm in the kitchen, and has put his own stamp on the cooking, winning two Michelin stars along the way. The tasting menu changes seasonally, but might include such delights as lobster sashimi or false popcorn.

Vadebaco

C/Campomanes 6 (680 132 538, www.vadebaco.com). Metro Ópera. **Open** noon-4.30pm, 6pm-midnight Mon-Sat; noon-4.30pm Sun. €€.
Modern Spanish. Map p51 B2 ⑭
With more than 350 wines – at least 40 by the glass – you'll probably spend longer choosing what to drink than what to eat at Vadebaco. One wall is a huge blackboard listing just some of the food and wine on offer. Share a few things to get the best experience: maybe slices of cured beef from León, a really excellent tortilla, lamb meatballs or oyster mushroom ravioli. Stick around after dinner for a cocktail too.

Shopping

Antigua Casa Talavera

C/Isabel la Católica 2 (91 547 34 17). Metro Santo Domingo. **Open** 10am-1.30pm, 5-8pm Mon-Fri; 10am-1.30pm Sat. Map p51 B2 ⑮
This long-standing family business specialises in traditional blue and white Spanish ceramics. Every available space is crammed with hand-painted designs, all sourced from small Spanish producers. The charming owner speaks good English.

Área Real Madrid

C/Carmen 3 (91 521 79 50). Metro Sol. **Open** 10am-9pm Mon-Sat; 10am-7pm Sun. Map p51 C3 ⑯
A true emporium for the Real Madrid-inclined. On sale are, naturally, replica shirts and all manner of other stuff bearing the club's logo, from ashtrays to mouse mats, bath towels to undies.

Casa de Diego

Puerta del Sol 12 (91 522 66 43, www.casadediego.com). Metro Sol. **Open** 9.30am-8pm Mon-Sat. Map p51 C3 ⑰
This much-loved shop specialises in hand-painted fans, umbrellas and classy walking sticks.

La Casa del Libro

Gran Vía 29 (91 521 66 57, www.casadellibro.com). Metro Gran Vía. **Open** 9.30am-9.30pm Mon-Sat; 11am-9pm Sun. Map p51 C2 ⑱
Madrid's most comprehensive bookshop by far, La Casa del Libro covers just about every subject imaginable in Spanish, but also has good sections of literature, reference and teaching material in English and other languages.

El Corte Inglés

C/Preciados 1-3 & 9 (all branches 91 379 80 00/Tel-entradas ticket phoneline 90 240 02 22, www.elcorteingles.es). Metro Sol. **Open** 10am-10pm Mon-Sat; 11am-9pm 1st Sun of mth except Aug. Map p51 C3 ⑲

San Pedro el Viejo p68

Joy Eslava

Spain's biggest retail concern has blown all the rest of the competition out of the water. El Corte Inglés is the solution when all else fails for some, but the first choice for many. You can get practically everything you need, be it clothes, household goods, books or multimedia products, and the store also offers a range of services from cutting keys to booking tickets. Most outlets also have well-stocked, if expensive, supermarkets.

FNAC

C/Preciados 28 (91 595 61 00/ 91 595 62 00, www.fnac.es). Metro Callao. **Open** 10am-9.30pm Mon-Sat; 11.30am-9.30pm Sun, public hols. **Map** p51 C2 ⓴
The French giant offers a huge range of CDs, DVDs, videos and books, plus computer hardware and software, all at competitive prices. Downstairs there's a ticket booking service, a café and a paper shop with a good range of foreign press and magazines.

Librería San Ginés

Pasadizo de San Ginés 2 (91 366 46 86). Metro Ópera or Sol. **Open** 11am-8pm Mon-Sat. **Map** p51 B3 ㉑
This Old Curiosity Shop-type place, in an atmospheric passageway, sells everything from scruffy English paperbacks to antique editions.

Madrid al Cubo

C/Cruz 35 (627 45 20 53, www.madridalcubo.com). Metro Tirso de Molina. **Open** 10.30am-2pm, 5-10pm Mon-Sat; 11am-3pm, 6-11pm; 11am-3pm Sun. **Map** p51 C3 ㉒
New tourist shop Madrid al Cubo sells cool alternative souvenirs, including graphics-based prints, T-shirts and mugs, coffee-table books, tote bags and original postcards.

Petra's International Bookshop

C/Campomanes 13 (91 541 72 91). Metro Ópera or Santo Domingo. **Open** 11am-9pm Mon-Sat. **Map** p51 B2 ㉓

A great range of second-hand books in English and other languages is on offer in this laid-back little shop. Here you can offload excess books or trade them for others. Petra the cat, who gave the shop its name, has now passed on.

Nightlife

Adraba

C/Alcalá 20 (902 49 99 94). Metro Sevilla. **Open** 12.30am-6am Wed-Sun. **Admission** varies. **Map** p51 D3 ㉔
Adraba opened in spring 2010, on the site of the former Alcalá 20 club – the place where 81 people tragically died in a fire in 1983. Huge sums of money have been spent to ensure that the club is now one of the safest – and most aesthetically impressive – in Europe. Inside the modern space, DJs spin commercial house and a sophisticated clientele knocks back classy cocktails.

La Bodeguita de Beny

C/Tres Cruces, 8 (91 521 34 82). Metro Gran Via. **Open** 7pm-3am daily. **Admission** free. **Map** p51 C2 ㉕
This rather narrow bar, adorned with pictures of Beny Moré, specialises in Cuban cocktails and sounds, and attracts a lively crowd. From Wednesday through to Sunday there are performances on the tiny stage. Expect to find acoustic duos and trios (there's no space for full bands) playing *son, guaracha* and Latin jazz.

Joy Eslava

C/Arenal 11 (91 366 54 39/ reservations 91 366 37 33, www.joy-eslava.com). Metro Ópera or Sol. **Open** Club nights midnight-5.30am Mon, Tue, Sat. **Admission** €12 Mon-Thur, Sun; €15 Fri, Sat (incl 1 drink). **Map** p51 B3 ㉖
Unusual in that it retains some original trappings of its former incarnation as a 19th-century theatre, in every other respect this is an ordinary high-street club. The vast crammed dancefloor runs

the gamut from teenage tribes through housewives, enjoying staple disco house. Also a concert venue and cinema.

Ocho y Medio

C/Mesonero Romanos 13 (91 541 35 00, www.tripfamily.com). Metro Callao or Gran Via. **Open** 1-6am Fri. **Admission** €10-€12 (incl 1 drink). **No credit cards. Map** p51 C2 ㉗
Although somewhat anachronistic, Ocho y Medio is the perfect stop on your hedonistic tour of the town if you're looking for an alcohol-fuelled mass of party energy. DJ Smart makes it all sound very '80s and '90s, thrashing out an eclectic mix of indie, electroclash, electro-pop, new wave and New York rock. It takes a master to meld Blur and Depeche Mode.

Ohm

Bash, Plaza Callao 4 (91 541 35 00, www.tripfamily. com). Metro Callao. **Open** midnight-6am Fri, Sat. **Admission** (incl 1 drink) €10. **No credit cards. Map** p51 C2 ㉘
While some nights come and go with alarming frequency, Trip Family's Ohm is one that's here for the duration. Strictly speaking it's a gay night, but it's too much fun (and too central) for the straight crowd to stay away. The result is a friendly party atmosphere with soulful, vocal-driven house tracks mixed to perfection by residents Kike Boy and Tetsu.

Sala Cool

C/Isabel la Católica 6 (91 542 34 39). Metro Santo Domingo. **Open** midnight-6am Fri, Sat; 9pm-2am Sun. **Admission** (incl 1 drink) €10-€15. **Map** p51 B2 ㉙
The *número uno* gay place to be on Friday and Saturday nights. Snarling caged gogos, preening Muscle Marys, serious shirtless studs with sweaty torsos, spaced-out twentysomethings and gorgeous waiters are all part of the coolture at this slick, designerish two-floored club.

Sala de Nombre Público

Plaza de los Mostenses 11 (no phone, www.intromusica.com). Metro Plaza de España. **Open** 12.30am-6am Fri, Sat. **Admission** (incl 1 drink) €13. **No credit cards. Map** p51 B1 ㉚
A nice and grimy basement club, of which the main room is Low Club – capitalising on the recent interest in the experimental side of electronica. The DJs – resident and otherwise – spin a varied mix, taking in everything from electro to indie, and making the venue one of the most forward-thinking in the city when it comes to dance music. The large venue doesn't fill up until 3am, though, so don't rush. The building also houses the Pop Room club.

Sala Wind

Plaza del Carmen s/n (no phone, www.salawind.com). Metro Gran Via or Sol. **Open** midnight-6am, Thur-Sat. **Admission** (incl 1 drink) €10-€14. **Map** p51 C2 ㉛
This old venue has had a serious makeover and flung open its doors four nights a week. Wednesdays see drum and bass or hip hop, Thursdays are turned over to tech and electro house, Fridays are gay night Spank, while Saturdays are Elástico, mixing up rock, electro, indie and everything in between.

El Sol

C/Jardines 3 (91 532 64 90, www.elsolmad.com). Metro Gran Via or Sol. **Open** 11pm-5.30am Tue-Sat. **Admission** (incl 1 drink) €9. **Map** p51 D2 ㉜
To call this music joint and club 'no-frills' is an understatement – as its faded yellow walls and middle-aged bar staff attest. However, it's the music and crowd that make a night, and that's where El Sol is a winner. A steady flow of live acts passes through its doors: local outfits producing rock, rhythm and blues, punk, soul

A marketing success

Don't miss the revamped Mercado de San Miguel.

One of Madrid's biggest success stories of recent times, **El Mercado de San Miguel** (see p73) is the daily food market/tapas emporium in Plaza de San Miguel – immediately south-west of the Plaza Mayor – which reopened its polished glass doors in May 2009 after a decade-long restoration. The 1915 wrought-iron and glass structure, with boutique-like food stands inside, has created a new culinary buzz in the city; the place is often heaving at lunchtimes and in the evening, and it continues in this vein until well after midnight (when you can nab bargain tapas). Some say it's lost some of its original soul and that it's overpriced, yet the slick operation – one of the few covered markets in the city – is always rammed with smart-looking madrileños and tourists enjoying bacalao pinchos (saltcod on bruschetta), oysters, tortillas, sushi, olives, wine, sherry, vermouth and, just as importantly, conversation.

An excellent starting-point is vermouth and sherry specialist **El Yantar de Ayer** (www.elyantar deayer.es). With 15 different types of vermút, it's an excellent place to initiate yourself in the quintessential madrileño tradition.

Other hightlights include saltcod specialist **La Casa de Bacalao**, offering €1 pinchos (small rounds of toast) topped with puréed bacalao in a range of different guises; **Ostra Sorlut** (www.ostra sorlut.com), a great spot in which to undertake the oyster rite of passage, knocked back with a cold glass of white wine; and artisan ice-cream specialist the **Horno San Onofre**, offering original flavours such as cava and lemon, as well as meringues, sugared almonds and more.

Take your tapas selection to one of the perches in the centre, which are also great people-watching spots.

MADRID BY AREA

and hip hop, complemented by visits from international acts such as the Bellrays, Snow Patrol and Gigolo Aunts. At other times, the DJ serves up an eclectic selection of unmixed rock, soul, funk and R&B. The classic climax to a big night out.

Terraza Atenas

C/Segovia & C/Cuesta de la Vega (91 765 12 06, mobile 650 50 67 93). Metro Ópera or Puerta del Ángel. **Open** noon-3am daily. Closed Nov-Mar. **Admission** free. **No credit cards**. **Map** p51 A3 **33**

A super-cool terraza set in its own small park. The plentiful tables in the front bar are filled by midnight and the overflow swells on to the surrounding gentle slope of grass. With no complaining neighbours to worry about, the crowd can enjoy the easy sounds of Latin blue mixed by the DJ long after other terrazas have called it a night.

Weekend

Bash, Plaza Callao 4 (91 541 3500, www.tripfamily.com). Metro Callao. **Open** midnight-5am Sun. **Admission** (incl 1 drink) €10-€12. **No credit cards**. **Map** p51 C2 **34**

Weekend is one of the longest standing and most successful Sunday club nights, with a funky feel. Resident DJ Roberto Rodríguez downshifts a gear from the harder revolutions of his other appearances and cruises with Latin and nu jazz, taking the mixed gay and straight crowd through to Monday morning.

Arts & leisure

Café de Chinitas

C/Torija 7 (91 559 51 35/91 547 15 02, www.chinitas.com). Metro Santo Domingo. **Open** 8pm-1.30am Mon-Sat. Performances 8.30pm & 10.30pm. **Admission** (incl dinner) €65 and up; (incl drinks) €31. **Map** p51 A2 **35**

An indulgent evening of flamenco for those who like to play at being 19th-century aristocrats – and don't mind paying 21st-century prices. At least this self-styled 'Cathedral of Flamenco' makes an effort, with sumptuous decor that contributes to the experience.

Medina Mayrit

C/Atocha 14 (902 33 33 34, www.medinamayrit.com). Metro Sol or Tirso de Molina. **Open** 10am-2am (last entry midnight) daily. **Admission** Baths €24-€26. **Baths & massage** (from 4pm & all day Sat, Sun) €28-€38; before 4pm Mon-Fri €25; €23 concessions. **Credit** AmEx, DC, MC, V. **Map** p51 C3 **36**

See box p55.

Real Academia de las Bellas Artes de San Fernando

C/Alcalá 13, Sol & Gran Vía (91 524 08 64, http://rabasf.insde.es) Metro Sevilla or Sol. **Concerts** Sept-June noon Sat. **Admission** free. **Map** p51 D3 **37**

This beautiful building right in the heart of Madrid is a must for a concert experience. It hosts three or four cycles of free concerts a year, usually organised through the Radio Nacional de España for broadcast with musicians from the Escuela Superior de Música Reina Sofía. One well-reputed cycle is the short baroque season, which usually takes place in March.

Torres Bermejas

C/Mesonero Romanos 11 (91 532 33 22, www.torresbermejas.com). Metro Callao. **Open** 8.30pm-2am daily. Performance 9.30pm. **Admission** (incl drink) €35. **Map** p51 C2 **38**

Modelled somewhat kitschly on the Alhambra, this bar plays hosts to authentic Gypsy flamenco and a faithful in-crowd, managing to absorb the tour parties without spoiling the mood. The paella and the Rioja veal are, like the flamenco, rich and satisfying.

Teatro Real p74

Café de Oriente p77

Los Austrias

The oldest part of the city, site of the Muslim town and of most of medieval Madrid, falls between **Plaza de la Cebada**, **Plaza Mayor** and the **Palacio Real**. Like several other parts of the Old City, this area has been smartened up over the past decade, and is now home to a slew of wine bars and expensive restaurants.

The area's core is **Plaza Mayor**, archetypal creation of Castilian baroque. To the south-east of the square, at the **Plaza de la Provincia**, is another major work in the Herreran style: the squatly proportioned **Palacio de Santa Cruz**, built between 1629 and 1643. Originally a prison, it is now the Foreign Ministry. Madrid's oldest square, **Plaza de la Villa**, is to the west of Plaza Major, along C/Major.

The western end of C/Mayor, near the Palacio Real, has several old palaces and runs out west into **C/Bailén**, connected southwards to a splendid 1930s concrete viaduct that offers views of the sierra and the Casa de Campo. On C/Segovia beneath the viaduct, you pass a forlorn fragment of the ninth-century **Muralla Árabe** (Arab wall), the only substantial relic of Madrid's Muslim founders.

Sights & museums

Iglesia-Catedral de San Isidro (La Colegiata)

C/Toledo 37 (91 369 20 37). Metro La Latina or Tirso de Molina. **Open** Sept-July 7.30am-1.30pm, 6-9pm Mon-Sat; 8.30am-2.30pm Sun. Aug 7.30am-8.30pm Mon-Sat; 8.30am-1.30pm, 7.15-8.30pm Sun. **Map** p66 C3 ❸
Still popularly known as La Colegiata, this massive church, built in 1622-33 once formed part of an important Jesuit college. The high-baroque design by

Pedro Sánchez was inspired by the quintessential church of the Jesuits, the Gesù in Rome; the façade was completed by Francisco Bautista in 1664. In 1768, after Charles III expelled the Jesuits from Spain, the church was separated from the college, dedicated to San Isidro and altered by Ventura Rodríguez to house the remains of the saint and his wife.

Museo de los Orígenes (Casa de San Isidro)

Plaza de San Andrés 2 (91 366 74 15, www.munimadrid.es/museosanisidro). Metro La Latina. **Open** Sept-July 9.30am-8pm Tue-Fri; 10am-2pm Sat, Sun. Aug 9.30am-2.30pm Tue-Fri; 10am-2pm Sat, Sun. **Admission** free. **Map** p66 B3 ❹
Dedicated to the city's patron saint, the well-digger and labourer San Isidro, this museum sits on the spot where he supposedly lived and performed one of his most famous miracles: when his son, Illán, fell into a well, Isidro made the water rise and thus was able to rescue the unfortunate lad. The well – or a well, anyway – is preserved inside the house, as is the chapel built in 1663 on the spot where Isidro allegedly died and was buried. More interesting, however, are the finds from local archaeological digs. They include items from lower-Palaeolithic settlements in the area, as well as artefacts from the Roman villas along the Manzanares, and from the Muslim era.

Plaza Mayor

Metro Sol. **Map** p66 C2 ❹
The Plaza Mayor began life in the 15th century as a humble market square. In the 1560s, after Madrid was made capital of Spain by Philip II, architect Juan de Herrera drew up plans for it to be completely rebuilt, but the only part constructed immediately was the **Casa de la Panadería** ('the Bakery'). It is typical of the Herreran style, with grey slate roofs, spiky pinnacles and two towers that

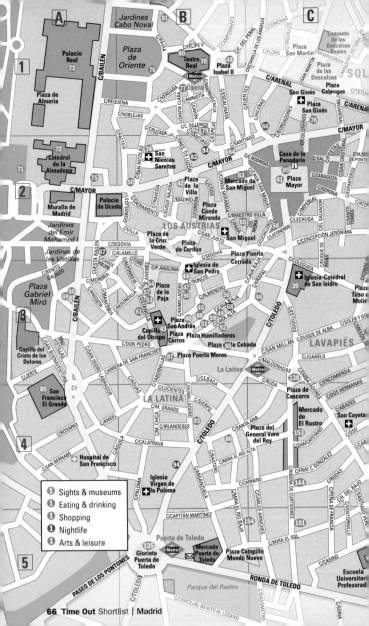

A

Jardines
Cabo Noval

Palacio
Real 73

Plaza de
Oriente 76

Plaza de
Almería

Catedral
de la
Almudena
72

C/MAYOR

Palacio
de Uceda

Muralla de
Madrid

Jardines
del Emir
Mohamed I

Jardines de
las Vistillas

Plaza
Gabriel
Miró 69 60

Capilla del
Cristo de los
Dolores

85 San
Francisco
El Grande

Hospital de
San Francisco

Iglesia
Virgen de
la Paloma

B

Teatro
Real 80

Plaza
Isabel II 48

San
Nicolás
Servitas 74

Plaza
de la
Villa

Mercado de
San Miguel 93

Plaza
Conde
Miranda

San Miguel 41

Plaza de
la Cruz
Verde

Plaza
de Cordón

Iglesia de
San Pedro 44

Plaza
de la
Paja 54 57

61

Plaza
San Andrés

Capilla
del Obispo 43

Plaza
Carros

Plaza Humilladeros

Plaza Puerta
Cerrada

Plaza Puerta
Moros 87

La Latina

LOS AUSTRIAS

LA LATINA

Plaza la Cebada 65

Plaza del
General Vara
del Rey

C

Convento
de las
Descalzas
Reales

Plaza
San Martín

Plaza de
las Descalzas

San Ginés
Plaza
San Ginés 78

Casa de la
Panadería
1

Plaza
Mayor 89

Iglesia-Catedral
de San Isidro 39

Mercado
de
El Rastro 153

Plaza de
Cascorro

LAVAPIÉS

San Cayeta

Puerta de Toledo

Glorieta
Puerta de
Toledo 135

Mercado
Puerta de
Toledo

Plaza Campillo
Mondo Nuevo

RONDA DE TOLEDO

Parque del Rastro

Escuela
Universita
Profesorad

1 Sights & museums
1 Eating & drinking
1 Shopping
1 Nightlife
1 Arts & leisure

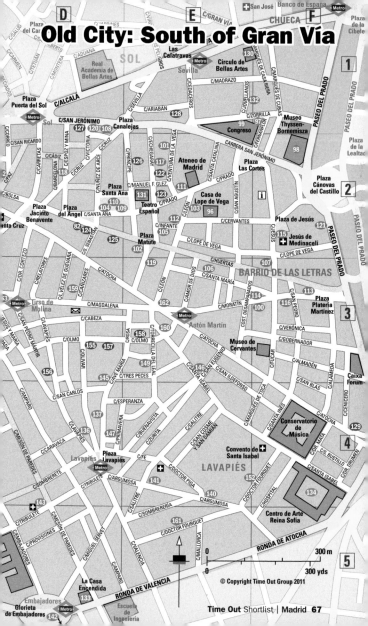

Old City: South of Gran Vía

dominate the square. In the early 1990s, in a move unlikely to be contemplated in most countries, this historic edifice was decorated with colourful psychedelic murals. The rest of the plaza was built by Juan Gómez de Mora for Philip III and completed in 1619 although large sections were destroyed by fire in 1790 and had to be rebuilt. Bullfights, carnivals and all the great ceremonies of imperial Madrid were held here. At its centre is a statue from 1616 of Philip III on horseback by Giambologna and Pietro Tacca. The square is still an important hub, with most Madrid-wide celebrations centred here.

Plaza de la Villa

Metro Ópera or Sol. **Map** p66 B2 ㊷
Madrid's oldest square, home to the city's main market place in Muslim and early medieval times, contains three noteworthy buildings. Dominant is the **Casa de la Villa**, or City Hall, designed in Castilian-baroque style by Juan Gómez de Mora in 1630. The façade was also altered by Juan de Villanueva in the 1780s. It contrasts nicely with the **Casa de Cisneros**, which was built as a palace by a relative of the great Cardinal Cisneros in 1537. It now also houses municipal offices. Opposite the Casa de la Villa is the simple **Torre de los Lujanes**, from the 1460s, where one of Madrid's aristocratic families once resided.

San Andrés, Capilla del Obispo & Capilla de San Isidro

Plaza de San Andrés 1 (91 365 48 71). Metro La Latina. **Open** 8am-1pm, 6-8pm Mon-Thur, Sat; 6-8pm Fri. **Open** for services only Sun. **Map** p66 B3 ㊸
The large church of San Andrés dates from the 16th century, but was badly damaged in the Civil War in 1936 and later rebuilt in a relatively simple style. Attached to it (but with separate entrances) are two of Madrid's most

historic early church buildings. The Capilla del Obispo (Bishop's Chapel, 1520-35), with its entrance on Plaza de la Paja, is the best-preserved Gothic building in the city. It contains finely carved tombs and a 1550 altarpiece by Francisco Giralte. Further towards Plaza de los Carros is the Capilla de San Isidro, built in 1642-69 by Pedro de la Torre to house the remains of the saint, which were later transferred to the Iglesia-Catedral de San Isidro.

San Pedro el Viejo

Costanilla de San Pedro (91 365 12 84). Metro La Latina. **Open** 6-8pm daily (phone to check). **Admission** free. **Map** p66 B3 ㊹
This impressive Mudéjar brick tower dates from the 14th century, although the rest of the church dates from much later, having been rebuilt in the 17th century.

Eating & drinking

El Almendro 13

C/Almendro 13 (91 365 42 52). Metro La Latina. **Open** 1-4pm, 7.30pm-12.30am Mon-Thur; 1-4pm, 7.30pm-1am Fri; 1-5pm, 8pm-1am Sat; 1-5pm, 8pm-12.30am Sun. **No credit cards.** **Tapas.** **Map** p66 B3 ㊺
A sleepy, traditional bar during the week, this place hots up at weekends, and drinkers often drift on to the pavements. A peculiar speciality is the *rosca*, a sort of oversized, filled bagel.

La Botillería de Maxi

C/Cava Alta 4 (91 365 12 49, www.labotilleriademaxi.com). Metro La Latina. **Open** 12.30-4pm, 8.30pm-12.30am Tue-Sat; 12.30-6pm Sun. Closed last 2wks Aug. €. **No credit cards.** **Castilian.** **Map** p66 C3 ㊻
Fashionably scruffy young waiting staff and blaring flamenco in a no-frills setting make for an unpretentious blend of old and new. While the *callos a la madrileña* (tripe in a spicy sauce) is acknowledged as the best in town,

Delic p71

El Viajero p81

there's no shame in going for the *pisto manchego* (aubergine, courgette, pepper and tomato stew) with fried eggs.

Café del Nuncio

C/Nuncio 12 & C/Segovia 9 (91 366 08 53). Metro La Latina. **Open** noon-1.30am Mon-Thur; noon-2.30am Fri, Sat; noon-1am Sun. **No credit cards.** **Café**. Map p66 B3 ③

Split into two halves at either end of the narrow Escalinata del Nuncio, the Café del Nuncio has lovely cool, dark interiors. The real charm of the place, however, lies in the terrace outside on the stepped slope dividing the two spaces; this is one of the most picturesque streets in the old city.

Café del Real

Plaza de Isabel II (91 547 21 24). Metro Ópera. **Open** 9am-1am Mon-Thur, Sun; 10am-3am Fri, Sat. **No credit cards. Café**. Map p66 B1 ④

This likeable, cramped café with a lovely façade is a good place to come for coffee and cake, though prices are a tad on the high side. Head upstairs to a low-beamed room with red leather chairs, overlooking the plaza. The café was a particular haunt of intellectuals, artists and actors in the '80s, but it's popular with a wider crowd these days.

La Camarilla

C/Cava Baja 21 (91 354 02 07, www.lacamarillarestaurante.com). Metro La Latina. **Open** 1.30-5.30pm, 9pm-midnight Mon, Tue, Thur; 1.30-5.30pm, 9pm-1am Fri; 1pm-1am Sat; 11.30am-midnight Sun. €€€.
Castilian. Map p66 B3 ④

Of the many traditional restaurants on this stretch of road, La Camarilla offers the most innovative versions of Spanish home cooking: *revuelto* (scrambled egg) with mushrooms and parmesan, and tasty cod dishes. The setting is reminiscent of a genteel 1930s hotel. Creative tapas and a

hearty *menú del día* are served in a relaxed front room and gourmet meals in an adjoining formal dining room.

Casa Ciriaco

C/Mayor 84 (91 548 06 20). Metro Ópera or Sol. **Open** 1-4.30pm, 8pm-12.30am Mon, Tue, Thur-Sun. €€.
Castilian. Map p66 B2 ⑩

Casa Ciriaco was a meeting place for the intelligentsia in pre-Civil War days, and the Castilian fare is a taste of days gone by. *Gallina en pepitoria* (chicken in an almond and white wine sauce) is the speciality. The waiters are generally very friendly.

Casa Lucio

C/Cava Baja 35 (91 365 32 52, www.casalucio.es). Metro La Latina. **Open** 1.15-4pm, 9pm-11.30pm Mon-Fri, Sun; 9pm-midnight Sat. Closed Aug.
€€€. **Castilian**. Map p66 B3 ⑪

A restaurant unsurpassed by any other in Madrid for its famous patrons: King Juan Carlos, Bill Clinton and Penélope Cruz among them. It also knows how to cook up one cracking *solomillo* (beef). Another star dish is a starter of fried eggs on top of a bed of crisp, thinly cut chips – the King always orders it.

La Casa de las Torrijas

C/Paz 4 (91 532 14 73). Metro Sol. **Open** 10am-4pm, 6-10pm Mon-Thur; 9.30am-4pm, 6-11pm Fri, Sat. Closed Aug. **No credit cards. Tapas.** Map p67 D2 ⑫

This is a charmingly old, unkempt bar, tiled and mirrored, with table-tops constructed from vintage enamel adverts. Since 1907, it has served little more than *torrijas* – bread soaked in wine and spices, coated in sugar and deep-fried – and house wine. There are other, simple, tapas, however, and a basic set lunch.

Delic

Costanilla de San Andrés 14, Plaza de la Paja (91 364 54 50). Metro La Latina. **Open** 10am-11.45pm

Mon-Thur; 10am-12.30am Fri, Sat. Closed last 2wks Aug. **Café**. **No credit cards**. Map p66 B3 ⑤③

A perennial favourite with seemingly everybody; from those looking for a peaceful morning coffee on the leafy Plaza de la Paja to those meeting up for a few bolstering cocktails before a big night out. A globe-trotting menu includes tabouleh, Japanese dumplings and filled ciabatta.

El Estragón

Costanilla de San Andrés 10, Plaza de la Paja (91 365 89 82, www.elestragon vegetariano.com). Metro La Latina. **Open** 1.30-4.15pm, 8-11.45pm Mon-Thur, Sun; 1.30-4.15pm, 8pm-12.45am Fri, Sat. **€€**. **Vegetarian**. Map p66 B3 ⑤④

While the menu features the likes of soya 'meatballs', 'hamburgers' and so on, where this place really excels is in its straightforward vegetarian dishes, such as a fabulous towering heap of risotto verde containing every green vegetable you can think of, topped with stringy Emmental. It's a delightful spot, with terracotta tiles and views over Plaza de la Paja, on which tables are set in summer.

La Fontanilla

Plaza Puerta Cerrada 13 (91 366 27 49). Metro La Latina. **Open** 11am-2am daily. **Bar**. Map p66 B2 ⑤⑤

It may be Madrid's smallest Irish pub, but La Fontanilla manages to cram in a couple of wooden tables alongside wide hatches opening on to the street. The myriad beers racked up the walls are sadly not for sale, but there is Murphy's and Guinness, along with some incongruous canapés to nibble at.

Julián de Tolosa

C/Cava Baja 18 (91 365 82 10, www.casajuliandetolosa.com). Metro La Latina. **Open** 1.30-4pm, 9pm-midnight Mon-Sat; 1.30-4pm Sun. **€€€**. **Basque**. Map p66 B3 ⑤⑥

Probably the most modern restaurant in the *barrio*, this Basque establishment is all smooth wood, glass and brick, housed in a 19th-century building. With a very limited, simple menu, the main attraction is the grilled steak (*chuletón de buey*). Try the smoky *idiazábal* sheep's cheese, a speciality from the little Basque town of the same name. There's an excellent selection of more than a hundred wines.

La Musa Latina

Costanilla San Andrés 12 (91 354 02 55, www.lamusalatina.com). Metro La Latina. **Open** noon-midnight Mon-Thur; noon-2pm Fri; 1pm-2am Sat; 1pm-1am Sun. **€**. **Global**. Map p66 B3 ⑤⑦

A laid-back vibe, tasty tapas and stir-fries, and a great location on the Plaza de la Paja all contribute towards making La Musa Latina into a tempting package. Try the fried green tomatoes and the prawn tempura with avocado. Waiters are supercool but friendly, and the diners well-heeled and hip (note the Junk Club downstairs).

El Sobrino de Botín

C/Cuchilleros 17 (91 366 42 17, 91 366 30 26, www.botin.es). Metro Sol. **Open** 1-4pm, 8pm-midnight daily. **€€€**. **Castilian**. Map p66 C2 ⑤⑧

The world's oldest restaurant is still coming up with the goods after nearly 300 years. Its nooks and crannies add up to an atmospheric – if cramped – dining spot over several floors. Ask for a table in the vaulted cellar for the full effect. Order the suckling pig or the lamb, which are roasted in a huge wood-fired oven.

Taberna Salamanca

C/Cava Baja 31 (91 366 31 10). Metro La Latina. **Open** 1-4pm, 8.30pm-midnight Tue-Thur; 1-4pm, 8.30pm-1am Fri, Sat; 1-4.30pm Sun. Closed mid July-mid Aug. **€€**. **Castilian**. **No credit cards**. Map p66 B3 ⑤⑨

On a street crammed with high-priced eateries, this is where the young and more frugal set come to eat. There are three lunch *menús* to choose from, offering the usual Spanish pickings – *croquetas*, courgette tortilla and endives with roquefort cheese are all pretty dependable. The staff are friendly, with a tendency to whack up the stereo.

El Ventorillo

C/Bailén 14 (91 366 35 78). Metro Ópera. **Open** 10am-1am daily.
No credit cards. Bar. Map p66 A3 🜄

Just down from the Palacio Real, this *terraza* offers the finest sunsets in Madrid, with a magnificent location looking out over the Casa del Campo and all the way to the Guadarrama. Not cheap, however.

Viva La Vida

Costanilla de San Andrés 16 (91 366 33 49). Metro La Latina. **Open** noon-midnight Mon-Wed; 11am-2am Thur-Sun. Closed last 2wks Aug. **Café. Map** p66 B3 🜄

This vegetarian café has been a great success. Take a plate (or take-away box) and make your selection from the buffet, which includes creative salads, sautéed vegetables, wholegrains, dips and hot meals, such as veggie lasagna. The staff then weigh the plate to get the price. A typical main course plate costs €10. There's also a good range of juices and sweet things.

Shopping

El Flamenco Vive

C/Conde de Lemos 7 (91 547 39 17, www.elflamencovive.es). Metro Ópera. **Open** 10am-2pm, 5-9pm Mon-Sat. **Map** p66 B1 🜄

Even if you harbour only a passing interest in flamenco, the brilliant range of CDs, guitars, books and other paraphernalia at this shop will lure you in.

El Mercado de San Miguel

Plaza de San Miguel (91 548 12 14). Metro Sol. **Map** p66 B2 🜄

This posh market, with a restored 19th-century wrought-iron façade, has been a huge success story since reopening in 2009. There's a good selection of quality produce that's perfect for gourmet gifts, and the market is a popular spot for tapas and aperitifs. See also box p61.

El Riojano

C/Mayor 10 (91 366 44 82, www.confiteriaelriojano.com). Metro Sol. **Open** Sept-July 10am-2pm, 5-9pm daily. Closed Aug.
Map p66 B2 🜄

El Riojano has been in business since 1885, selling irresistible cakes, pastries, meringues and seasonal goodies. All are made in the traditional way, with meringues a particular speciality. Enjoy one with a coffee in the café.

Taller Puntera

Plaza Conde de Barajas 4 (91 364 29 26, www.puntera.com). Metro Ópera, La Latina or Tirso de Molina. **Open** 10am-2pm, 5-9pm Mon-Sat; 10am-2pm Sun. **Map** p66 B2 🜄

This lovely leather accessories shop/workshop stocks stylish bags, satchels, rucksacks, wallets, notebooks and more, all in top-quality leather, in a range of tasteful colours. You can personalise your purchase by getting your name engraved for free. What's more, the staff are genuinely friendly and the prices excellent for this level of workmanship.

Nightlife

Garibaldi Café

C/San Felipe Neri 4 (91 559 27 33, www.salagaribaldi.com). Metro Ópera. **Open** 9.30pm-6am daily. **Admission** varies. **Map** p66 C1 🜄

A roomy venue with a good sound system and a varied programme. Its staple fare is new bands doing the rounds on the local scene, but in addition there are DJ sessions from Thursday to Sunday. Midweek you'll find stand-ups, storytelling, theatre and dance.

MADRID BY AREA

Marula

C/Caños Viejos 3 (91 366 15 96, www.marulacafe.com). Metro La Latina. **Open** 11pm-6am daily. **Admission** varies. **No credit cards. Map** p66 A2 ⑰

This small venue serves as bar, club and live music venue. Tuesday nights are concert nights, and there are late-night jams midweek, but the place really hots up at weekends, attracting DJ sessions from local talent such as Señorlobo, Chema Ama and Javi Kalero. The summertime terrace is a big pull.

La Soleá

C/Cava Baja 34 (91 366 05 34). Metro La Latina. **Open** 10pm-6am Tue-Sat. **Map** p66 B3 ⑱

This small but amiable bar boasts a constant babble of flamenco aficionados and a roster of performers that alternate with spontaneous (and variable) songs from the clientele. Great fun on a good night, but it can also be surprisingly dull. Watch out, too, for the occasional rough element.

Arts & leisure

Corral de la Morería

C/Morería 17 (91 365 84 46, www. corraldelamoreria.com). Metro La Latina. **Open** 8pm-2am daily. Performances from 10.30pm. **Admission** (incl drinks) €36-€41. **Map** p66 A3 ⑲

More serious and exacting than the tourist-packed Las Carboneras (Plaza del Conde de Miranda 1), this longstanding *tablao* sports seemingly authentic Arab decor and an atmosphere to match. A relaxed mix of tourists, fans and professionals enjoy a solid, expensive and sometimes exhilarating show.

Teatro Real

Plaza de Isabel II (information 91 516 06 60, box office 902 24 48 48, www. teatro-real.com). Metro Opera. **Open** Box office 10am-8pm Mon-Sat, from 2hrs before show Sun. Visits 10.30am-

1pm Mon, Wed-Fri; 11am-1.30pm Sat, Sun. Main season Sept-July. **Tickets** Ballet €10-€107. Opera €6-€156. Visits €5; concessions €3. **Map** p66 B1 ⑳

The interior of the city's opera house is breathtakingly ornate compared with its sombre façade, and one of the most technologically advanced in Europe. Productions are impressive, with complicated revolving sets and attention to detail in costume and props. Performances usually begin at 8pm, or 6pm on Sundays, with ballet and family opera matinées at noon. Tickets go on sale approximately ten days before the première, and stand-by tickets are available on the day.

Ópera

The area between **Plaza Mayor** and the **Palacio Real** is named after the **Teatro Real** opera house at its centre. As well as containing some of the city's most important buildings (the **cathedral** among them), this is one of the most elegant areas of Madrid.

A tunnel whisks traffic under the stunning **Plaza de Oriente**, making it a pleasant spot for coffee. At the square's centre is a fine equestrian statue of King Philip IV.

On the esplanade between the cathedral and palace, excavations have been undertaken to unearth the remains of the original Muslim fortress and the foundations of Philip II's Alcázar, covered over by the building of the later Palacio Real. Some of the discoveries, including Moorish arches, have been open to public view. Behind the palace, the **Campo del Moro** gardens run down towards the Manzanares and the Paseo de la Florida.

Sights & museums

Campo del Moro

Paseo de la Virgen del Puerto (91 454 88 00). Metro Príncipe Pío. **Open**

Taller Puntera p73

Oct-Mar 10am-6pm Mon-Sat; 9am-6pm Sun. Apr-Sept 10am-8pm Mon-Sat; 9am-8pm Sun. **Map** p66 A2 **71**

This vast garden is only accessible from the Paseo de la Virgen del Puerto side, requiring a fairly long walk down Cuesta de San Vicente or Cuesta de la Vega. As a reward, however, you will see two fine monumental fountains. Nearest the palace is Los Tritones, originally made in 1657 for the palace in Aranjuez; the other is Las Conchas, designed in the 18th century by Ventura Rodríguez. Both were moved here in the 1890s.

Catedral de la Almudena

C/Bailén 10 (91 542 22 00). Metro Ópera. **Open** 9am-8.30pm daily. **Map** p66 A2 **72**

This is not Spain's most impressive cathedral, and it's something of a miracle that it exists at all. For centuries, Church and State could not agree on whether Madrid should have a cathedral; once they did, it took 110 years to complete it. In 1883 work began on a neo-Gothic design by the Marqués de Cubas, but only the crypt was completed. Another architect, Fernando Chueca Goitia, took over in 1944, and introduced a neo-classical style. It was finally finished in 1993. The site once contained the church of Santa María de la Almudena, formerly the main mosque of Muslim Madrid. One of its more interesting pieces is the 13th-century polychromatic funerary chest of San Isidro.

Palacio Real (Palacio de Oriente)

Plaza de Oriente, C/Bailén (91 454 88 00). Metro Ópera. **Open** Oct-Mar 9.30am-5pm Mon-Sat; 9am-2pm Sun. Apr-Sept 9am-6pm Mon-Sat; 9am-3pm Sun. **Admission** €10 with guided tour; €8 without; €3.50 concessions. Free to EU citizens Wed. **Map** p66 A1 **73**

Commissioned by Philip V after the earlier Alcázar was lost to a fire in 1734, the architects principally responsible for the final design, which reflects the taste of the Spanish Bourbons, were Italian – Giambattista Sacchetti and Francesco Sabatini – with contributions by the Spaniard Ventura Rodríguez. Completed in 1764, the late-baroque palace is built almost entirely of granite and white Colmenar stone, and, surrounded by majestic gardens.

Inside you must keep to a fixed route, but are free to set your own pace rather than follow a tour. The entrance is awe-inspiring: you pass up a truly vast staircase and then through the main state rooms, the Hall of Halbardiers and Hall of Columns, all with soaring ceilings and frescoes by Corrado Giaquinto and Giambattista Tiepolo. In the grand Throne Room there are some fine 17th-century sculptures commissioned by Velázquez, which were saved from the earlier Alcázar. Other highlights are the extravagantly ornate private apartments of the palace's first resident, Charles III, again decorated by Italians. Particularly striking are the Gasparini Room, the king's dressing room, covered in mosaics and rococo stuccoes by Mattia Gasparini; and the Porcelain Room, its walls covered entirely in porcelain reliefs. A later addition is another giant: the State Dining Room, redesigned for King Alfonso XII in 1880 and still used for official banquets.

Another highlight is the Real Armería (Royal Armoury), reached via a separate entrance off the palace courtyard, with a superb collection of ceremonial armour, much of it actually worn by Charles V and other Habsburgs. Look out too for the suits of armour worn by El Cid and his horse, displayed on life-size statues.

The palace is closed to the public when official receptions or ceremonies are due, so it's a good idea to check before visiting. On the first Wednesday of each month the Royal Guard stages a ceremonial Changing of the Guard in the courtyard at noon. There are tours of the Palace throughout the day, but frequency depends on the volume of visitors.

San Nicolás de los Servitas

Plaza San Nicolás (91 559 40 64).
Metro Ópera. **Open** 8.30am-1.30pm,
5.30-8pm Mon; 8.30-9am, 6.30-8pm Tue-
Sat; 6.30-8.30pm Sun. Mass 8pm Mon;
9am & 8pm Tue-Sat; 10.30am, noon &
1pm Sun. **Map** p66 B2 ⓐ

The oldest surviving church in Madrid
stands just a few minutes from Plaza
de Oriente. Its 12th-century tower is
one of two Mudéjar towers (see
also p68 San Pedro el Viejo), built
by Muslim craftsmen living under
Christian rule, in the city. Most of the
rest of the church was rebuilt later, during the 15th and 16th centuries.

Eating & drinking

El Anciano Rey de los Vinos

C/Bailén 19 (91 559 53 32,
www.elancianoreydelosvinos.es).
Metro Ópera. **Open** 10am-midnight
Mon-Sun. Closed mid Feb-mid Mar.
No credit cards at bar. **Bar**.
Map p66 A2 ⓐ

Kept much as it has been for the last
century – very simple, but spacious
and light inside with a wide counter
and mirrored walls – the King of Wines
serves good canapés, and is a great
place for a drink after visiting the
cathedral. Prices are quite high, especially if you sit outdoors.

Café de Oriente

Plaza de Oriente 2 (91 541 39 74).
Metro Ópera. **Open** 8.30am-1.30am
Mon-Thur, Sun; 9am-2am Fri, Sat.
Café. **Map** p66 B1 ⓐ

The belle époque interior is entirely
fake yet entirely convincing, making
this one of the most peaceful and elegant spots to flick through the newspapers or recover from the exertions of
the Palacio Real opposite. Despite its
location, with tables outside on the
stunning Plaza de Oriente, the café
seems to be more popular with locals
than with tourists.

Casa Marta

C/Santa Clara 10 (91 548 28 25,
www.restaurantecasamarta.com).
Metro Ópera. **Open** 1.30-4pm Mon;
1.30-4pm, 9pm-midnight Tue-Sat.
Closed Aug. **€€**. **Castilian**.
Map p66 B1 ⓐ

Every Saturday, according to the
novel, Don Quixote ate *duelos y que-
brantes* (scrambled eggs, ham, bacon,
chorizo and brains) and you can still
try them at Casa Marta – although they
usually leave out the brains these days.
A quaint old place, it's been a favourite
since the beginning of the 20th century. The satisfying *platos de cuchara* –
warming bowls of *cocido*, beans and
lentils – are another star turn.

Chocolatería San Ginés

Pasadizo de San Ginés 5 (91 365 65
46). Metro Ópera or Sol. **Open** 9.30am-
7am daily. **No credit cards**. **Café**.
Map p66 C1 ⓐ

Serving chocolate and *churros* (deep-
fried batter sticks) to the city night and
day since 1894, this veritable institution has had to introduce a ticketing
system – pay before you order – to deal
with the 5am queues of exhausted club-
bers and chipper old ladies.

Marechiaro

C/Conde de Lemos 3 (91 547 00 42).
Metro Ópera. **Open** 9pm-midnight
Mon; noon-4.30pm, 9pm-1am Tue-Sat.
Closed 2wks Aug. **€€**. **Italian**. **Map**
p66 B1 ⓐ

Two Neapolitans are behind this mod-
est little restaurant that provides some
of the best pizzas in the city. Cooked in
wood-fired ovens, they have thin,
flavourful crusts and fresh ingredients.
Pastas are good too. Decor is pungent-
orange walls sporting a mix of Venetian
masks and old photos of Maradona.

La Taberna del Alabardero

C/Felipe V 6 (91 547 25 77,
www.alabardero.eu). Metro Ópera.
Open 1-4pm, 9pm-midnight daily.
€€€. **Basque**. **Map** p66 B1 ⓐ

MADRID BY AREA

Father Lezama first started up his traditional tavern in 1974, when he put underprivileged boys to work as waiters in this converted 16th-century townhouse. With a quiet terraza on the street that runs along the north side of the Teatro Real, it is still one of the most popular post-theatre dining spots, serving traditional tapas at the bar and Basque cuisine in the restaurant in the back.

Shopping

Tiempos Modernos

C/Arrieta 17 (91 542 85 94, www.tiempos-modernos.com). Metro Ópera. **Open** 11am-2pm, 5-8.30pm Mon-Fri; 11am-2pm Sat. Closed 1st 3 wks of Aug. **Map** p66 B1 ③

Tiempos Modernos deals in modern Spanish painting and hosts temporary shows and exhibitions of photography and artwork. The main line of business, though, is the great range of 1940s, '50s and '60s furniture.

Nightlife

La Coquette

C/Hileras 14 (91 530 80 95). Metro Ópera or Sol. **Open** Sept-Apr 8pm-3am Mon-Thur, Sun; 8pm-3.30am Fri, Sat; May-July 9pm-3am Mon-Thur, Sun; 9pm-3.30am Fri, Sat. Closed Aug. **Admission** varies. **Map** p67 D2 ③

This basement bar, going for some 20 years now, was Madrid's first dedicated exclusively to blues. Run by a Swiss-Spanish guy called Albert, who has a large collection of old records that won't disappoint, there are live acts featuring local bluesers from Tuesday to Thursday.

Kathmandú

C/Señores de Luzón 3 (no phone, http://kathmanduclub.com). Metro Ópera or Sol. **Open** midnight-6am Thur-Sat. **Admission** (incl 1 drink) €10 Fri, Sat; free Thur. **No credit cards. Map** p66 B2 ③

This basement club is cosy, friendly and nicely chilled. The DJs spin a delicious mix of funk, soul, jazz and hip hop, luring the friendly clientele on to the dancefloor by about 3am. Non-dancers take to ample seating in the cave-like venue and nod along.

El Nuevo Barbú

C/Santiago 3 (91 542 56 98, www.elbarbuclub.com). Metro Ópera or Sol. **Open** 10.30pm-3.30am Mon-Thur; 10.30pm-4am Fri, Sat. **Admission** free. **Map** p66 B2 ③

A sumptuous red velvet curtain separates the chilled front bar from two spacious candlelit chambers at the back, where a swirling wash of intensely coloured psychedelic projections bathe the walls and ceilings. The DJ keeps the easygoing, urbane crowd happy with a slick mixture of funk, salsa and African beats.

La Latina

La Latina is officially the area below Plaza de la Cebada, but many people think of the squares north of here as being part of it. La Latina remains a popular Sunday outing for madrileños of all stripes. The tradition is to start at El Rastro flea market, and then to head to the tapas bars around Cava Baja, Plaza de la Paja, Plaza San Andrés and Calle Humilladero for an aperitif of vermouth and some tapas.

Sights & museums

Basílica de San Francisco el Grande

Plaza de San Francisco (91 365 38 00). Metro La Latina. **Open** Sept-June 11am-12.30pm, 4-6.30pm Tue-Fri; 11am-1.30pm Sat. July-Sept 11am-12.30pm, 5-7.30pm Tue-Sun. Last admission half hr before closing. **Admission** (guided tour only) €3; €2 concessions. **Map** p66 A4 ③

La Torre del Oro p81

Teatro La Latina p82

This huge, multi-tiered church between Puerta de Toledo and the Palacio Real is difficult to miss. A monastery on the site, reputedly founded by Saint Francis of Assisi, was knocked down in 1760; this neo-classical church was built in its place. Most challenging was the construction of the spectacular dome, with a diameter of 33m (108ft). The dome was restored fairly recently, and work on the rest of the basilica has now been completed. Inside there is an early Goya, *The Sermon of San Bernardino of Siena.*

Eating & drinking

La Cabra en el Tejado

C/Santa Ana 29 (91 142 46 43).
Metro La Latina. **Open** 6-11pm daily.
No credit cards. Tapas. **Map**
p66 B4 ⑥

A clear fave among creative types, 'The Goat on the Rooftop' is a little hidden away, but worth seeking out for its selection of good, cheap and unusual tapas – including quiches, houmous, crêpes, *tostas*, salads, and sweet options. The space is nicely decorated, with a huge mural painted on one wall, and a retro feel.

Juanalaloca

Plaza Puerta de Moros 4 (91 364 05 25). Metro La Latina. **Open** 1.30-5.50pm, 8.30pm-12.30am Mon-Thur; 1.30-5.30pm, 8.30pm-1am Fri-Sun. No credit cards. **Tapas. Map** p66 B3 ⑥

Where the hip go to *tapear*, this Uruguayan-run tapas bar attracts a stylish mix of Argentinians, Uruguayans, locals and tourists. It's kind of pricey, but offers undeniably creative cooking – such as wild mushroom and truffle croquettes and vegetables in a 'Hindu tempura'. Its delicious tortilla is also renowned.

El Tempranillo

C/Cava Baja 38 (91 364 15 32).
Metro La Latina. **Open** 1-4pm, 8pm-midnight Tue-Sun. Closed Aug.
Tapas. Map p66 B3 ⑥

Never less than rowdy, decorated in bullring ochre and bare brick, with flamenco on the sound system, El Tempranillo offers an impressive range of labels from nearly every wine-producing region in Spain. The tapas are addictive too: try the wild mushrooms in scrambled egg or the sweetbreads.

La Torre del Oro

Plaza Mayor 26 (91 366 50 16).
Metro Sol. **Open** noon-1am daily.
Tapas. **Map** p66 C2 ⑥

It's smack on the Plaza Mayor, so don't expect any bargains, but this Andalucian bar is the real deal, with bullfighting memorabilia and incomprehensible waiters. Ask for prawns or whitebait (*pescaitos*), and accompany them with a cold, dry fino.

Txirimiri

C/Humilladero 6 (91 364 11 96, www.txirimiri.es). Metro La Latina.
Open noon-4.30pm, 8.30pm-midnight Mon-Sat; 11am-midnight Sun. Closed Aug. **Tapas. Map** p66 B3 ⑥

The popular Txirimiri specialises in Basque pintxos, and despite its aspirational-sounding tag line of 'haute cuisine in miniature', it's a laid-back, friendly place. The thirtysomething crowd is drawn by the excellent, well-priced tapas and sociable atmosphere. There's a restaurant area at the far end.

El Viajero

Plaza de la Cebada 11 (91 366 90 64).
Metro La Latina. **Open** 2-4.30pm, 9pm-12.30am Tue-Thur; 2-4.30pm, 9pm-1am Fri, Sat; 2-4.30pm Sun. Closed 3wks Jan & last 2wks Aug. €€. **Mediterranean**. **Map** p66 B3 ⑥

La Latina scenesters in retro couture still flock to this three-storey bar/restaurant famous for its rooftop terraza. The food, a mixed array of Mediterranean dishes and barbecued meats, is delicious, if a little expensive. The carpaccios are melt-in-the-mouth and the pastas, particularly the taglioni marinera, drip with flavour.

MADRID BY AREA

Viuda de Vacas

C/Águila 2 (91 366 58 47). Metro La Latina. **Open** 1.30-5pm, 9pm-1am Mon-Wed, Fri, Sat; 1.30-4.30pm Sun. Closed July. **€€. Castilian. Map** p66 B3 ㉜
Offering classic Castilian home cooking, Viuda de Vacas has been in the Canova family for three generations; the restaurant was established (at a different location) by the feisty grandmother – widow of Señor Vacas. Favourite dishes include stuffed courgettes and baked hake or sea bream.

Xentes

C/Humilladero 13 (91 366 42 66). Metro La Latina. **Open** 2-5pm, 9pm-midnight Tue-Sat; 12.30-5pm Sun. Closed Aug. **€€. Galician. Map** p66 B4 ㉝
With the TV blaring and some half-hearted nautical decor, this is a rather strange setting for some of the best seafood in Madrid. But the Galician patrons at the bar happily gulp down oysters and beer, and the diners in the back are delighted with their *pulpo a gallega* (octopus with paprika) and *arroz con bogavantes* (lobster paella).

Nightlife

Shôko Restaurant & Lounge Club

C/Toledo 86 (91 366 87 41, www.shokomadrid.com). Metro Puerta de Toledo. **Open** midnight-6am Thur-Sat. **Admission** varies. **Map** p66 B4 ㉞
This popular space houses an Oriental restaurant (at the top) and slick lounge-club with high ceilings and minimalist decor made up of bamboo, water pools, Japanese panels and contemporary furniture. DJs spin 1990s disco, deep house and electronica. There's sometimes a dress code of shirts (for men) and no trainers. Events are often held here.

Arts & leisure

Teatro La Latina

Plaza de la Cebada 2 (91 365 28 35, www.teatrolalatina.net). Metro La Latina or Tirso de Molina. **Open** Box office 5-8pm Tue; 11am-1pm, 5pm until performance Wed-Sun. **Tickets** €15-€30. **No credit cards**. **Map** p66 B3 ㉟
Previously known for its homespun comic theatre (plenty of star names in farcical situations and lots of banging of doors), this comfortable venue has undergone a slight shift of image in recent years. Although the programme now mainly consists of quality drama (most of it 20th century), the theatre also sometimes hosts less highbrow productions, such as *Peter Pan*.

Barrio de las Letras

Spain has more bars and restaurants per capita than anywhere in the world, and you can get the impression that most of Madrid's are crowded into the wedge-shaped swathe of streets between Alcalá and C/Atocha. **Plaza Santa Ana**, at the core of the area, has some of the city's most popular bars and pavement terraces, while **Calle Huertas**, the artery of this neighbourhood, is home to several more.

The **Carrera de San Jerónimo**, one of the centres of official Madrid, borders the north of the district. On one side is the **Congreso de los Diputados**, Spain's parliament building. At the bottom of this stretch, where it meets the Paseo del Prado at the last corner of the neighbourhood, is the world-famous **Museo Thyssen-Bornemisza**.

Sights & museums

Casa-Museo Lope de Vega

C/Cervantes 11 (91 429 92 16). Metro Antón Martín. **Open** 10am-3pm Tue-Sun. Closed Aug. **Admission** €2; €1 students, over-65s. Free to all Sat. **No credit cards. Map** p67 E2 ㊱
Spain's most prolific playwright and poet, Félix Lope de Vega Carpio (1562-

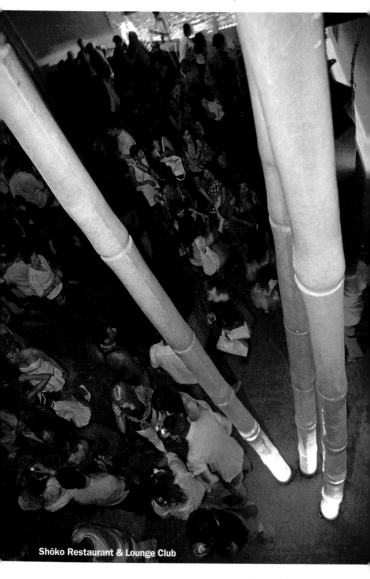

Shôko Restaurant & Lounge Club

Museo Thyssen-Bornemisza

1635) spent the last 25 years of his life in this simple, tranquil three-storey house. Guided tours are available for groups of no more than ten people. Tours last around 45 minutes and leave roughly every half an hour. Some guides speak English; call in advance to check.

Museo Colecciones Instituto de Crédito Oficial (ICO)

C/Zorrilla 3 (91 420 12 42, www. fundacionico.es). Metro Banco de España. **Open** 11am-8pm Tue-Sat; 10am-2pm Sun. **Admission** free. **Map** p67 F1 ☜

This small museum is run by the ICO, a state bank. Its collection has three main parts: most important among them is Picasso's Suite Vollard series, a milestone in 20th-century prints, dating from 1927 to 1937. There is also a fine selection of modern Spanish sculpture and some international painting from the 1980s.

Museo Thyssen-Bornemisza

Palacio de Villahermosa, Paseo del Prado 8, Barrio de las Letras (91 369 01 51, 91 420 39 44, www.museo thyssen.org). Metro Banco de España. **Open** *Permanent collection* 10am-7pm Tue-Sun. *Temporary exhibitions* Sept-mid July 10am-7pm Tue-Sun. Mid July-Aug 10am-11pm daily. **Admission** €8; €5.50 concessions; free under-12s. *Paseo del Arte ticket* €17.60. *Temporary exhibitions* €8; €5.50 concessions. **Map** p67 F2 ☜

Consisting of some 800 paintings, the private art collection of the late Baron Hans-Heinrich Thyssen-Bornemisza – purchased by the Spanish state in 1993 – is widely considered the most important in the world. The collection is housed in the Palacio de Villahermosa. In 2004, the museum unveiled a new wing, containing some 200 works from the collection of the Baron's wife, Carmen Cervera.

Works are displayed in chronological order. Beginning on the second

floor, you'll find 13th-century paintings, notably by the early Italians, such as Duccio di Buoninsegna. You finish the tour on the ground floor, where Roy Lichtenstein's *Woman in Bath* is on show. Along the way, you'll have seen examples of all the major schools.

The Thyssen is recognisably a personal collection that reflects a distinct taste, as seen in the room dedicated to early portraits, with works by Antonello da Messina and Hans Memling. Equally quirky is the section on early North American painting, including the *Presumed Portrait of George Washington's Cook* by Gilbert Stuart. But it also has its share of real masterpieces. Among the Old Masters, the works of Duccio, van Eyck and Petrus Christus stand out. The museum's most famous painting, however, is the great Florentine master Domenico Ghirlandaio's idealised *Portrait of Giovanna Tornabuoni* (1488) in the Portrait Room. Two rooms further on is Vittore Carpaccio's allegorical *Young Knight in a Landscape* (1510), another gem. Among the masters of the Flemish School represented is the sublime *Annunciation* diptych by van Eyck. The Thyssen is also strong in the German Renaissance, with works by Cranach the Elder and Albrecht Dürer.

From the later 16th century and baroque there are superb paintings, such as Titian's *Saint Jerome in the Wilderness*. There are also representative works by El Greco, Rubens and Tintoretto, and a Bernini marble, *St Sebastian*.

The German Expressionists are well represented too, with powerful works by Emil Nolde, Ernst Ludwig Kirchner, Otto Dix, Max Beckmann and Blue Rider group artists Franz Marc and Kandinsky. Also present, on the ground floor, are some more familiar modern masters – Braque, Mondrian, Klee, Max Ernst and Picasso (in the shape of his 1911 *Man with a Clarinet*), among others. The last few rooms

MADRID BY AREA

focus on the USA, with works by Georgia O'Keeffe and Edward Hopper, among others.

The Carmen Thyssen-Bornemisza collection

The space exhibits some 220 works from the private collection of 'Tita' Cervera. Access is from Room 18 on the second floor, which leads straight into rooms with early Italian and Flemish works by the likes of Jan Breughel and van Dyck. Moving on, you will enter a gallery that contains landscapes by Canaletto, Constable, Guardi and van Gogh. In the next room is 18th-century French and Italian painting and beyond that a selection of 19th-century paintings from North America. Downstairs on the first floor you'll find North American Impressionists. Two rooms are given over to Gauguin and other post-Impressionists. From then on, you move into German Expressionists, Fauvists and the early 20th-century avant-garde. The collection also contains four Rodin sculptures.

Palacio del Congreso de los Diputados (Las Cortes)

Carrera de San Jerónimo (information 91 390 60 00, guided tours 91 390 65 25, www.congreso.es). Metro Banco de España or Sevilla. **Open** Guided tours 10.30am-12.30pm Sat. Closed Aug. **Admission** free. **Map** p67 E1 ⓺⓽

Spain's parliament, the Cortes, was built in 1843-50 by Narciso Pascual y Colomer. A classical portico gives it a suitably dignified air, but the building is best distinguished by the handsome 1860 bronze lions that guard its entrance. Tourists can only visit on Saturdays, on the popular free guided tours, which cannot be booked in advance. You'll need to wait outside the iron gates on the Carrera de San Jerónimo to join a tour. Groups of more than 15, however, can book tours for visits between 9am and 2.30pm and 4pm and 6.30pm on weekdays.

Eating & drinking

Arrocería Champagneria Gala

C/Moratín 22 (91 429 25 62, www.arroceriagala.hostoi.com). Metro Antón Martín. **Open** 1-4pm, 8.30-10.30pm Tue-Thur; 1.30-3.30pm, 8.30-11pm Fri-Sun. **€€. Paella. No credit cards. Map** p67 F3 ⓵⓪⓪

This garden atrium, dripping in ivy and gaudy chandeliers, is a festive place to enjoy 28 varieties of paella. But it's the *porrón* – a long-spouted jug from which you pour a stream of wine down your throat – that makes it really fun. The place has ever so slightly become a victim of its own success, however, and the quality of the food has diminished in recent years.

Artemisa

C/Ventura de la Vega 4 (91 429 50 92, www.restauranteartesmisa.com). Metro Sevilla. **Open** 1.30-4pm, 9pm-midnight daily. **€. Vegetarian. Map** p67 E2 ⓵⓪⓵

With the nondescript decor typical of Madrid's vegetarian restaurants, Artemisa might seem like all the rest. But the salads are bigger and more creative, and the soy burgers have more flavour. The *menú de degustación* lets you try it all: veggie paella, croquetas, aubergine salad and more. There are a few non-veggie options.

Casa Alberto

C/Huertas 18 (91 429 93 56, www.casaalberto.es). Metro Antón Martín. **Open** Sept-June noon-1.30am daily. July noon-1.30am Mon-Sat. Closed Aug. **Tapas. Map** p67 E2 ⓵⓪⓶

One of the city's most evocative *tabernas*, hung with oil paintings and presided over by a septuagenarian. It still has its old zinc bar complete with running water trough to keep the wine cool and a draught beer head with five founts. Try lambs' trotters, garlicky prawns, chorizo in cider or oxtail stew as tapas, or as more substantial dishes in the restaurant at the back.

Casa Pueblo

C/León 3 (91 420 20 38). Metro Antón Martín. **Open** 5pm-2.30am daily. **Bar. Map** p67 E2 `103`

A handsome, old-fashioned jazz bar, Casa Pueblo is popular with a slightly older crowd that knows its whisky. Occasional live music includes jazz and tango (on a Wednesday).

Cervecería Alemana

Plaza Santa Ana 6 (91 429 70 33). Metro Sol. **Open** 11am-midnight Mon-Thur, Sun; 11am-2am Fri, Sat. **Bar. Map** p67 E2 `104`

Famous for being Ernest Hemingway's daily haunt. The decor is fin-de-siècle German *bierkeller*, with dusty old paintings and dark wood. The tapas can be uninspired and the waiters are unfailingly gruff, but for many this will be an essential stop.

Come Prima

C/Echegaray 27 (91 420 30 42). Metro Antón Martín. **Open** 9pm-midnight Mon; 1.30-4pm, 9pm-midnight Tue-Sat. Closed 3wks Aug. €€€. **Italian. Map** p67 E2 `105`

The toothsome risottos and own-made pastas here are a godsend: don't miss the risotto with mushrooms, parmesan and white-truffle oil, or the perfectly executed pasta with lobster. With white curtains and tablecloths, green wood-panelled walls and Italian opera posters, you could almost be in the Tuscan countryside.

Dos Gardenias

C/Santa María 13 (mobile 627 003 571). Metro Antón Martín. **Open** Oct-May 8pm-2am Tue-Sun. June-Sept 10pm-2am Tue-Sun. **No credit cards. Bar. Map** p67 E3 `106`

There's no sign on the door – just look out for this mellow little space painted in warm yellow, orange and blue and the emanating chilled-out vibes, soft

flamenco and Brazilian jazz. Kick back on a velvet sofa with the house speciality: a mojito made with brown sugar and Angostura bitters.

Los Gatos

C/Jesús 2 (91 429 30 67). Metro Antón Martín or Sevilla. **Open** 11am-2am daily. **Tapas. Map** p67 F3 `107`

With their reputation for staying out all night, *madrileños* are popularly known as *'los gatos'* (the cats) and there's nowhere better than here to begin a night prowling the tiles. The bar is hung with all manner of paraphernalia from gramophones to choirboy mannequins. Here you can get a selection of tasty canapés, and a good frothy beer. The owners opened La Anchoita bar next door in early 2011.

Lhardy

Carrera de San Jerónimo 8 (91 521 33 85, www.lhardy.com). Metro Sol. **Open** 1-3.30pm, 8.30-11pm Mon-Sat; 1-3.30pm Sun. Closed Aug. €€€€. **Castilian/French. Map** p67 D1 `108`

This landmark restaurant opened in 1839, and is credited with having introduced haute cuisine to Madrid. These days, it's rated as much for its history and belle-époque decor as for the food. The menu is as Frenchified as ever, although there's also a very refined *cocido*, good game and *callos* (tripe), in addition to an excellent, if pricey, wine list.

Midnight Rose

Hotel ME Madrid, Plaza Santa Ana 14 (91 701 60 20, www.memadrid.com/MidnightRose.html). Metro Sol or Sevilla. **Open** 1-4pm, 9pm-12.30am daily. €€€. **Fusion. Map** p67 D2 `109`

With shimmering scarlet lamps and shimmying gorgeous staff, Midnight Rose is fashionista heaven. The restaurant is located on the ground floor of the ultrahip ME hotel and if there isn't a famous face dining at the next table, you should ask for your money back. And the food? Surprisingly good, in a sort of Mediterranean-Asian fusion way.

MADRID BY AREA

Naturbier

Plaza Santa Ana 9 (91 429 39 18,
www.naturbier.com). Metro Antón
Martín or Sol. **Open** 11am-12.30am
Mon-Thur, Sun; 11am-1.30am Fri, Sat.
Bar. Map p67 D2 **110**

The least exciting-looking of all the beer
cellars lining this side of the Plaza Santa
Ana, Naturbier's big draw is its own-
made organic beer – in fact, it's the only
place in Madrid to brew its own. The
tapas are also worth checking out,
despite the somewhat creative pricing.

Olsen

C/Prado 15 (91 429 36 59,
www.olsenmadrid.com). Metro Antón
Martín or Sevilla. **Open** 1-5pm, 8pm-
2am Mon-Thur, Sun; 1-5pm, 8pm-
2.30am Fri, Sat.* **€€. Scandinavian.**
Map p67 E2 **111**

Olsen is a hugely successful, if rather
strange-sounding, Argentinian-run but
Scandinavian-flavoured restaurant
and vodka bar. The decor is all moulded beech and snow scenes. Somehow it
all serves to throw into sharper relief a
selection of the freshest food ideas
around. Especially good are the hot
corn blinis served with dishes of
caviar, sour cream, smoked salmon
and shredded wild trout.

Pizzeria Cervantes

C/León 8 (91 420 12 98). Metro Antón
Martín. **Open** 9am-1pm Mon, Wed-
Sun; 6pm-1am Tue. Closed 2wks July.
€€. Italian. Map p67 E2 **112**

Despite the name, this place exceeds
the definition of pizzeria, with a long
list of salads, crêpes, risottos and standard fare such as roast beef and
solomillo. The neighbourhood regulars are fans of the cheap breakfast
deal and love to linger over *café con*
leche and the papers.

La Platería

C/Moratín 49 (91 429 17 22). Metro
Antón Martín. **Open** 7.30am-1am
Mon-Fri; 9.30am-2am Sat, Sun. **Tapas.**
Map p67 F3 **113**

Everything from the smoked salmon
and red peppers to *caldo gallego*, grilled
asparagus or baked potatoes with eggs
and garlic, is available in half portions,
so this is a perfect place for a quick
snack 'twixt two of the big three museums. The bar is rather cramped, but
there are tables outside.

Taberna de Conspiradores

C/Moratín 33 (91 369 4741, www.
conspiradores.com). Metro Antón
Martín. **Open** 1pm-1am Mon-Thur,
Sun; 1pm-2am Fri, Sat. **Tapas.**
Map p67 F3 **114**

The food, wine and liqueurs on offer
here are all from Extremadura, unusually. The speciality is *migas* – fried
breadcrumbs baked with sausage, garlic and pancetta – and a dense venison
stew. The small space occasionally
hosts world music or flamenco gigs.

Taberna La Dolores

Plaza de Jesús 4 (91 429 22 43). Metro
Antón Martín. **Open** 11am-1am Mon-
Thur; 11am-2am Fri-Sun. **No credit**
cards. Tapas. Map p67 F2 **115**

Another Madrid classic, with wonderful tiling outside and rows of dusty
beer steins inside, La Dolores has been
serving ice-cold frothy beer since the
1920s. There's a short list of tapas,
which are good if a bit expensive.
Specialities are smoked fish, anchovies
and *mojama* (wind-dried tuna).

La Vaca Verónica

C/Moratín 38 (91 429 78 27, www.
lavaca veronica.es). Metro Antón
Martín. **Open** 1-4.30pm, 8.30pm-
12.30am Mon-Sat; 1-4.30pm Sun. **Pan-**
European. €€€. Map p67 F3 **116**

With canary-yellow walls, bright
paintings and a certain Gallic charm,
Veronica the Cow attracts business
types and hipsters alike. It's a fine
choice for a quality *menú del día*. Pesto
pasta, the abundant 'cow's platter' of
chorizo, *morcilla* (black blood sausage)
and other meats, and various salads
are just some of the options.

Olsen

La Venencia

C/Echegaray 7 (91 429 73 13). Metro Sevilla or Sol. **Open** 1-3.30pm, 7.30pm-1.30am daily. **No credit cards. Bar.** **Map** p67 E2 117

Totally unreconstructed, La Venencia is gloriously shabby, with old, peeling sherry posters, barrels behind the bar and walls burnished gold by decades of tobacco smoke. It serves only sherry, along with manchego cheese, *cecina* (air-dried beef) and chorizo by way of tapas. Orders are still chalked up on the bar, and an enamel sign asks customers not to spit on the floor.

Shopping

Guantes Luque

C/Espoz y Mina 3 (91 522 32 87). Metro Sol. **Open** 10am-1.30pm, 5-8pm Mon-Sat. **Map** p67 D2 118

This old-fashioned glove shop has been open for more than 125 years. Luque sells gloves in all sizes, colours and materials, covering all types of wool, silk and leather. Prices range from €20 to €300.

Libreria Desnivel

Plaza Matute 6 (91 429 97 40, www.libreriadesnivel.com). Metro Antón Martín. **Open** 10am-2pm, 4.30-8pm Mon-Sat. **Map** p67 E3 119

An excellent travel and adventure bookshop. Desnivel's own publications include walking and climbing guides, and the shop also has information on organised hikes and so on.

Museo del Jamón

Carrera de San Jerónimo 6 (91 521 03 46, www.museodeljamon.es). Metro Sol. **Open** 9am-midnight daily. **Map** p67 D1 120

Dotted around town, the various branches of the 'Ham Museum' are a sight to behold, with dozens of hams dangling from the ceiling. Sample their wares at the bar or in their restaurants.

Objetos de Arte Toledano

Paseo del Prado 10 (91 429 50 00, www.armasmedievales.com). Metro Banco de España. **Open** 10am-7.45pm Mon-Sat. **Map** p67 F2 121

Located across from the Prado, this souvenir shop par excellence sells traditional *españoladas* such as fans, flamenco and bullfighting dolls. A great place to find that gift for your kitsch-loving friends.

Nightlife

La Boca del Lobo

C/Echegaray 11 (91 429 70 13, www.labocadellobo.com). Metro Sevilla. **Open** midnight-3.30am Tue, Thur-Sun. **Admission** (incl 1 drink) €5-€10, otherwise free. **Map** p67 E2 122

Unselfconsciously hip and unremittingly friendly, La Boca del Lobo combines live bands with a heady mix of house, breakbeats and R&B. Emerge from the sweaty downstairs dancefloor to the cramped bar area by the entrance or retire upstairs to watch the DJ spin a beguiling cocktail of music.

El Burladero

C/Echegaray 19 (no phone, www.elburladerocopas.com). Metro Sevilla or Sol. **Open** 8pm-4am daily. **Admission** free. **No credit cards.** **Map** p67 E2 123

A cosmopolitan crowd, buzzing to the sound of flamenco and rumba, throngs the Moorish arches. Upstairs the rumba rumbles but doesn't dominate. Head up here for respite and a chat with the languid barman, but the frenzied guitar and pistol-shot handclapping will eventually lure you back.

Café Central

Plaza del Ángel 10 (91 369 41 43, www.cafecentralmadrid.com). Metro Antón Martín or Sol. **Open** 1.30pm-2.30am Mon-Thur, Sun; 1.30pm-3.30am Fri, Sat. Concerts 10pm-midnight. **Admission** *Gigs* €7-€12. **Map** p67 D2 124

For many years now, this beautiful place with high ceilings and elegant decor has been *the* place to get your jazz fix in Madrid. George Adams, Don Pullen, Ben Sidran and Bob Sands have all taken the stage, as well as Spanish stalwarts such as Chano Dominguez, Jorge Pardo and the oldest and greatest of them all, Pedro Iturralde.

Café Populart

C/Huertas 22 (91 429 84 07, www.populart.es). Metro Antón Martín. **Open** 6pm-2.30am Mon-Thur, Sun; 6pm-3.30am Fri, Sat. Concerts 10.15pm-11.30pm. **Admission** free. **Map** p67 D2 **125**

Escape from the beer-crawl route that is Huertas by slipping into this superb jazz club. There's no cover charge, but the drinks are a bit pricey. A strong backer of Spanish jazz and host to many an international artist, Populart features jazz and blues every night with two shows, one at 11.30pm and the other at 12.30am.

Las Cuevas de Sésamo

C/Príncipe 7 (91 429 65 24). Metro Sevilla or Sol. **Open** 7pm-2am Mon-Thur, Sun; 7pm-3am Fri, Sat. **Admission** free. **No credit cards**. **Map** p67 E2 **126**

It's easy to find this basement cavern at weekends – just look for the queue that snakes out of the door. But it's well worth the wait for what's inside: Las Cuevas is a sit-down affair, with live piano music from 9pm (except Monday), where punters take advantage of the cheapish drinks (the place is famous for its sangria) and friendly atmosphere. A good choice to start the night rather than a final destination.

La Fontana de Oro

C/Victoria 3 (91 531 04 20, www.la fontanadeoro.es). Metro Sol. **Open** noon-6am daily. **Admission** free. **Map** p67 D1 **127**

As Madrid's oldest bar, this place used to be a real institution. These days, it's an Irish theme bar. It's run-of-the-mill by day, but everything changes when night falls. Then the crowd packs in, fuelling up for the night ahead and losing themselves to a mix of classic beer anthems and a variety of live music.

Mondo

C/Arlabán 7 (91 523 86 54/91 522 88 26, www.web-mondo.com). Metro Sevilla. **Open** 1am-6am Thur; 12.30am-7am Sat. **Admission** (incl 1 drink) €13 (€11 before 2.30am) Thur; €14 (€12 before 2.30am) Fri, Sat. **Map** p67 E1 **128**

Mondo has become one of the most lauded spots in the city for electronica and techno, but you can also hear funk, house and disco. A regular stable of high-profile guest DJs play here, with previous guests including Carl Craig, Layo & Bushwacka and Alex Guerra.

Teatro Kapital

C/Atocha 125 (91 420 29 06, www.grupo-kapital.com). Metro Atocha. **Open** 11.30pm-6am Thur-Sun. **Admission** €12-€16. **Map** p67 F4 **129**

The Godzilla of Madrid clubs. Each of the seven storeys has something different to offer: the main dancefloor and bars are at ground level; the first floor has karaoke; the second R&B and hip hop; the third cosy cocktail bars; the fourth is Spanish disco; the fifth has a cinema and more cool sounds, and at the top is a terrace with a retractable roof. No trainers.

Arts & leisure

Cine Estudio de Bellas Artes

C/Alcalá 42 (91 360 54 00, www.circulobellasartes.com). Metro Banco de España. **Tickets** €5; €3.40 members and concessions. **No credit cards**. **Map** p67 E1 **130**

Originally a theatre, this repertory cinema is part of the grand Círculo de

Museo Nacional Centro de Arte Reina Sofía p94

Bellas Artes building. The sound system is excellent, and the programme of themed film seasons goes down well with the trendy audience.

Teatro Español

C/Príncipe 25(box office 91 360 14 84, information 91 360 14 80). Metro Sevilla or Sol. **Tickets** €3-€20. **No credit cards. Map** p67 E2 **131**

This grand theatre on Plaza Santa Ana dates back to 1745, but that doesn't mean it's old-fashioned – in fact it has enjoyed some fairly radical programming in recent years. In 2010, the varied programme included a production of *Macbeth* and a modern tango show by the Mora Godoy Tango Company.

Teatro de la Zarzuela

C/Jovellanos 4, Barrio de las Letras (box office 91 524 54 10, http:// teatrodelazarzuela.mcu.es). Metro Banco de España. **Main season** Sept-July. **Tickets** €5-€42. **Map** p67 E1 **132**

The Teatro de la Zarzuela, which served as an opera house for many years previous to the Teatro Real's renovation, is now principally devoted to its raison d'être – staging *zarzuela*, home-grown Spanish operetta. Despite its uncool image, it retains considerable popularity. Accompanying the Teatro's packed *zarzuela* programme are performances of dance (often by the Ballet Nacional), music, plays, conferences and special family-orientated shows.

Lavapiés

South of Sol and the Plaza Mayor is the area traditionally considered the home of Madrid's *castizos*, rough-diamond chirpy types straight out of a Spanish *My Fair Lady*. Since the end of the 1990s, however, Lavapiés has taken on a new characteristic: as a big recipient of non-Spanish immigration and thus one of the city's most multicultural areas.

East of neighbouring La Latina is the **Rastro**, Madrid's Sunday flea market. It runs all the way down Ribera de Curtidores to the Ronda de Toledo from Plaza Cascorro.

If, on the other hand, you head from Plaza Cascorro slightly eastwards down **C/Embajadores**, you will enter Lavapiés proper. The area has sometimes been portrayed as an urban crime zone. However, while there are places in Lavapiés it's probably best to steer clear of (the small square halfway down Mesón de Paredes, by C/Cabestreros, is the most obvious example), it would be a shame if this led anyone to avoid the whole neighbourhood, for this web of sloping, winding streets remains one of the most characterful parts of Old Madrid.

The recently renovated **Plaza de Lavapiés** has several good cafés and restaurants. Running away from the south-east corner of the Plaza de Lavapiés is **C/Argumosa**, with shops, restaurants and outdoor-terrace bars. Argumosa leads towards Atocha and the **Museo Nacional Centro de Arte Reina Sofía** (see p94).

Sights & museums

La Casa Encendida

Ronda de Valencia 2 (90 243 03 22, www.lacasaencendida.com). Metro Embajadores. **Open** 10am-9.45pm daily. **Admission** free. **Map** p67 D5 **133**

This exciting new multidisciplinary centre in a large neo-Mudéjar building was conceived as a space for cultural interchange. Spread over four floors, the 'Burning House' has exhibitions principally by emerging artists working in all genres, but also features cutting-edge performance art and music (including short seasons of video artists) and activities for kids. The centre also includes a Fairtrade shop, a library and classrooms for courses in, above all, IT and languages.

Museo Nacional Centro de Arte Reina Sofía

Edificio Sabatini C/Santa Isabel 52. Edificio Nouvel Plaza del Emperador Carlos V s/n (91 774 10 00, www. museoreinasofia.es). Metro Atocha. **Open** 10am-9pm Mon, Wed-Sat; 10am-2.30pm Sun. **Admission** €6; €3 groups of 15 or more; free students, under-18s, over-65s. Free to all 7-9pm Mon, Wed-Fri; 2.30-9pm Sat; all day Sun. *Paseo del Arte ticket* €17.60. **Map** p67 F4 ⓵⓷⓸

The Reina Sofía's great jewel is unquestionably *Guernica*, Picasso's impassioned denunciation of war and fascism, a painting that commemorates the destruction in 1937 of the Basque town of Guernica by German bombers that flew in support of the Francoist forces in the Spanish Civil War.

The rest of the museum's permanent collection has been criticised as being merely a reasonable collection of Spanish modern art, with some thin coverage of non-Spanish artists, rather than an outstanding international collection. It certainly contains works by practically all the major Spanish artists of the 20th century – Picasso, Dalí, Miró, Julio González, Tàpies, Alfonso Ponce de León and Antonio Saura are all present – but even here there are few major works.

The collection has recently been reorganised in a way that interweaves common influences, themes and ideas; so works by Luis Buñuel are now displayed alongside works by Picasso, Goya, Solana and even African art. The permanent collection is spread over the first, second and fourth floors of the Sabatini building, while increasingly international temporary shows are weaved throughout. The ground floor also features Espacio Uno, a space for

more cutting-edge work. The second floor is still the most important, housing Collection 1 – Historical Avant-Garde. This includes 'Guernica and the 1930s' in Room 206, with works by Juan Miró, Oskar Schlemmer, Torres García, and, of course, Picasso. Other themes explored on this floor include Modernity, Progress and Decadentism, with works by Picasso and José Gutiérrez Solana; the New Culture in Spain; Dalí, Surrealism and Revolution; Juan Gris; and Cubism, with more works by Picasso, as well as Georges Braque and Sonia Delaunay.

Collection 2 – Triumph and Failure of Modernity: the 1950s and 1960s, is on the fourth floor, in Room 405. This section explores themes such as European art after World War II, and the 'End of Painting', with more works by Picasso and Miró.

Collection 3 – Paradigm Shift is in Room 104 on the first floor, with works by Yves Klein, Robert Rauschenberg, Eduardo Arroyo and Raymond Hains, mainly from the 1960s and '70s.

Puerta de Toledo

Glorieta de la Puerta de Toledo. Metro Puerta de Toledo. **Map** p66 B5 ⓵⓷⓹

Slightly swallowed up in the traffic at the meeting point of the Old City and the roads in from the south-west, this neo-classical gate was one of the monuments commissioned by Napoleon's brother Joseph in his brief span as King of Spain. After his departure, it was rejigged to honour the delegates from the Cortes in Cádiz, and then King Fernando VII.

Eating & drinking

Baisakhi

C/Lavapiés 42 (91 521 80 31). Metro Lavapiés. **Open** 12.30pm-4pm, 8pm-midnight daily. **€**. **Indian**. **Map** p67 D4 ⓵⓷⓺

For good-value Indian food, Baisakhi is probably the best bet along what has become Madrid's answer to Brick

Lane. The waiters all speak English, and the dishes on the menu include all the old faves. The terrace is preferable to the slightly shabby interior.

Café Melo's

C/Ave María 44 (91 527 50 54). Metro Lavapiés. **Open** 8pm-1.30am Tue-Sat. Closed Aug. **No credit cards. Tapas.** **Map** p67 D4 **137**

It's got all the aesthetic charm of a kebab shop, but this bright little bar is something of a classic. It's famous for its *zapatillas* – huge, open sandwiches (the word, like ciabatta, means 'slipper') with a variety of toppings. A big favourite for late-night munchies with the bohemian element of the *barrio*.

Casa Amadeo Los Caracoles

Plaza de Cascorro 18 (91 365 94 39). Metro La Latina. **Open** 10.30am-3.30pm, 7-10.30pm Tue-Sat; 10.30am-4pm Sun. **No credit cards. Tapas.** **Map** p66 C3 **138**

Again, this is no looker, but it's a popular post-Rastro stop. Its specialities include the eponymous snails in spicy sauce, knuckle of ham, and *zarajo*, the lamb's intestines wrapped round sticks without which your Madrid trip would not be complete.

Casa de Granada

C/Doctor Cortezo 17 (91 369 35 96/reservations 91 420 08 25). Metro Tirso de Molina. **Open** noon-midnight Mon-Sat; 11am-8pm Sun. **Tapas.** **Map** p327 G/H13 **139**

A very ordinary bar serving very ordinary food, which has an extraordinary view. To get in, ring the buzzer on street level, and then ride the lift all the way up to the sixth floor – in summer you'll have to fight tooth and nail for a seat on the terrace.

La Casa de las Tostas

C/Argumosa 29 (91 527 08 42). Metro Lavapiés. **Open** noon-4pm, 7.30pm-1am Tue-Thur, Sun; 7.30pm-

2am Fri, Sat. **No credit cards. Tapas. Map** p67 E4 **140**

Welcome to the House of Toast. Toast with scrambled eggs, prawns and wild mushrooms; toast with salmon in white vermouth; toast with gammon and melted cheese; toast with anchovies and roquefort. And most importantly, toast with wine, many available by the glass.

El Económico Soidemersol

C/Argumosa 9 (91 528 16 55, http://restauranteeleconomico.es). Metro Atocha. **Open** 9am-2am Tue-Sun. **€€. Castilian. Map** p67 E4 **141**

Also confusingly known as Los Remedios (turn it backwards to see why), the Soidemersol is something of an institution. In recent years, the premises have had a bit of a facelift, but it retains a friendly neighbourhood feel, along with the wooden furniture and original tiling. Try the seafood risotto, calf's liver and onions, or beef ragoût with vegetables. There are tables outside in summer.

Freiduría de Gallinejas

C/Embajadores 84 (91 517 59 33, www.mformacion.com/gallinejas). Metro Embajadores. **Open** 11am-11pm Mon-Sat. Closed 3wks Aug. **€. Castilian. No credit cards. Map** p67 D5 **142**

Still going strong after a century, this offal institution offers superbly prepared testicles, glands and stomach linings, all accompanied by strong red wine. Worth checking out just for the lively scene and for a taste of Old Madrid's innard circle.

Gaudeamus Café

C/Tribulete 14 (91 528 25 94, www.gaudeamuscafe.com). Metro Lavapiés. **Open** 6pm-midnight Mon-Sat. **No credit cards. Café. Map** p67 D5 **143**

Gaudeamus attracts cultured types in their droves. They come for the large roof terrace and the 'in-the-know' vibe (the place isn't visible from the outside

– you have to walk through the university building to reach the lift that takes you up to the café). The partitioned-off restaurant area has two seatings – at 8.30pm and 10.15pm.

Los Hermanos

C/Rodas 28 (91 468 33 13). Metro Tirso de Molina. **Open** 7am-11pm Mon-Fri; 7am-5pm Sun. Closed Aug. **Tapas. Map** p66 C4 **144**

Just off the main drag of the Rastro is this bar with a strong neighbourhood feel, generous complimentary tapas, a huge range of raciones or a great selection of *bocadillos*, including a hangover-busting bacon and egg. On Sundays, there's a well-priced *menú del día* for the market crowd.

Moharaj

C/Ave María 26 (91 467 86 02, http://moharajcomidaindiamadrid.com). Metro Lavapiés. **Open** noon-5pm, 8pm-midnight daily. **€. Indian. Map** p67 D3 **145**

It may not look fancy, but among curry lovers Moharaj is widely believed to serve the best Indian food in Madrid. If there are four of you, order the Moharaj platter to start, which has samosas, bhajis and more, then maybe prawn rezala, lamb jalfrezi, beef madras and matar paneer. But everything is tasty.

La Musa de Espronceda

C/Santa Isabel 17 (91 539 12 84). Metro Antón Martín. **Open** 1.30-4pm, 8pm-midnight daily. **Tapas. Map** p67 E3 **146**

La Musa is known for its *pinchos* – don't miss the butternut squash, goat's cheese and caramelised onion version, or the brie wrapped in bacon. The tortilla is also excellent, while the mojitos are well made and priced. Blackboards, literary posters and globe lights around a central bar lend the place an arty vibe.

Nuevo Café Barbieri

C/Ave María 45 (91 527 36 58). Metro Lavapiés. **Open** 4pm-2am Tue-Thur, Sun; 4pm-2.30am Fri, Sat. **No credit cards. Café. Map** p67 D4 **147**

An airy and peaceful space with high ceilings and a dusty elegance. A favourite haunt of journos and wannabe travel writers, Barbieri has plenty of newspapers and magazines, but its ordinary coffee comes at a premium and the service lacks much verve.

La Taberna de Antonio Sánchez

C/Mesón de Paredes 13 (91 539 78 26). Metro Tirso de Molina. **Open** noon-4pm, 8pm-midnight Tue-Sat; noon-4pm Sun. **Tapas. Map** p66 C3 **148**

Little changes at this historic bar, from the zinc bar to the bull's head on the wall. Its various owners have all been involved in bullfighting, and *tertulias* of critics, *toreros* and aficionados are still held here. It's local and friendly, with superior tapas (the best is the scrumptious salad you get free with a drink).

Taberna El Sur

C/Torrecilla del Leal 12 (91 527 83 40). Metro Antón Martín. **Open** 8pm-midnight Tue-Thur; 1-5pm, 8pm-1am Fri-Sun. **Tapas. Map** p67 E3 **149**

Named after Victor Erice's seminal film, decorated with cinematic posters and popular with long-haired soulful types from the nearby Filmoteca. Juan, the friendly owner, offers an interesting selection of raciones: try *ropa vieja* (shredded beef, Cuban style) with fried potatoes or 'Arabian' lentils.

Shopping

Fotocasión

C/Ribera de Curtidores 22 (91 467 64 91, www.fotocasion.es). Metro Puerta de Toledo. **Open** 10am-2pm, 4.30-8.30pm Mon-Fri; 10am-2pm Sat, Sun. **Map** p66 C5 **151**

A treasure trove for photographers and camera collectors. Owner José Luis Mur is a walking encyclopedia on cameras; he also has great offers on spare parts and new and second-hand cameras.

Pepita is Dead

C/Doctor Fourquet 10 (91 528 87 88, www.pepitaisdead.es). Metro Atocha. **Open** 11am-2pm, 5-8.30pm Mon-Sat. Closed 3wks Aug. **Map** p67 F4 ⓲

Pepita is Dead specialises in vintage clothing. These items – mens-, womens- and childrenswear, plus accessories – are all unworn originals, carefully chosen from the '60s to the '80s.

El Rastro

C/Ribera de Curtidores, between Plaza de Cascorro & Ronda de Toledo (no phone, www.elrastro.org). Metro La Latina. **Open** dawn-approx 2pm Sun. **Map** p66 C4 ⓲

Stalls start setting up from 8am at the city's most famous fleamarket, with the hardcore bargain-hunters arriving soon afterwards, though trading officially begins at 9am. In truth, there are few real deals to be had these days, but in among the tat are Moroccan stalls selling lovely leather bags (though be sure to haggle hard), and antiques stalls and shops that are worth a trawl. In any case, it's still a quintessential stop on the tourist map. Do keep an eye on your bag though.

El Transformista

C/Mirà el Rio Baja 18 (91 539 88 33). Metro Puerta de Toledo. **Open** 11am-2pm Tue-Sun. **No credit cards.** **Map** p66 B5 ⓲

Original '50s and '60s furniture and collectibles are up for grabs at this shop. Almodóvar is rumoured to source items for his movies here.

Nightlife

Candela

C/Olmo 2 (91 467 33 82). Metro Antón Martín. **Open** 11pm-5.30am Mon-Thur, Sun; 11pm-6am Fri, Sat. **No credit cards.** **Map** p67 D3 ⓲

An ideal place to soak up flamenco atmosphere, though performances are impromptu and only take place downstairs and after hours. Still, this in-the-know watering hole for professional musicians and amateurs is welcoming to knowledgeable and respectful aficionados.

El Juglar

C/Lavapiés 37 (91 528 43 81, www.salajuglar.com). Metro Lavapiés. **Open** 9.30pm-3am Mon-Wed, Sun; 9.30pm-3.30am Thur-Sat. Concerts usually start at 10pm. **Admission** €5-€10. **No credit cards.** **Map** p67 D3 ⓲

A bohemian, laid-back hangout, the bare red brick and chrome front bar providing a chilled background for a soundtrack of jazz and soul. After midnight the rhythm speeds up in the back as the resident DJ Señores de Funk spins a mix of souped-up soul, Latin and funk. Sunday nights see flamenco performed by students from the Amor de Dios school.

El Mojito

C/Olmo 6 (no phone). Metro Tirso de Molina or Antón Martín. **Open** 9pm-2.30am daily. **Admission** free. **No credit cards.** **Map** p67 D3 ⓲

This cute Lavapiés locale has a retro vibe (Barbie dolls in compromising positions are part of the decor) and excellent cocktails. It attracts a friendly, mixed crowd of both gays and metrosexuals.

La Ventura

C/Olmo 31 (no phone). Metro Antón Martín. **Open** 10.30pm-2.30am Tue-Thur; 11pm-3am Fri, Sat; 8pm-2.30am Sun. **Admission** free. **No credit cards.** **Map** p67 E3 ⓲

If you've been in Madrid a while, you're sure to have been here at least once. Lounge on full-length floor cushions while soaking up the measured sounds of trip hop and dub. Later the pace hots up a little with breakbeat, electronica and house thrown in, and the dancefloor is filled by a cosmopolitan crowd of students, ex-students and the casually hip.

Arts & leisure

Casa Patas

C/Cañizares 10 (91 369 04 96, www.casapatas.com). Metro Antón Martín. **Open** 1-4.30pm, 8pm-midnight Mon-Thur; 1-4.30pm, 7.30pm-1am Fri, Sat. Performances 10.30pm Mon-Thur; 9pm, midnight Fri, Sat. Closed 3 wks Aug. **Admission** (incl 1 drink) €31. **Map** p67 D3 ⓵⓹⓽

A plush and somewhat pricey place to savour traditional or *nuevo* flamenco. Recent topliners have included Chaquetón, Remedios Amaya and Niña Pastori. With a reputation to maintain, Casa Patas is deservedly proud of its standing and treats its loyal, knowledgeable and sometimes intimidating audience with a great deal of respect.

Cine Doré (Filmoteca Española)

C/Santa Isabel 3 (box office 91 369 11 25, information 91 369 21 18, bookshop 91 369 46 73). Metro Antón Martín. **Open** Bar-cafés 5pm-12.30am Tue-Sun. Bookshop 5.30-10pm Tue-Sun. **Tickets** €2.50; €2 concessions. 10 films €20, €15 concessions. **No credit cards. Map** p67 E3 ⓵⓺⓪

Featured in films by Almodóvar, the art nouveau national film theatre was founded more than 50 years ago. A fold-out monthly programme features details of its eclectic seasons of films from the Spanish National Archive and world cinema. The outdoor rooftop cinema and bar are open – and unsurprisingly very popular – in the summer. Note that the box office opens at 5.15pm and stays open until 15 minutes after the start of the last performance of the night. Advance tickets can only be bought for the following day's performance and then only up until a third of capacity has been booked. Note also that you can only buy three tickets per person for each performance.

Sala Mirador

C/Doctor Fourquet 31 (91 539 57 67, www.cnc-eca.es). Metro Atocha or Lavapiés. **Open** Box office 1hr before performance Thur-Sun. Closed Aug. **Tickets** €13-€16. **No credit cards. Map** p67 E5 ⓵⓺⓵

Doubling as theatre/dance school and performance space, this is also the site of the long-running *La Katarsis del Tomatazo*, performed every Friday and Saturday night at 10.30pm. The audience are given tomatoes as they enter, which they can use to express their feelings on this singing and dancing cabaret.

Teatro Monumental

C/Atocha 65s (91 429 12 81, www.rtve.es). Metro Antón Martín. **Open** Box office 11am-2pm, 5-7pm daily. Concerts Oct-May 8pm Thur, Fri. Main season Oct-March. **Tickets** €9-€22. **Map** p67 E3 ⓵⓺⓶

The Monumental's main purpose is to record broadcast concerts by the RTVE Orchestra and Choir – consequently it may not have the glitz of the Teatro Real, but it does have excellent acoustics and high-quality performances. The principal diet here is generally concerts, with a side order of opera and *zarzuela*.

Teatro Nuevo Apolo

Plaza de Tirso de Molina 1 (91 369 06 37). Metro Tirso de Molina. **Open** Box office 11.30am-1.30pm, 5-9pm Tue-Sat; 5-7pm Sun. Closed mid July-mid Aug. **Tickets** €20-€30. **No credit cards** (except for purchases exceeding €150). **Map** p67 D3 ⓵⓺⓷

In recent seasons, this venue has welcomed such exciting acts as dancer Joaquin Cortes and the Mayumana dance-percussion troupe. One of the big shows in 2010 was a production of Bizet's *Carmen* by the Ballet Flamenco de Madrid.

Gaudeamus Café p95

Malasaña p112

Old City: North of Gran Via

Chueca & Alonso Martínez

Bounded by the Gran Vía, the Paseo de Recoletos and C/Fuencarral, Chueca has undergone a spectacular revival since the 1980s, due, above all, to it becoming the gay centre of Madrid. The epicentre of the scene is **Plaza de Chueca**; its terraces are packed on summer nights.

The north side of the district, above C/Fernando VI, is often referred to as **Alonso Martínez**, after the metro station. It's not so much part of 'gay Chueca' but instead is one of the foremost preserves of Madrid's teen scene.

Sights & museums

Museo de Historia

C/Fuencarral 78 (91 588 86 72, www.munimadrid.es/museomunicipal).
Metro Tribunal. **Open** Closed at time of writing; call or see website for future opening times. **Admission** free. **Map** p103 D3 ①

This museum – previously the Museo Municipal – has been closed for several years for renovation work. Parts of the building may be reopening in 2011; call or see the website for details. The building itself boasts an exuberantly ornate entrance by Pedro de Ribera, one of the finest examples of baroque architecture in Madrid, and worth seeing in itself. For pre-Habsburg Madrid, visit the Museo de los Orígenes (see p68).

Museo del Romanticismo

C/San Mateo 13 (91 448 10 45, http://museoromanticismo.mcu.es).
Metro Tribunal. **Open** *May-Oct* 9.30am-8.30pm Tue-Sat; 10am-3pm Sun. *Nov-Apr* 9.30am-6.30pm Tue-Sat; 10am-3pm Sun. **Admission** €3; €1.50 concessions. Free to all from 2pm Sat. **Map** p103 E3 ②

The newly reopened Museo del Romanticismo contains a charming collection of furniture, paintings, ornaments, early pianos and other pieces that evoke the Romantic period of 19th-century Spain. As well as these objets d'art there are a paintings from the likes of Francisco Goya and Vicente López Portaña, thousands of prints and lithographs and a substantial number of antique photographs.

Sociedad General de Autores y Editores (Palacio Longoria)

C/Fernando VI 4 (91 349 95 50). Metro Alonso Martínez. **Map** p103 E3 ❸
Given the extraordinary output of Catalan modernista architects such as Gaudí in Barcelona in the early 20th century, it is remarkable that there is not a single example of their work in Madrid. The only thing at all like it is this building in Chueca, designed by José Grasés Riera in 1902 as a residence for banker Javier González Longoria. The voluptuous façade looks as if it was formed out of wet sand, moulded by an expert in giant cake decoration.

Eating & drinking

Ángel Sierra

C/Gravina 11 (91 531 01 26). Metro Chueca. **Open** 12.30pm-2.30am Mon-Sat; 12.30pm-2am Sun. **No credit cards. Bar. Map** p103 E4 ❹
This battered old bar with its tiled walls, zinc bar top, overflowing sink and glasses stacked on wooden slats has become the Chueca meeting-place par excellence, thanks to its position overlooking the main square. A newer room at the back, however, has a faux-pub look enhanced with amplified MOR radio and a rule that only doubles and pints are served after midnight.

Bar Cock

C/Reina 16 (91 532 28 26, www.barcock.com). Metro Gran Via.
Open *Sept-June* 7pm-3am Mon-Thur,

Vinoculture

Fine wines, fine prices.

Madrid is an oenophile's playground, with none of the solemnity and hefty price-tags attached to wine-drinking elsewhere. Everyone drinks it here, from builders to nuns.

Wine-lovers around the globe have now caught on to the fact that Spanish labels are the best value for your euro. The sad fact remains, however, that a lot of bars serve plonk. To taste the good stuff, get thee to a wine bar. Madrid has a number of cosy little *enotecas* where you can settle in at the bar and try different wines by the glass. **La Cruzada** (C/Amnistía 8, 91 548 01 31), for example, offers a great selection of reasonably priced *vinos*. King Alfonso XII reportedly used to frequent this bar when he needed to escape the nearby royal palace for a clandestine tipple. Other spots for quality wines include **La Taberna de Cien Vinos** (C/Nuncio 17), **González** (see p89), **Entrevinos** (C/Ferraz 36, 91 548 31 14) and **Vinoteca Barbechera** (see p89).

An entertaining way to dive into Spanish wine is to attend one of Madrid's wine-tasting classes, known as *cursos de cata*, which get you happily swirling, sniffing and sipping good wine. The city's best wine shops, **Reserva y Cata** (see p110), **Lavinia** (see p145) and **Bodegas Santa Cecilia** (www.santacecilia.es) offer regular *cursos de cata* in Spanish; for English courses, try **AtSpain** (91 547 50 91, www.atspain.com).

Old City: North of Gran Vía

CHAMBERÍ

C/MELÉNDEZ VALDÉS
C/ARAPILES

C/F. GARRIDO

C/GAZTAMBIDE
C/ANDRÉS MELLADO
C/GUZMÁN EL
C/BLASCO DE GARAY
C/VALLEHERMOSO
PLAZA DEL CON

C/RODRÍGUEZ SAN PEDRO
C/RODRÍGUEZ SAN PEDRO
C/RODRÍGUEZ SAN PEDRO

C/GAZTAMBIDE
C/GALILEO

Argüelles
Metro

C/FRANCISCO DE RICCI
C/E. CARRERE

Juzgado
Municipal

Plaza
Conde
del Valle
Suchil

C/SAN BERNARDO
C/J. DE LA
QUINTANA
C/MONTERLEON
C/SANDOVAL

San Bernardo 61
Metro

C/ALBERTO AGUILERA

Buen
Suceso
Metro

C/SANTA CRUZ DE MARCENADO
C/SERRANO JOVER
C/BERNARDO LÓPEZ

Glorieta de
Ruíz Jiménez

C/CARRANZA

C/QUINTANA

93

C/MANUELA MALASAÑA

C/SANTA CRUZ DE MARCENADO

C/SANTA CRUZ DE MARCENADO
C/SAN HERMENEGILDO

C/MONTSERRAT

C/MONTELEON
C/G. ROBLES
C/DIVINO PASTO

Convento Santa María
La Real de Monserrat

C/NOBLES
C/ALTAMIRANO
C/REY FRANCISCO

Palacio
Duque
de Liria

55

Centro Cultural
del Conde Duque

108

Convento
Comendadoras
Plaza de
las Comendadoras

64
153

C/QUIÑONES
C/CHRISTO

Convento de
la Visitación

C/DAOIZ

Plaza
Dos de Mayo

C/EVARISTO SAN MIGUEL

Metro
Ventura
Rodríguez

C/QUINTANA
C/DUQUE DE LIRIA

Antiguo
Cuartel
del Conde
Duque

94
95
85

Plaza
Guardías
de Corps

98
105

104

C/CACHERO
C/PALMA

73
Las Maravillas

C/SAN DIMAS
C/CAMANIEL

65

CONDE
DUQUE

C/SAN VICENTE FERRER
66

101

C/CINTOR
C/RODRÍGUEZ
C/AMANIEL

Plaza de
Cristino Martos

71

TRAVESÍA DEL CONDE DUQUE

C/SAN BERNARDO

92
Noviciado
Metro

C/NOVICIADO
C/ESPÍRITU SANTO

89

C/POZAS

Plaza
Juan Pujol

C/TESORO

106 San
Marcos

C/SAN LEONARDO
C/LOS AMIGOS

C/GUERRERO

57

80

C/SAN BERNARDINO

C/DOS DE
JUNIO

C/PEZ

C/LAS MINAS

C/MARQUÉS DE SANTA ANA

102

C/JESÚS DEL VALLE

MALASAÑA

Convento de
San Plácido

59

Plaza
Conde
Toreno

C/LOS REYES

C/MANZANA

C/AMANIEL

Plaza
Mostenses

C/A. GRILO

C/CRUZ VERDE
C/PIZARRO

C/BORREGO
C/LUNA

C/MADERA
C/SAN ROQUE
C/CORREDER

91

Museo
Cerralbo

Jardines
Ferraz

Plaza de España

Plaza
de España
Metro

C/LOS REYES

C/CARBONAL MATEO
C/LEÓN

C/R. LEÓN

C/SAN BERNARDO

TRAVESÍA
PARADA

C/ESTRELLA

San Martín

C/BAILÉN

CUESTA DE SAN VICENTE

C/FLOR BAJA

C/GRAN VÍA

100

C/MARQUÉS LEGANÉS

C/FLOR ALTA

C/SILVA

C/GRAN VÍA

C/TUDESCOS

C/M. MOYA

Palacio
del Senado

C/IRIO

PLAZA DE LA M. ESPAÑOLA
C/LA ENCARNACIÓN

C/CEBADA
C/SILVA

C/JACOMETREZO

Metro

C/PRECIADOS

Plaza
Callao
Metro
Callao

C/CARMEN
C/CARMEN

Palacio
Marqués
Grimaldi

Jardines
Sabatini

C/BAILÉN

Convento de
la Encarnación

Santo
Domingo
Metro

C/PRECIADOS
C/TETUÁN

❶ Sights & museums
❶ Eating & drinking
❶ Shopping
❶ Nightlife
❶ Arts & leisure

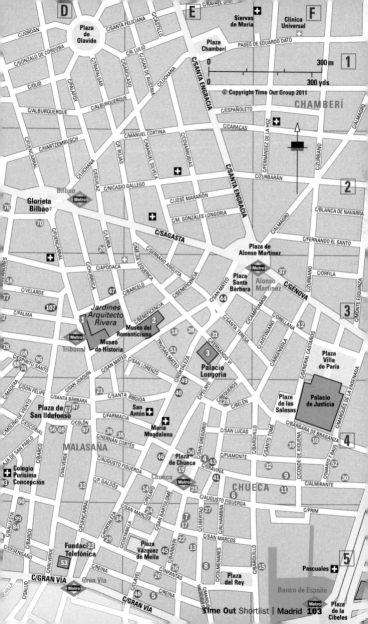

Stop Madrid p107

Sun; 7pm-3.30am Fri, Sat. *July, Aug* 9pm-3am Mon-Thur, Sun; 9pm-3.30am Fri, Sat. **Bar. Map** p103 E5 ⑤
A former brothel, Bar Cock is pricey and very stagey, furnished in what Spaniards think to be the style of an 'English pub' (red-velvet curtains, embossed leather armchairs and a fake half-timbered effect), and it still continues to attract those who like to think of themselves as being in the know. As a result it can get extremely crowded.

La Bardemcilla

C/Augusto Figueroa 47 (91 521 42 56, www.labardemcilla.com). Metro Chueca. **Open** noon-5pm, 8pm-2am Mon-Fri; 8pm-2am Sat. **Tapas. Map** p103 E4 ⑥
A fun, mellow place, owned by the royal family of Spanish cinema, the Bardems. There are filmic references everywhere, from the doll's house set from *Before Night Falls* to the names of the tapas. Jamón, Jamón is *croquetas* (geddit?); Víctor o Victória is gazpacho or consommé, depending on the season.

El Bierzo

C/Barbieri 16 (91 531 91 10). Metro Chueca. **Open** 1-4pm, 8-11.30pm Mon-Sat. Closed Aug. **€€. Castilian. Map** p103 E5 ⑦
El Bierzo is one of the best of Madrid's long-established *casas de comida* – honest, dependable neighbourhood joints where you can get a good *menú del día* at a reasonable price. It buzzes, particularly during lunch, with a loyal crowd feasting on simple dishes: roast chicken, seven types of tortilla and excellent *setas al ajillo* (wild mushrooms fried in garlic).

El Bocaíto

C/Libertad 4-6 (91 532 12 19, www.bocaito.com). Metro Chueca. **Open** 1-4.30pm, 8-30pm-midnight Mon-Fri; 8.30pm-midnight Sat. Closed Aug. **Tapas. Map** p103 E5 ⑧
Film-set traditional, from the bullfight posters and Andalucian ceramics to the old-school tapas and unsmiling,

white-jacketed waiters. If you're famous, though, they'll grin for the camera, just as they did with Pedro, Hugh and, goddammit, Mark Knopfler.

El Bogavante del Almirante

C/Almirante 11 (91 532 18 50, www.bogabar.com). Metro Banco de España or Chueca. **Open** 1.30-5.30pm, 9pm-12.30am Mon-Sat; 1-4pm Sun. Closed 2wks Aug. **€€€. Seafood. Map** p103 F4 ⑨
Set in a cave-like basement, where a ponderous lobster claw hangs from the ceiling and black outlines of sea creatures swirl across shrimp-pink walls, this place wins the prize for fanciful design. Seafood is the forte. The fish specials are always excellent, but the *arroz con bogavante* (lobster paella) takes the prize.

Le Cabrera

C/Bárbara de Braganza 2 (91 319 94 57, www.lecabrera.com). Metro Colón. **Open** *Cocktail bar* 4pm-2am Mon-Thur; 4pm-2.30am Fri, Sat. *Gastro bar* 1.30-4pm; 8.30pm-midnight Tue-Thur; 1.30-4pm, 8.30pm-2am Fri, Sat. **Bar. Map** p103 F4 ⑩
This excellent new cocktail bar opened in 2010, employing the heady talents of barman Diego Cabrera. The ground-floor bar serves wine and quality tapas, while the basement area has a hidden, intimate feel and is the place to sample the bar's long list of both classic and innovative cocktails.

Café Oliver

C/Almirante 12 (91 521 73 79, http://cafeoliver.com). Metro Colón. **Open** 1.30-4.30pm, 9pm-midnight Mon-Thur; 1.30-4.30pm, 9pm-1am Fri, Sat; 11.30am-4pm Sun. **€€€. Pan-European. Map** p103 F4 ⑪
Café Oliver runs the gamut of French, Spanish, Italian and Moroccan without falling into the dreaded (con)fusion trap. The plush red velvet banquettes and large windows looking out on the street make it an ideal place for Chueca

people-watching. Ideal on a Sunday for American brunch. The downstairs cocktail bar is cool and loungey.

Casa Manolo

C/Orellana 17 (91 308 73 78, www. comidascasamanolo.es). Metro Alonso Martínez. **Open** 1.30-4.30pm Mon-Thur; 1.30-4.30pm, 9pm-midnight Fri; 2-4.30pm, 9pm-midnight Sat. Closed Aug. €€€. **Castilian. Map** p103 F3 ⑫
One of the best sources of *cocina casera*, or home cooking, in Madrid, Casa Manolo has an endearing, homely atmosphere. Although traditional, its creative mouthwatering salads put the usual *ensalada mixta* to shame – the aubergine with tomato and goat's cheese, for example, must be one of the best in the city. And then there's lentil soup, *cocido* and other hearty stews, all supremely well prepared.

Extremadura

C/Libertad 13 (91 531 82 22, www.restauranteextremadura.com). Metro Chueca. **Open** 1.30-4.30pm Mon; 1.30-4.30pm, 9pm-midnight Tue-Sun. Closed 3wks Aug. €€€. **Extremaduran. Map** p103 E5 ⑬
With live piano accompaniment, this is the spot to try out specialities from one of Spain's least-known regions, Extremadura. The place is both classy and country – beautifully set tables with enormous glasses (for the excellent wines) combine with painting and pottery from the region. The trademark dish, *migas*, is a mix of breadcrumbs, chorizo and peppers that shepherds concocted to make use of old bread.

Gastromaquia

C/Pelayo 8 (91 522 64 13). Metro Chueca. **Open** 1-4pm, 9-11.30pm Tue-Sat; 1-4pm Sun. €€€. **Spanish fusion. Map** p103 E4 ⑭
Gastromaquia has been getting rave reviews since opening a few years ago. The compact interior is minimalist in style, and the Spanish-fusion food is expertly executed and beautifully pre-

sented: guacamole and plantain chips, and grilled octopus with potato foam are among its most celebrated dishes. The set lunch menu is great value, and this is also a popular spot for tapas.

Indochina

C/Barquillo 10 (91 524 03 17). Metro Banco de España. **Open** noon-4pm, 8pm-midnight daily. €€. **Asian. Map** p103 F5 ⑮
Yes, it's Asian fusion with modern design, but Indochina is more relaxed and less style-conscious than most. It's best for a lunchtime *menú del día*: enjoy piquant sweet and sour soup followed by decent pad thai and then green-tea ice-cream with caramelised walnuts on top (trust us, it's good). Ask for a table in the front, near the tall windows looking out on C/Barquillo.

Isolée

C/Infantas, 19 (91 524 12 98, www.isolee.com). Metro Banco de España. **Open** 10am-10pm Mon-Wed; 10am-9pm Thur-Sat; 3.30pm-10.30pm Sun. **Café. Map** p103 E5 ⑯
Isolée is a multi-faceted café, CD, clothes and kitchenware shop. The café is a little on the pricey side, but it does serve decent sushi and bagels. Mostly, though, it's a place for the hip to sip espressos and make use of the Wi-Fi.

Los Jiménez

C/Barbieri 14 (91 521 11 86, http://losjimenez.restaurantesok.com). Metro Chueca. **Open** 12.30-4pm, 9pm-midnight Tue-Sat; 12.30-4pm Sun. Closed Aug. €€. **Andalucian. Map** p103 E5 ⑰
Refreshingly unpretentious, Los Jiménez was serving no-frills food long before Chueca became the gay capital of Spain. There are ghastly fluorescent lights overhead and a persistent smell of frying – basically, it's a good old-fashioned greasy spoon. Old-time locals and new kids come here for all the Andalucian staples: oxtail stew, tripe, *cocido* and generous, if basic, salads.

Olé Lola

C/San Mateo 28 (91 310 66 95, www. lamordida.com). Metro Tribunal. **Open** noon-2am Mon-Thur, Sun; noon-2.30am Fri, Sat. **Bar/Tapas**. **Map** p103 E3 ⑱
This stylish cocktail bar – decked out with portraits of bullfighters and velvet sofas – blends modernity with tradition perfectly, and has become a popular lounging spot. Presentation is key when it comes to the tapas, which include mini chicken burgers with a tomato compote.

La Piazzetta

Plaza Chueca 8 (91 523 83 22). Metro Chueca. **Open** 1.30-4pm, 8pm-12.30am Tue-Sat; 1.30-4pm Sun. **€**. **Italian**. **Map** p103 E4 ⑲
Plaza Chueca has plenty of bars, but only one great restaurant, and this is it. The menu boasts simple but tasty Italian fare, with starters such as buffalo mozzarella with tomato and aubergine salad, and great pasta main courses like tortellini with pumpkin and mushrooms. It's perfect for summer evenings, when you can dine on the terrace.

El Puchero

C/Larra 13 (91 445 05 77, www.elpuchero.com). Metro Bilbao or Tribunal. **Open** 2-4pm, 9pm-midnight Mon-Sat. Closed Aug. **€€€**. **Castilian**. **Map** p103 D2 ⑳
Excitingly for El Puchero, red gingham is making a comeback after 30 years in the cold. Here it had never gone away – in tablecloths, lampshades and curtains. Almost unchanged too are the tasty country classics – from *civet de liebre* (hare stew) to *criadillas* (don't ask) – and some excellent seafood. It's a good idea to reserve at lunchtime.

Ribeira Do Miño

C/Santa Brígida 1 (91 521 98 54, www.marisqueriaribeiradomino.com). Metro Tribunal. **Open** 1-4pm, 8-11.30pm Tue-Sun. Closed 2wks Jan & all Aug. **€€**. **No credit cards**. **Map** p103 D4 ㉑
Galician in origin, this one's for seafood lovers, with heaped platters of prawns, crab, goose-necked barnacles, lobster and other sea creatures. Other typical *gallego* dishes that add to the fun are pancakes doused in *orujo* (a fiery spirit similar to grappa) and set aflame, and *queimada* – a bowl of *orujo* set on fire and then cooled with black coffee. No reservations are allowed.

Salvador

C/Barbieri 12 (91 521 45 24). Metro Chueca. **Open** 1.30-4pm, 9pm-midnight Mon-Sat. Closed Aug. **€€€**. **Castilian**. **Map** p103 E5 ㉒
Every inch of this old classic is crammed with bullfighting memorabilia. You'll find good traditional fare – lentil soup, *revueltos* (scrambled egg, often with seafood or asparagus), hake, *solomillo* (sirloin steak) with french fries – but the real treat is the atmosphere.

Stop Madrid

C/Hortaleza 11 (91 521 88 87, www.stopmadrid.es). Metro Chueca or Gran Via. **Open** noon-2am daily. **Bar**. **Map** p103 D5 ㉓
When it opened in 1929, this was the first ham and charcuterie shop in Madrid. It's undergone a few changes since then, but many of the original fittings have been retained, and great pride is taken in sourcing the best ingredients for tapas. Of the 50-strong wine list, all are available by the glass.

Tepic

Pelayo 4 (91 522 08 50, www.tepic.es). Metro Chueca. **Open** 1.15-4.30pm, 9pm-midnight Mon-Thur, Sun; 1.15-4.30pm, 9pm-12.30am Fri, Sat. **€€**. **Mexican**. **Map** p103 E5 ㉔
The name comes from the capital of Nayarit state in Mexico and a huge photo of a typical Mexican takes up one wall of this chic restaurant. There is no doubt about what you're going to eat here: quesadillas, guacamole, tacos, enchiladas, enmoladas… all of a much higher standard than at most Mexican joints in Madrid.

Tienda de Vinos (El Comunista)

C/Augusto Figueroa 35 (91 521 70 12). Metro Chueca. **Open** noon-4pm, 8pm-midnight Mon-Sat. Closed mid Aug-mid Sept. **€. Castilian. No credit cards. Map** p103 E4 **25**

This restaurant's popular name comes from its role as a lefty meeting-place under Franco (but Tienda de Vinos is all you'll see above the door). It's a Madrid classic, but no one makes any grand claims about its unchanging menu: soups, followed by liver and onions, lamb cutlets, kidneys in sherry and plenty of fish. Service is known for being deadpan, but if you're lucky, you'll get one of the two charming great-grandsons of the original owner.

El Tigre

C/Infantas 30 (91 532 00 72). Metro Banco de España or Chueca. **Open** 10.30am-2am Mon-Thur, Sun; 12.30pm-2.30am Fri, Sat. **Tapas. Map** p103 E5 **26**

If you can actually make it through the door, order a beer or cider and marvel at the hefty tapas that come with it – *patatas bravas, jamón serrano,* tortilla… it's all free, and each plate varies with each round. The bar itself is noisy, smoky and always rammed.

El 26 de Libertad

C/Libertad 26 (91 522 25 22). Metro Chueca. **Open** 1-4pm Mon, Sun; 1-4pm, 8pm-11pm Tue-Thur; 1-4pm, 9pm-midnight Fri, Sat. **€€. Castilian/ International. Map** p103 E5 **27**

With its deep colours and lavishly set tables, El 26 de Libertad is over-the-top elegance bordering on the camp. The food is Spanish, but dishes such as *morcilla* (black pudding), and cannelloni and anchovies filled with spinach and pine nuts have a creative edge. It's just a simple *menú* for lunch, so book for dinner to put the kitchen through its paces.

Zanzíbar

C/Regueros 9 (91 319 90 64, http://212.34.146.165/~zanzibar).
Metro Alonso Martínez. **Open** *Sept-July* 8pm-3am Mon-Thur, Sun; 8pm-3.30am Fri, Sat. *Aug* 8pm-2am Thur; 8pm-3.30am Fri, Sat. **No credit cards. Bar. Map** p103 E4 **28**

Good causes and ethnic chic combine to create a cute and colourful hangout for right-on revellers. On a small stage at the back there are frequent appearances by bossa nova bands, singer-songwriters and storytellers; at other times soft flamenco and reggae tickle the speakers. A few bar snacks are available, along with fairtrade coffee.

Zara

C/Infantas 5 (91 532 20 74, http://restaurantezara.com). Metro Chueca or Gran Vía. **Open** 1-5pm, 8.30-11.30pm Mon-Fri. Closed Aug. **€. Cuban. Map** p103 D5 **29**

Inés, the owner of this Little Havana, left her home city over 30 years ago, but brought the best Cuban recipes with her – try the 'Typically Tropical' dishes like *ropa vieja* (shredded beef), black beans and rice with pork, and minced beef with fried bananas. Daiquiris are the drink of the house. You may have to wait in line as they don't take reservations.

Shopping

Almirante 23

C/Almirante 23 (91 308 12 02, www.almirante23.net). Metro Chueca. **Open** 11am-1.30pm, 5-7.30pm Mon-Fri; 11am-1.30pm Sat. **Map** p103 F1 **30**

This curiosity shop is packed with all manner of old stuff, including toys, tacky postcards, prints, cameras, watches, bullfighting programmes and more. Brilliant for browsing.

La Duquesita

C/Fernando VI 2 (91 308 02 31). Metro Alonso Martínez. **Open** 9.30am-2.30pm, 5-9pm Tue-Sun. Closed Aug. **Map** p103 E3 **31**

This traditional *pastelería*, dating from 1914, has featured in lots of period-

Tepic p107

piece movies. Gorgeous chocolates and cakes are up for grabs, along with *turrón* in the run-up to Christmas.

Expresión Negra

C/Piamonte 15 (91 319 95 27, www.expresionnegra.org). Metro Chueca. **Open** 11am-2.30pm, 5-8.30pm Mon-Sat. **Map** p103 F4 ㉜
As well as breathing new life into recycled objects – briefcases, lamps and other objects made from used Coke cans, sardine tins and so on – the shop puts a different spin on African handicrafts, with brightly coloured throws, textiles and metalwork.

Hakei

C/Fuencarral 35 (91 522 09 34, www.hakei.com). Metro Chueca. **Open** 11am-9pm Mon-Sat; noon-8pm Sun. **Map** p103 D4 ㉝
Clothes, shoes and accessories from this nationwide womenswear chain are stylish, feminine and well-priced; there's a large range of leather bags too.

HAND

C/Hortaleza 26 (91 521 51 52, www.hand-haveaniceday.com). Metro Chueca. **Open** 11am-2.30pm, 5-9pm Mon-Sat. **Map** p103 D5 ㉞
This interesting boutique mixes French labels with bits and pieces brought back from the owners' travels.

Lotta

C/Hernán Cortés 9 (91 523 25 05, www.lottavintage.com). Metro Chueca or Tribunal. **Open** *Sept-July* 11am-2.30pm, 5-8.30pm Mon-Sat. *Aug* 6-10pm Mon-Sat. **Map** p103 D4 ㉟
Lotta carries vintage clothing and accessories from the 1950s to the 1980s and also stocks colourful dresses designed by the owner herself.

Panta Rhei

C/Hernán Cortés 7 (91 319 89 02, www.panta-rhei.es). Metro Chueca. **Open** 10.30am-8.30pm Mon-Fri; 11am-8pm Sat. **Map** p103 D4 ㊱

This friendly bookshop sells an excellent range of illustrated and photography books, many in English and many with a humorous bent. Its stylish cotton totes make nice, cheap souvenirs.

Pasajes

C/Génova 3 (91 310 12 45, www.pasajeslibros.com). Metro Alonso Martínez. **Open** 10am-8pm Mon-Fri; 10am-2pm Sat. **Map** p103 F3 ㊲
This linguists' treasure trove sells a great range of fiction and non-fiction, language-learning materials, maps, audio books and DVDs. Most are in English, French, German and Spanish.

Patrimonio Comunal Olivarero

C/Mejía Lequerica 1 (91 308 05 05, www.pco.es). Metro Alonso Martínez. **Open** 10am-2pm, 5-8pm Mon-Fri; 10am-2pm Sat. Closed Aug. **Map** p103 E3 ㊳
Olive oil from every region of Spain that produces the stuff is sold here, from two-litre bottles to five-litre cans, and some make lovely gifts.

Reserva y Cata

C/Conde de Xiquena 13 (91 319 04 01, www.reservaycata.com). Metro Chueca. **Open** 11am-2.30pm, 5-9pm Mon-Fri; 11am-2.30pm Sat. **Map** p103 F4 ㊴
This shop is crammed full of wines from Spain and abroad, all displayed with helpful information and often at prices lower than in the supermarkets. There are tasting sessions too.

Nightlife

Areia

C/Hortaleza 92 (91 310 03 07, www.areiachillout.com). Metro Chueca. **Open** 1pm-3am daily. **Admission** free. **Map** p103 E4 ㊵
Areia has all the angles covered: by day it's somewhere to get lunch or a snack, in the afternoon it becomes a place to chill, and by the evening the vibe hots up. The sofas and cushions on which to lounge, can make it difficult to leave.

Black & White

C/Libertad 34 (91 531 11 41, www. discoblack-white.net). Metro Chueca. **Open** 10pm-5.30am Mon-Thur, Sun; 10pm-6am Fri, Sat. **No credit cards.** **Map** p103 E4 ④

The grubby upstairs bar is a hit with cocky *latino* rent boys and their older prospective patrons, and plays host to some of the best cabaret shows in town. Downstairs things really liven up in the heaving *discobar*. A classic.

Búho Real

C/Regueros 5 (91 308 48 51, www.buhoreal.com). Metro Alonso Martínez or Chueca. **Open** 7pm-3am daily. Closed Aug. **Map** p103 E4 ②

The lights go down very low in the Búho Real, and the spots come up on a tiny stage. The size limitations here dictate the acts – expect local jazz or acoustic groups, most of them just two- or three-piece bands.

Escape

C/Gravina 13 (91 532 52 06, www. escapechueca.com). Metro Chueca. **Open** midnight-5.30am Mon-Thur, Sun; midnight-6am Fri, Sat. **Admission** (incl 1 drink) €8-€10. **Map** p103 E4 ③

This cavernous dancehall is one of the most popular destinations for lesbian women and is filled to the brim with the sexiest *chicas* in the city at the weekends. In fact, its popularity has spiralled to the extent that it's now one of the more boisterous clubs around Plaza de Chueca.

El Junco

Plaza Santa Bárbara 10 (91 319 20 81, www.el junco.com). Metro Alonso Martínez. **Open** 11pm-6am daily. **Map** p103 E3 ④

This is the late-night jazz spot in the city, boasting jam sessions on Sundays and Tuesdays, and gigs on most other weeknights. When there are no live musicians, a carefully selected roster of DJs will be spinning vinyl with just the right amount of off-beats.

Liquid

C/Barbieri 7 (91 523 28 08, www.liquid.es). Metro Chueca. **Open** 9pm-3am Mon-Thur; 9pm-3.30am Fri, Sat. **Map** p103 E5 ④

A cool, happening gay bar in which to see and be seen, with a contemporary, minimalist interior, lit up with mega-screens showing the latest dance music videos. It might be a bit tame for some, but it's a friendly crowd.

Muse

C/Pelayo 31 (mobile 600 265 236). Metro Chueca. **Open** 10pm-3.30am Mon-Sat. **Admission** varies. **No credit cards.** **Map** p103 E4 ④

Britney and Madonna engaging in that famous kiss take pride of place on the wall at Muse, which is a mostly lesbian disco-bar on bustling Calle Pelayo. Be sure to get there for around 1am, when the venue starts to pack out, and get your groove on to the house classics that roar out of the bar's sound system.

Pachá

C/Barceló 11 (91 447 01 28, www.pacha-madrid.com). Metro Tribunal. **Open** 11pm-6am Wed-Sat. **Admission** (incl 1 drink) €12-€17. **Map** p103 D3 ④

In a club scene that ditches the glitz, Pachá is the black sheep. Dress up to get in, and expect glamorous go-gos, on-stage dance routines and themed parties, enacted to a soundtrack of soulful house. Wednesdays are hip hop nights, with appearances from the likes of local star Jotamayuscula.

Rick's

C/Clavel 8 (91 531 91 86). Metro Gran Vía. **Open** 11.30pm-5.30am daily. **Admission** (incl 1 drink) €8. **No credit cards.** **Map** p103 E5 ④

Expensive drinks and an expensive, older crowd are the hallmarks of this gay-friendly late-night alternative to the discos. With hi-NRG beats and camp Spanish hits, it's standing-room only at weekends.

MADRID BY AREA

Stromboli

C/Hortaleza 96 (91 319 46 28). Metro Alonso Martínez. **Open** 6.30pm-3.30am daily. **Map** p103 E3/E4 ⓰

A very cool little lounge that's perfect for a mid-week drink or as a stop on your weekend tour of the town. Very much part of the hip scene around C/Hortaleza and C/Fuencarral, and a place where the club DJs of Madrid drop their big-room style and spin something a little more intimate.

Truco

C/Gravina 10 (91 532 89 21, www.trucochueca.com). Metro Chueca. **Open** 5pm-3am Mon-Thur; noon-3am Fri, Sat. **Map** p103 E4 ⓾

Truco is often very crowded and usually with an extremely young and loud crowd. No matter: this high-octane corner joint remains the place for gals who are looking for gals in the earlier part of the evening. It's a stone's throw from the popular girl bar Escape (see p111).

Arts & leisure

La Enana Marrón

Travesía de San Mateo 8 (91 308 14 97, www.laenanamarron.org). Metro Tribunal. **Tickets** €4; €2.60 members. **No credit cards. Map** p103 E3 ⓾

A side-street in Chueca is the hip and lively location of the strangely named Brown Dwarf microcinema, specialising in experimental films, retrospectives, shorts and repertory classics. Films are shown in their original language.

Teatro María Guerrero

C/Tamayo y Baus 4 (box office 91 310 15 00, information 91 310 29 49, http://cdn.mcu.es). Metro Colón. **Tickets** €11-€18; half- price concessions Wed. **Map** p103 F4 ⓾

This late 19th-century theatre is home to the state-run Centro Dramático Nacional (CDN). Having reopened after full renovations, it's retained its red-velvet plushness and is to host, among other works, Büchner's *Woyzeck* in 2011.

Malasaña & Conde Duque

By day, the neighbourhood of **Malasaña**, between C/Fuencarral and San Bernardo, still has a laid-back neighbourhood feel. By night, though, this has long been the epicentre of Madrid's bar culture. Although less showy than Chueca, this is the city's hipster barrio, albeit with a grungy edge. However, the tentacles of Old City gentrification are beginning to take hold, with new boutiques, cafés and bars opening up in the area in the past few years – especially on **Calle Espíritu Santo**.

The area west of C/San Bernardo is most commonly known as **Conde Duque**, after its finest monument, the **Centro Cultural Conde Duque**, which occupies the giant barracks (*cuartel*) built in 1717-54. It was wonderfully renovated in the 1980s as an arts centre (see p124).

Sights & museums

Fundación Telefónica

C/Gran Vía 28, Malasaña (entrance at C/Valverde 2) (91 522 66 45, www.fundacion.telefonica.com/ arte_tecnologia). Metro Gran Vía. **Open** 11am-9pm Tue-Sun. Closed Aug. **Admission** free. **Map** p103 D5 ⓾

This place functions on several levels. The Museo de las Telecomunicaciones is a permanent exhibition illustrating the history of telecommunications. Another large space is used to display selections from its permanent collection of Spanish art, including various works by Eduardo Chillida, Luis Fernández, Miró, Picasso and Tàpies and it also has a permanent show based around post-Civil War Spanish artists of the so-called Madrid and Paris schools, the latter in exile. Temporary exhibitions feature both the arts and technology.

Museo Municipal de Arte Contemporáneo

C/Conde Duque 9 & 11, Conde Duque (91 588 58 61). Metro Noviciado. **Open** *Closed until May 2011. Sept-June* 10am-2pm, 5.30-9pm Tue-Sat; 10.30am-2.30pm Sun. *July, Aug* 10am-2pm, 6-9pm Tue-Sat; 10.30am-2pm Sun. **Admission** free. **Map** p102 B3 ⑤④

The council's contemporary art collection is currently closed for reparations and expected to reopen in May 2011. It covers painting and graphic work, along with sculpture, photography and drawing. Highlights include work by Eduardo Arroyo, Ouka Lele, Eduardo Úrculo, Jorge Oteiza and Eva Lootz.

Palacio de Liria

C/Princesa 20 (91 547 53 02). Metro Ventura Rodríguez. **Open** *Guided tours* 10am, 11am, noon Fri. Booking essential. Closed July-Oct. **Admission** free. **Map** p102 B2 ⑤⑤

This neo-classical palace, completed in 1783 and refurbished in the 1910s by Edwin Lutyens, is the private property of Spanish aristocrat, the Duchess of Alba. The extraordinary collection includes work by Rembrandt, Titian and Rubens, and one of the most important Goyas in private hands: his portrait of an earlier Duchess of Alba in red and white. The problem is, the current duchess has no need to open her palace to public view. The guided tours must be booked in advance. Bookings can be made by email and should be sent to visitas@funacioncasadealba.com. There is currently a waiting list of over a year!

Eating & drinking

La Ardosa

C/Colón 13, Malasaña (91 521 49 79, www.laardosa.com). Metro Tribunal. **Open** 8.30am-2am Mon-Fri; 11.50am-2.30am Sat, Sun. **No credit cards. Bar. Map** p103 D4 ⑤⑥

Having an affair? Then simply duck under the counter to find the most intimate bar-room you could wish for. Out front, meanwhile, this is a lovely old tiled *taberna* lined with dusty bottles, old black-and-white lithographs and beer posters. The speciality of the house is its draught beer – Bombardier, Budvar and, especially, Guinness.

Adrish

C/San Bernardino 1, Conde Duque (91 541 15 41, www.restauranteadrish. com). Metro Noviciado or Plaza de España. **Open** 1-4pm, 8.30pm-midnight Mon-Thur, Sun; 1-4pm, 8.30pm-1am Fri, Sat. **€€**. **Indian**. **Map** p102 B4 ⑤⑦

The place may look a tad dreary, but you'll forget all about the mauve tablecloths when you taste the tandoori chicken with almonds. The large tandoori oven and charcoal grill produce some tasty dishes and a variety of naan breads, even if the spiciness has dropped to a level acceptable to local palates.

Bar El 2D

C/Velarde 24, Malasaña (91 448 64 72). Metro Tribunal. **Open** *Sept-June* 1pm-2am Mon-Wed, Sun; 1pm-3am Thur-Sat. *July, Aug* 6pm-2am Mon-Wed, Sat; 1pm-3am Thur, Fri. **No credit cards. Bar. Map** p103 D3 ⑤⑧

The emblematic Malasaña hang-out, packed at weekends and drowsily mellow in the afternoons, with a tiled bar and engraved mirrors, nicotine-stained walls and lazily circling ceiling fans. To drink there's vermouth, lager and Beamish on tap, plus plenty of bottled beers and a small range of wines, served (if you dare) in *porrones*, long-spouted drinking jars.

Bar El Palentino

C/Pez 12, Malasaña (91 532 30 58, www.myspace.com/barpalentino). Metro Callao or Noviciado. **Open** 8.30am-2am Mon-Sat. **No credit cards. Bar. Map** p102 C4 ⑤⑨

Something of a Madrid institution, this old-school neighbourhood bar is popular with seemingly everyone – the place is always packed in the evenings. Wooden panelling, fluorescent strip

MADRID BY AREA

Grassroots revival

Madrid's squat-led cultural scene has been reignited.

Squats that function as arts centres have existed in Spain – and particularly in Madrid and Barcelona – for decades; but with the recent economic crisis, the phenomenon has gained more impetus, with squatted buildings around the Madrid barrios of Malasaña and Lavapiés housing organisations that offer activities such as yoga and art classes.

Squatting first arose in Madrid during the rural exodus of the 1960s and '70s, and was later revived as the *okupa* movement during *La Movida Madrileña*. Over the last few years of rising prices and unemployment, the movement has been reignited, with various squatted buildings being turned into grassroots cultural centres.

One of the most famous of these highly politicised *centros sociales okupados* is **Patio Maravillas** (www.patiomaravillas. net) in Malasaña, which runs a bike repair shop, an internet café, exhibitions, English and art classes, concerts and more from its (new) home in Calle de Pez.

It started in a former school building on Calle del Acuerdo (No.8) – famous for its exterior graffitti (pictured above) – but the organisation was evicted by police in January 2010.

Another recent 'arts squat' is **CSO Casablanca** (www.csocasa blanca.org) on Calle Santa Isabel (No.23), on the border of Lavapiés (just down from the Cine Doré). It offers empowering courses in yoga, digital photography, acting, dance, self-defence and Marxist studies, as well as films and talks.

The cultural centres have been so successful that even the Spanish Ministry of Culture has got in on the action. In winter 2010, it handed over a huge 18th-century Lavapiés building to local artists. The building will in the future house a National Centre for Visual Arts, but as the project has been delayed, it was decided that temporary management be undertaken by the artists – who opened **La Tabacalera** (http://la tabacalera.net), a centre offering social and cultural activities.

ceiling lamps, a much-loved owner and notoriously cheap (but good) drinks attract punters of all ages. Sandwiches help to soak up the *cañas*.

Bufalino

C/Puebla 9, Malasaña (91 521 80 31, www.bufalino.es). Metro Gran Via or Tribunal. **Open** 1pm-1am Tue-Sat. Closed 1wk Aug. **€. Argentinian/ Italian.** Map p103 D4 ⑥⓪
Run by an Italian and Argentine couple, Bufalino takes the cuisines of their countries and fuses them, offering a fine selection of fresh pastas, along with panini and polenta. The restaurant gets packed at around 11pm as regulars pop by for a few drinks.

Café Comercial

Glorieta de Bilbao 7, Malasaña (91 521 56 55). Metro Bilbao. **Open** 7.30am-midnight daily. **No credit cards.** **Bar**. Map p102 C2 ⑥①
Café Comercial still rates as one of the classic Madrid bars, with its original battered brown leather seats, revolving doors and marbled walls. A cursory nod to the modern age comes in the shape of the internet terminals upstairs, where American gap-year students write home about the old men playing chess alongside them.

Café Isadora

C/Divino Pastor 14, Malasaña (91 445 71 54). Metro Bilbao. **Open** 4pm-2am Mon-Thur, Sun; 4pm-2.30am Fri, Sat. **No credit cards.** **Bar**. Map p102 C2 ⑥②
An elegant shrine to the dancer Isadora Duncan, this café also hosts frequently changing exhibitions. Along with a range of *patxaráns*, many of them own-made, is a list of *'aguas'* (cocktails made with cava). Agua de Valencia is the original and best, featuring orange juice, gin, Cointreau and vodka.

Café Manuela

C/San Vicente Ferrer 29, Malasaña (91 531 70 37). Metro Tribunal. **Open** *Oct-May* 6pm-2am Mon-Thur;

4pm-2am Fri, Sat. *June-Sept* 6pm-2.30am daily. **Café**. Map p103 D3 ⑥③
Stacked to the rafters with board games, Café Manuela has been a hive of activity since the Movida days. Its handsome art nouveau decor and conveniently nicotine-coloured walls are still the backdrop to occasional live music and other performances, but otherwise it's a great place to reacquaint yourself with Cluedo and Mastermind.

Café El Moderno

Plaza de las Comendadoras 1, Conde Duque (91 531 62 77, 91 522 48 35). Metro Noviciado. **Open** *Sept-July* 3pm-1.30am Mon-Thur, Sun; 3pm-2.30am Fri, Sat. *Aug* 5.30pm-1.30am Mon-Thur, Sun; 5.30pm-2.30am Fri, Sat. **No credit cards.** **Café**. Map p102 B3 ⑥④
El Moderno's art deco look is entirely fake, but none the worse for it, and, along with its large terrace, attracts a mixture of local characters and curious tourists. The specialities are teas, milkshakes and hot chocolates, with an impressive 30 varieties of each. Fans of *Sex and Lucia* will recognise the building as Lorenzo's apartment block.

Café Rustika

C/Limón 11, Conde Duque (91 542 15 67, www.rustikacafe.es). Metro Noviciado. **Open** 6.30pm-midnight Tue-Thur, Sun; 6.30pm-2.30am Fri, Sat. **Café**. Map p102 B3 ⑥⑤
Whimsical interiors, funky lo-fi music and lots of hanging lanterns make this one of the most relaxing cafés in a neighbourhood full of them. New ownership brings a randomly international menu with dishes from couscous to chop suey to chocolate cake and a wide selection of teas.

Casa do Compañeiro

C/San Vicente Ferrer 44, Malasaña (91 521 57 02). Metro Noviciado. **Open** 1.30pm-2am Tue-Sun. **No credit cards.** **Tapas**. Map p102 C3 ⑥⑥
A tiny jewel among tapas bars, with wonderful tiling. The tapas are mainly

from Galicia, with lots of octopus, gammon, pig's ear and, of course, *caldo gallego*, a broth made with cabbage and pork. A glass of crisp, dry fino makes the perfect accompaniment.

Conache

Plaza de San Ildefonso, C/Santa Barbara 11, Malasaña (91 522 95 00). Metro Tribunal. **Open** 10am-1am Mon-Thur; 10am-2am Sat; 11-6pm Sun. **Tapas.** Map p103 D4 **⑥⑦**

The Conache look is casually hip, even though the bright lighting and fruit machines keep scenesters at bay. The food, however, is absolutely where it's at. Try stir-fried vegetables with prawns, little rolls of venison and apple, or spinach and brie with figs, and be sure to finish with the cheese mousse with fruits of the forest.

Home

C/Espíritu Santo 12, Malasaña (91 522 97 28, www.homeburgerbar.com). Metro Tribunal. **Open** 1.30-4pm, 9pm-midnight Tue-Sat; 1-4pm, 8.30pm-midnight Sun. **€. Burger bar.** Map p103 D3 **⑥⑧**

If you associate burger bars with junk food, then this restaurant's aim is to make you think again. The carefully thought-out menu uses 100% organic produce. The attention to detail is fantastic, from the diner-style decor to the menus. There are quite a few vegetarian dishes, and even vegans can enjoy a marinated tofu club sandwich.

La Ida

C/Colón 11, Malasaña (91 522 91 07). Metro Tribunal. **Open** 1pm-2am daily. Closed Aug. **No credit cards. Café.** Map p103 D4 **⑥⑨**

Everybody knows everybody else here. This is where the painfully cool neo-punks from the nearby Mercado Fuencarral come to let their guard down, tucking into courgette tart and canapés at the scrubbed pine tables amid perky green walls.

La Isla del Tesoro

C/Manuela Malasaña 3, Malasaña (91 593 14 40, www.isladeltesoro. net). Metro Bilbao or San Bernardo. **Open** 1.30-4pm, 9pm-midnight daily. **€. Vegetarian.** Map p103 D2 **⑦⓪**

One of Madrid's few vegetarian eateries not stuck in a circa-1978 time warp, La Isla del Tesoro matches the international collectibles decor with dishes from across the globe. Try the locally renowned couscous *seitan* or the *buen rollito* (fresh pasta stuffed with spinach, apple, leek, cheese and nuts). The *menú del día* features dishes from a different nation each day.

El Jardín Secreto

C/Conde Duque 2, Conde Duque (91 541 80 23). Metro Plaza de España or Ventura Rodríguez. **Open** 6.30pm-1.30am Mon-Thur; 6.30pm-2.30am Fri, Sat; 5.30pm-12.30am Sun. **Café.** Map p102 B3 **⑦①**

El Jardín Secreto – decked out with mismatched furniture and arty knick-knacks – is most popular as a *merienda* (afternoon tea) spot, although it also functions as a restaurant. Crowds tend to show up right when it opens at 6.30pm. Its cakes and desserts are much talked about, and there's a large selection of chocolate drinks, teas and coffees on the menu. It's also popular as a cocktail spot.

Laydown

Plaza Mostenses 9, Conde Duque (91 548 79 37, www.laydown.es). Metro Plaza de España. **Open** 9.30pm-2.30am Tue-Sat; noon-6pm Sun. **Bar.** Map p102 B4 **⑦②**

This flashy, minimalist bar, restaurant and club is known for its chic lounge chairs with comfy mattresses (the clue is in the name). Dinner is a set meal and there are live music or theatre performances most nights. Once dinner is over, it's DJ time. The Sunday brunch is very popular.

Lola Loba

C/Palma 38, Malasaña (91 522 96 16).
Metro Noviciado. **Open** noon-2am Mon-
Sat. **No credit cards. Bar/Café.**
Map p102 C3 ⑦

Lola Loba is named after a *copla* singer
who ran away from her abusive
American millionaire husband and
opened this bar. In 1872 he found her
and murdered her, and 'tis said her
ghost still prowls within the red-brick
walls. What is not known is whether
she approves of the jazz, funk and
house, or the fab *tostas*, slathered
in mozzarella, tomato and basil;
caramelised onion with brie, or smoked
salmon with camembert.

Lolina Vintage Café

Espíritu Santo 9, Malasaña (91 523
58 59, www.lolinacafe.com). Metro
Tribunal. **Open** 9am-2am Mon-Thur,
Sun; 9am-2.30am Fri, Sat. **Café.**
Map p103 D3 ⑦

The cute, retro space – with its 1970s
wallpaper and vintage floor lamps – is
a popular hangout for arty types and
young expats, drawn by its pan-
European vibe, brunch-style menu and
large selection of teas, coffees and
juices. If you visit in the evening, be
sure to order a mojito or caipirinha –
the house specialities.

La Palmera

C/Palma 67, Conde Duque (mobile 630
884 470). Metro Noviciado. **Open** 8pm-
2am Mon-Thur; 8pm-2.30am Fri, Sat.
No credit cards. Bar. Map p102 B3 ⑦

The tiles in this tiny, crowded bar date
back to its opening at the beginning
of the last century, and have featured
in various magazines. For years it lay
in terminal decline, until it was bought
in the late 1990s by a long-term regular. It almost exclusively serves vermouth and beer to a loyal crowd of
locals and expats.

El Parnasillo

C/San Andrés 33, Malasaña (91 447 00
79). Metro Bilbao. **Open** 2.30pm-3am

Food forward

Madrid has embraced the new wave.

Over the past decade, Spain's
new wave of experimental
cooking known as *nueva cocina*
has been shaking things up
in the Madrid restaurant world.
Spearheaded by Catalan
culinary legend Ferran Adrià,
and renowned for its improbable
pairings of flavours and twists of
texture and temperature, *nueva
cocina* was previously restricted
to restaurants in Catalonia and
the Basque country, with Madrid
chefs shunning the movement
by sticking rigidly to *madrileño*
old faves such as *cocido*,
suckling pig and offal.

But, despite the slow start,
nueva cocina got a foothold
in Madrid when *madrileño*
Paco Roncero opened the
now Michelin-starred **La Terraza
del Casino** (see p56). Overseen
by Adrià, the place is renowned
for its whimsical creations like
'lollipop' parmesan wafers.
Madrid has witnessed a
widespread shift in attitude
since its opening, with a wave
of new places offering a more
watered-down version of
nueva cocina in the form
of '*cocina creativa*'.

This culinary revolution has
made its mark on the city's
tapas bars too, with one
of the most recent 'cocina
creativa' openings being
Rancero's **Estado Puro** (see
p135), a chic diner-style
restaurant offering upmarket
tapas with a modern twist.

MADRID BY AREA

Mon-Thur, Sun; 2.30pm-3.30am Fri, Sat. **No credit cards. Bar/café.** Map p103 D2 ⑰

The art nouveau El Parnasillo was at the centre of Madrid's cultural renewal in the 1970s and '80s, to the extent that it was bombed by a far-right group. It's unlikely to excite the same emotion these days, but is still an evocative place for a cocktail, sarnie or *pa tumaca* (bread rubbed with tomato) topped with cheese, ham or smoked salmon.

Pepe Botella

C/San Andrés 12, Malasaña (91 522 43 09). Metro Tribunal. **Open** *Sept-July* 10am-2am Mon-Thur; 11am-3am Fri, Sat; 11am-2am Sun. *Aug* 3pm-2am Mon-Thur, Sun; 3pm-3am Fri, Sat. **No credit cards. Café.** Map p103 D3 ⑰

A cineaste's delight, the colourful Pepe Botella is frequented by the likes of director Alejandro Amenábar and actor Eduardo Noriega. For all that, it's wonderfully unpretentious, and attracts an intelligent bunch of mainly thirty- and fortysomethings, who engage in lively debate while smoking for Spain. The place has free Wi-Fi.

El Rincón

C/Espíritu Santo 26, Malasaña (91 522 19 86). Metro Tribunal. **Open** 10am-2am daily. **Café.** Map p103 D3 ⑰

Laid-back El Rincón has a classic new-wave Malasaña feel, with chequered floors, powder-blue walls, black-and-white photos on the walls, mismatched wooden tables and a boho vibe. For a bite to eat, try the house gazpacho or the quality sandwiches and cakes.

Siam

C/San Bernardino 6, Conde Duque (91 559 83 15). Metro Noviciado or Plaza de España. **Open** noon-4.30pm, 8pm-midnight daily. **€€. Thai.** Map p102 B4 ⑰

Texan David Haynes has poured his heart and the experience of years spent in Thailand into this restaurant, and the investment has paid off with a loyal and enthusiastic clientele. Authenticity is his thing and he imports vegetables and spices that he can't get hold of in the city. There is also a fabulous range of cocktails and special teas.

Subiendo al Sur

C/Ponciano 5, Conde Duque (91 548 11 47, www.subiendoalsur.org). Metro Noviciado or Plaza de España. **Open** *Food served* 2-5pm Mon; 2-5pm, 9pm-midnight Tue-Sat. **No credit cards. €. International.** Map p102 B3 ⑳

Easily missed, this co-operative-run fair trade café-restaurant and shop is a gem. All profits go to good causes, and the charming co-owners take turns in the kitchen, each lending ideas from their home country to the daily-changing menu. A wide selection of empanadas and pastries sit alongside Zambian *babotie*, Peruvian ceviche, Brazilian *moqueca*, and kebabs.

Taberna Agrado

C/Ballesta 1, Malasaña (91 521 63 46). Metro Gran Vía or Callao. **Open** 10am-2.30am Mon-Sat. **€. Nueva cocina.** Map p103 D5 ㉛

Agrado opened in early 2010 and immediately caused a bit of a stir. The chef, Byron Canning, is British, with experience in some of London and Madrid's top restaurants. Behind the bar, Héctor Monroy from Mexico shakes up some mean cocktails. The speciality is the melt-in-the-mouth beef and Iberian pork hamburger. There's also octopus carpaccio and, of course, fish and chips.

Taberna El 9

C/San Andrés 9, Malasaña (91 319 29 46). Metro Tribunal. **Open** *Sept-June* 7.30pm-1am Tue-Thur, Sun; 7.30pm-2.30am Fri, Sat. *July, Aug* 8.30pm-2am Tue-Thur, Sun, 8pm-2.30am Fri, Sat. **No credit cards. Tapas.** Map p103 D3 ㉜

Fun, funky and very much of its neighbourhood, with a young crowd.

Laydown p116

Taberna Agrado p118

Taberna El 9 has a straightforward list of canapés, including good scrambled egg with chorizo, and serves house wine by the very cheap *chato* – a small glass.

La Tabernilla del Gato Amadeus

C/Cristo 2, Conde Duque (91 541 41 12). Metro Noviciado. **Open** 1pm-midnight Mon-Wed, Sun; 1pm-1am Thur-Sat. **No credit cards. Tapas.** **Map** p102 B3 ㉝

Named after a late, great, Persian cat, this is a tiny, welcoming bar, whose *croquetas* are legendary. The other favourite is the *patatas con mojo picón* (baked new potatoes with a spicy sauce). Although there's not much seating inside the premises (the sister bar nearby is bigger), in summer there are tables outside.
Other location C/Limón 32, Malasaña (91 542 54 23).

La Tasquita de Enfrente

C/Ballesta 6, Malasaña (91 532 54 49, www.latasquitadeenfrente.com). Metro Gran Via or Callao. **Open** 1.30-3.30pm, 8.30-11pm Tue-Sat. Closed Aug. **Nueva cocina.** €€€€. **Map** p103 D5 ㉞

One of Madrid's best restaurants, La Tasquita de Enfrente has only half a dozen tables, so you need to book well ahead. The menu changes seasonally, but don't miss the *pochas* (white beans) with clams, if they're available. Also fabulous are the squid gnocchi, and the slow-cooked acorn-fed Iberian pork cheeks. But the best idea is to go for the special menu of the day.

Toma

C/Conde Duque 14, Conde Duque (91 547 49 96). Metro Noviciado or Plaza de España. **Open** 9pm-12.30am Tue-Fri; 1-4.30pm, 9pm-12.30am Sat, Sun. Closed 1wk end Dec, 1wk Jan. €€. **International. Map** p102 B3 ㉟

A tiny restaurant with cherry-red walls and an informal feel, Toma's homely, laid-back atmosphere can make the prices seem rather high, especially if you end up having to sit at the bar. But the food is commensurately good. From duck magret with pak choi to tuna tartare with lemon and soy, or rack of lamb with honey and mustard, the preparation is equally assured, and the results often divine.

Shopping

Antigua Casa Crespo

C/Divino Pastor 29, Malasaña (91 521 56 54, www.alpargateriacrespo.com). Metro Bilbao. **Open** Sept-Apr 10am-1.30pm, 5-8pm Mon-Fri. May-Aug 10am-1.30pm, 5-8.30pm Mon-Fri; 10am-1.30pm Sat. Closed last 2wks Aug. **No credit cards. Map** p103 D2 ㊱

This perfectly preserved, old-fashioned, family-run store, founded in 1863, is dedicated to espadrilles (*alpargatas* in Spanish) of all sizes and colours.

Bunkha

C/Santa Bárbara 6, Malasaña (91 522 09 50, www.bunkha.com). Metro Tribunal or Gran Via. **Open** 11am-9pm Mon-Sat. **Map** p103 D4 ㊲

This stylish boutique stocks a host of upmarket yet hip labels, such as Danish brand Won Hundred, Spanish brand Marlota and Italian label Camo.

Happy Day

C/Espíritu Santo 11, Malasaña (91 522 91 33). Metro Tribunal. **Open** 10am-2pm, 5-8pm Mon-Sat. **Map** p103 D3 ㊳

Happy Day is aiming to bring the cupcake phenomenon to Madrid. The 1950s-style *pastelería* is kitted out in pastel shades, and has a café table if you want to indulge your sweet tooth in-store.

J&J Books & Coffee

C/Espíritu Santo 47, Malasaña (91 521 85 76, www.jandjbooksandcoffee.com). Metro Noviciado. **Open** 11am-midnight Mon-Thur, Sat; 11am-2am Fri; 4-10pm Sun. **Map** p103 C3 ㊴

J&J Books & Coffee is both a relaxing little café and a well-stocked second-hand bookshop. Activities held here include open-mic sessions, language exchanges (8pm Wednesdays and Thursdays) and quizzes (11pm Fridays). The daily 'happy hour' is from 4pm to 7pm.

Los Mostenses

Plaza de Los Mostenses, Malasaña (no phone). Metro Plaza de España. **Map** p102 B4 ⑨

A huge market in Malasaña with an international atmosphere: Chinese and Mexican products are very much in evidence.

Nonstop Sneakers

C/Pez 14, Malasaña (91 523 26 46). Metro Callao or Noviciado. **Open** 11am-2.30pm, 5-8.45pm Mon-Sat. **Map** p102 C4 ㉛

Madrid's best trainers shop sells a good range of New Balance and Nike, with plenty of rare editions and exclusive models.

Peseta

C/Noviciado 9, Conde Duque (91 521 14 04, www.peseta.org). Metro Noviciado or Plaza de España. **Open** 10am-8.30pm Mon-Fri; 10am-3pm Sat. **Map** p102 B3 ㉜

This cute shop-atelier in a creative quarter of Conde Duque sells artisan bags, purses, laptop and passport cases, handkerchiefs, keyrings and badges from the Peseta range, all made using vintage-style fabrics. It also sells Harinezumi 2 Japanese digital cameras. The shop itself is lovingly kitted out with retro furniture, and its owners, Laura and Jaime, are often at work in the attached atelier. Collaborations with Marc Jacobs have raised the brand's profile of late.

Popland

C/Manuela Malasaña 24, Malasaña (91 591 21 20, www.popland.es). Metro Bilbao. **Open** 11am-8.30pm Mon-Sat. **Map** p102 C2 ㉝

For times when only a Jesus action figure will do, Popland saves the day. The shop is packed with all things pop-culture and plastic, but also film posters, shower curtains and T-shirts.

Radio City

Plaza Guardias de Corps 1, Conde Duque (91 547 77 67, www.radio citydiscos.com). Metro Noviciado or Plaza de España or Ventura Rodriguez. **Open** 11am-2pm, 5-9pm Mon-Sat. **Map** p102 B3 ㉞

One of the city's best record shops, with a host of independent labels covering everything from indie folk to rare soul and R&B via Latin beats, on both vinyl and CD. A selection of vintage LPs is also stocked.

Sportivo

C/Conde Duque 20, Conde Duque (91 542 56 61, www.grupsportivo.com). Metro San Bernardo. **Open** 10am-9pm Mon-Sat. **Map** p102 B3 ㉟

With a great range of menswear labels, including Cantskate, Burro, Levi's Red and Vintage, New York Industries, YMC and Duffer of St George, Sportivo is an unmissable stop. The staff are extremely helpful.

Up Beat Discos

C/Espiritu Santo 6, Malasaña (91 522 76 60, www.upbeat.es). Metro Noviciado or Tribunal. **Open** 11am-2pm, 5-8.30pm Mon-Sat. **Map** p103 F1 ㊱

Soul, jazz and reggae dominate the shelves here, with a hand-picked collection of CDs and vinyl, along with a sideline in donkey jackets, parkas, Dr Martens, and so on. The shop has a fab '60s feel.

Vialis

C/Colón 3, Malasaña (91 575 99 33, www.vialis.es). Metro Tribunal. **Open** 10am-2pm, 5-8pm Mon-Sat. **Map** p103 D4 ㊲

This is Madrid's only branch of the stylish Spanish footwear brand that's become popular worldwide in the last few years. Expect chunky but hip shoes and boots in solid shapes, and a small selection of high-quality leather bags.

Nightlife

Café la Palma

C/Palma 62, Conde Duque (91 522 50 31, www.cafelapalma.com). Metro Noviciado. **Open** 4pm-3am Mon-Thur, Sun; 4pm-4am Fri, Sat. *Concerts & club nights* from 10pm & midnight Thur-Sat. **Admission** *Concerts* (minimum consumption) €7. **No credit cards. Map** p102 B3 ⓸

A longstanding favourite among the Malasaña crowd. Choose from an area with tables, a chill-out zone where everyone lazes on cushions on the floor or the main room, where from Thursday to Saturday you can catch concerts from local up-and-comers.

Démodé

C/Ballesta 7, Malasaña (mobile 678 50 52 37). Metro Chueca. **Open** 11pm-3.30am Tue-Sat. **Admission** free. **No credit cards. Map** p103 D5 ⓹

This pre-club joint is housed in an old brothel. Faux oil paintings still adorn the walls, and red lighting, sofas and an ample sound system have transformed it into one of the coolest nightspots of the moment. DJs spin both underground house and electro for a mixed gay/straight crowd.

Morocco

C/Marqués de Leganés 7, Malasaña (91 531 51 67, www.moroccoclub.es). Metro Santo Domingo. **Open** midnight-3am Thur; midnight-6am Fri, Sat. **Admission** (incl 2 drinks) €10. **No credit cards. Map** p102 C4 ⓸⓸⓸

Morocco has two feet firmly planted in the past. From its '80s decor and crowd, everything here smacks of days gone by. The DJ mixes mainly classic Spanish pop with today's nu flamenco. It's great fun, completely free of pretension and brimming with dancefloor energy.

Nasti

C/San Vicente Ferrer 33, Malasaña (91 521 76 05, http://nasti.es). Metro Tribunal. **Open** midnight-6am Fri, Sat. **Admission** (incl 1 drink) €10. **No credit cards. Map** p102 C3 ⓸⓸⓸

The remit here is simple – pack out a small and smoky *sala* with a fiercely loyal crowd, and play anything from the Sex Pistols to Joy Division to make them dance. A riotous, grungy and alternative crowd find their home here, enjoying the live acts such as Fanny Pack or Humbert Humbert and the guest DJs such as 2 Many DJs.

Oui

C/Marqués de Santa Ana 11, Malasaña (no phone). Metro Noviciado. **Open** 11pm-3am Thur; 11pm-3.30am Fri, Sat. Closed mid Aug. **Admission** free. **No credit cards. Map** p102 C4 ⓸⓸⓸

A truly unique bar, Oui is damn difficult to find but worth the search. Its bizarre shape and eclectic music policy – expect anything from early techno to present-day electronica – together with a knowledgeable and loyal clientele, make this a gem among the sometimes mediocre bars of Malasaña.

El Perro de la Parte Atrás del Coche

C/Puebla 15, Malasaña (no phone, www.myspace.com/elperroclub). Metro Gran Via. **Open** 9.30pm-3.30am daily. **Admission** €6. **No credit cards. Map** p103 D4 ⓸⓸⓸

As the unusual name (it means the 'nodding dog') suggests, everything about El Perro is different. The music policy is a mix-up of everything, with hip hop, house, soul and funk played by the resident DJs. The live acts take in heavy metal, so you might hear Aretha Franklin songs one night and a Metallica tribute band the next. A mix that shouldn't work, but really does.

Radar

C/Amaniel 22, Conde Duque (no phone). Metro Noviciado or Plaza de

España. **Open** 9.30pm-3.30am Wed-Sun. **Admission** free. **No credit cards**. Map p102 B3 ⓄⒶ

For those who get off on experimental electronic music, this is a must-visit venue. Small and dark, the decor – along the lines of minimalist 1980s computer-game chic – forms the perfect backdrop.

Siroco

C/San Dimas 3, Conde Duque (91 593 30 70, www.siroco.es). Metro Noviciado. **Open** 9.30pm-5am Thur; 9.30pm-6am Fri, Sat. Closed 3 wks Aug. **Admission** (incl 1 drink) €8-€10. **No credit cards**. Map p102 C3 ⓄⓈ

A steady schedule of well-established local rock, indie, pop and funk outfits perform here, and Siroco also provides a stage for young hopefuls. In addition, there are late-night DJ sessions. Things start to hot up after the concerts finish at around 2am, when a crowd of wannabe b-boys, club kids and beardy young students get down to the soul, funk and rare groove seven-inchers.

Tempo

C/Duque de Osuna 8, Conde Duque (91 547 75 18, www.tempoclub.net). Metro Plaza España. **Open** Café 5pm-3am daily. Nightclub 10pm-6am Thur-Sat. Closed Aug. **Admission** *Café* free. *Nightclub* €3 or free. Map p102 B3 ⓄⓄ

A very cool little venue that doubles as a café by day and a venue at night for live acts and DJs. In the pleasant upstairs café you can sit and have a bite, but as the night wears on, head downstairs, either to the dimly lit chill-out room or the dancefloor bathed with psychedelic projections.

Tupperware

C/Corredera Alta de San Pablo 26, Malasaña (no phone). Metro Tribunal. **Open** 9pm-3.30am daily. **Admission** free. **No credit cards**. Map p103 D3 ⓄⓄ

Truly postmodern, this bar is outrageously kitsch but with a pop art sen-

sibility that saves it from crossing over too far into tackiness. The fake fur, *Star Wars* pictures, 1970s toys and faux-cool psychedelia hang together surprisingly well, and there's a pleasant anything-goes music policy. The slightly older and sociable crowd tend to chill out in the easygoing vibe. Something of a neighbourhood institution.

Arts & leisure

Centro Cultural Conde Duque

C/Conde Duque 11, Conde Duque (91 588 58 34, www.munimadrid.es/condeduque). Metro Noviciado or Ventura Rodríguez. **Open** 10am-2pm, 6-9pm Tue-Sat; 10.30am-2pm Sun. **Admission** free. Map p102 B2 ⓄⓄ

Housed in a former barracks, built in the 18th century for Philip V's guard by Pedro de Ribera, the magnificent Conde Duque is a multi-purpose cultural centre. Around a dozen shows, both artistic and historical, are held annually in the two exhibition spaces and the two vast patios. Open-air concerts in summer bring in a range of acts. Also housed here is the Museo Municipal de Arte Contemporáneo (see p113). Both centres have been undergoing refurbishments but are due to reopen in summer 2011.

Teatro Alfil

C/Pez 10, Malasaña (box office 91 521 58 27, information 91 521 45 41, www.teatroalfil.com). Metro Callao or Noviciado. **Open** Box office 1hr before performance daily. Tickets €9-€12. **No credit cards**. Map p102 C4 ⓄⓄ

Madrid's renegade theatre, the Alfil has been threatened with closure but has battled on, and produces increasingly radical plays – both *The Vagina Monologues* and *Puppetry of the Penis* have been staged here. It's also one of the few venues to host stand-up comedy, including the Giggling Guiri English comedy nights (www.comedyinspain.com).

Películas and print

Madrid's specialist film bookshop is a gem.

Cinéfilos will find a mecca of moviedom at Madrid's **Ocho y Medio** bookshop (C/Martín de los Heros 11, Argüelles, 91 559 06 28, www.ochoymedio.com). Rolling since 1996, in larger premises near Plaza de España since 2006 and renovated with the addition of a smart café in 2009, the store's empire is now well established.

Stock includes over 20,000 books in Spanish, English, Italian, French and even Japanese, and anything not on the shelves can be ordered. The DVD section is also excellent and visitors will find film posters, T-shirts, calendars and all sorts of filmic gadgets. Not surprisingly, the shop has become something of a living museum for lovers of Spanish cinema – even the bags, re-designed every few months by an actor or director, have become collectors' items.

Frequent guest signings and launch parties, too, have made the store the hub of the Spanish film industry.

Given its reputation, it's not surprising that Ocho y Medio's enthusiastic owners, Jesús Robles and María Silveyro, have been awarded several prestigious prizes and are often recipients of thanks during film awards ceremonies. Both of them speak English and are founts of information.

Just across the street are some of the city's best multi-screen arthouse and VO cinemas – the Golem, the Renoir Plaza de España and the Renoir Princesa – while a range of tapas bars, tabernas and restaurants serves the film-going crowds. So the location is perfect for when the shop closes and you're turfed onto the streets... at 8.30pm, in line with the Felliniesque name.

Puerta del Europa

The Retiro & Salamanca

Most visitors encounter the area around the Retiro within the first few days of a trip to the city, seeing as it's home to Madrid's star attraction, the **Museo del Prado**. The famous art museum is often referred to in relation to the 'Golden Triangle' it forms with the nearby Thyssen and Reina Sofía (covered in the Old City chapters).

To the east of the museum district is the **Retiro park**, a verdant oasis of old-fashioned delights, and a perfect post-museum respite. North of here is the *barrio* of **Salamanca**, an area known for its designer shopping, expensive restaurants and, along the Paseo de la Castellana, futuristic architecture, including the **Puerta del Europa** towers (known at the *Torres KIO*). But the neighbourhood is also home to some fascinating small museums.

Paseo del Prado & the Retiro

The most attractive section of Madrid's north–south avenue is the oldest: the Paseo del Prado, from Atocha up to Plaza de Cibeles. Despite the traffic, the tree-lined boulevard has many attractions on and around it, most notably Madrid's 'big three' great art museums: the **Museo Thyssen-Bornemisza** (see p83); the **Museo del Prado** (see p131); and, at the very bottom, in the south-east corner of Lavapiés, the **Museo Nacional Centro de Arte Reína Sofía** (see p92). Together with the cutting-edge **CaixaForum** (see p136), these spaces form what the local council has coined the 'Paseo del Arte' (see box p130).

In the 1630s, the area that now lies to the east of the Prado was made into gardens that became part of the **Palacio del Buen Retiro**. However, it was after it became a park open to all that the Retiro acquired most of its many statues, particularly the giant 1902 monument to King Alfonso XII presiding over the lake.

The **Parque del Retiro** has a special place in the hearts and habits of the people of Madrid and is particularly popular for Sunday strolls. During the week it's emptier, and it's easier to take a look at some of the 15,000 trees, the rose garden and the park's exhibition spaces.

The greatest curiosity of the park is Madrid's monument to Lucifer, in the moment of his fall from heaven. Known as the *Angel Caído* (Fallen Angel), this bizarrely unique statue on the avenue south of the Palacio de Cristal is thought to be the only monument to the devil in the world.

Sights & museums

Banco de España
Plaza de Cibeles. Metro Banco de España. **Map** p128 A1 ❶
This grandiose pile on the corner of Calle Alcalá was designed in 1882 by Eduardo Adaro and Severiano Saínz de la Lastra to house the Bank of Spain. The eclectic style was most influenced by French Second Empire designs, with a few Viennese touches. The decorative arched window and elaborate clock above the main entrance are best appreciated from a distance.

Bolsa de Comercio de Madrid
Plaza de la Lealtad 1 (91 589 22 64, www.bolsamadrid.es). Metro Banco de España. **Open** (By guided tour only) Sept-June *Individuals* noon Thur. *Groups* 10am Mon-Fri. **Admission** free. **Map** p128 B2 ❷

In the same plaza as the Hotel Ritz, Madrid's stock exchange is a landmark as well as a business centre. Enrique María Repullés won the competition to design it in 1884, with a neo-classical style chosen to reflect that of the nearby Prado. The building has two distinct areas: one is the trading area; the other, open to the public, houses an exhibition on the market's history.

Estación de Atocha
Glorieta del Emperador Carlos V. Metro Atocha. **Map** p128 B5 ❸
Madrid's classic wrought-iron and glass main rail station was built in 1888-92, to a design by Alberto del Palacio. It remained much the same, gathering a coating of soot, until the 1980s, when Rafael Moneo – he of the Thyssen and Prado extensions – gave it a complete renovation in preparation for Spain's golden year of 1992. Entirely new sections were added for the AVE high-speed trains to Andalucia and Barcelona and the *cercanías* local rail network, and an indoor tropical garden was installed.

Museo Nacional de Antropología
C/Alfonso XII 68 (91 539 59 95, http://.mn antropologia.mcu.es). Metro Atocha. **Open** 9.30am-8pm Tue-Sat; 10am-3pm Sun. **Admission** €3; €1.50 students; free under-18s, over-65s. Free to all 2-8pm Sat & all Sun. **No credit cards. Map** p128 C5 ❹
This three-storey building between the Retiro and Atocha station houses several levels, each devoted to a specific region or country. Among the bizarre highlights are a 19th-century Philippine helmet made from a spiky blowfish, shrunken human heads from Peru and the skeleton of Don Agustín Luengo y Capilla, an Extremaduran who was 2.25m (7ft 4in) tall.

Museo Nacional de Artes Decorativas
C/Montalbán 12 (91 532 64 99, http://mnartesdecorativas.mcu.es).

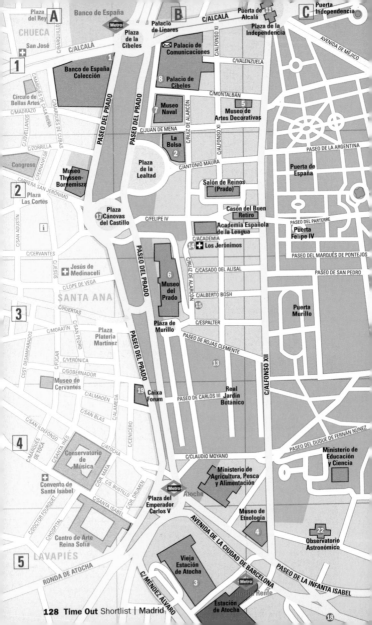

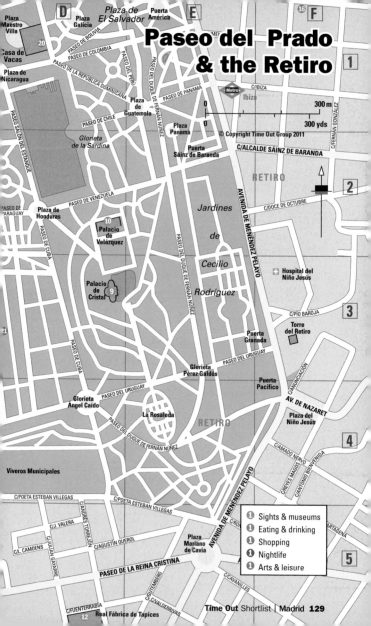

Paseo del Prado & the Retiro

The Paseo del Arte

Madrid's key art museums are just a stroll apart.

In the **Prado** (see right), the **Thyssen-Bornemisza** (see p85) and the **Reina Sofía** (see p94), Madrid has three art palaces that are quite simply world class. You'll find them dotted along the Paseo del Prado, in what has increasingly come to be known as the 'Golden Triangle'. This formidable trio of museums has made Madrid the world's capital of art for many people, and, with extensive revamps of all three museums over the past decade (reckoned to have cost some €150 million), the label is set to stick more firmly.

The city council initiative known as the **Paseo del Arte** ('art stroll') takes advantage of the proximity of the three art collections, promoting the fact that they are barely ten minutes' walk from one another. The idea echoes Berlin's 'Museum Island', London's 'Museum District' or Washington's 'Museums on the Mall'. The axis that unites the big three – as well as newcomer the **CaixaForum** (see p136) – is the Paseo del Prado, which is currently being remodelled by a team of architects under the leadership of Álvaro Siza. The team wants to reclaim the area for pedestrians by widening the pavements, planting new trees and, most controversially, reducing traffic lanes.

Of course, it would be far too tiring to approach the Paseo del Arte as a one-day itinerary – a visit to just one of the three museums is likely to take up several hours, and plenty of energy. The idea is more to familiarise visitors with the area so that the museums can be understood within a historical, geographical and cultural context, and for visits to then be undertaken at one's leisure.

A joint ticket, the Paseo del Arte, gives entry to the Prado, the Reina Sofía and the Thyssen for €17.60. It is available from the ticket desks at all three museums; after visiting one you can visit the other two at any time in the same calendar year.

Metro Banco de España. **Open**
9.30am-3pm Tue-Sat; 10am-3pm Sun.
3rd and 4th floors closed July, Aug.
Admission €3; €1.50 students; free
under-18s, over-65s. Free to all Sun.
No credit cards. **Map** p128 C1 ⑤
The Decorative Arts Museum houses
more than 15,000 *objets d'art*, furniture
and tapestries from all over Spain, plus
many from China. One of the most
prized rooms is the fifth-floor tiled
kitchen, painstakingly transferred
from an 18th-century Valencian palace,
whose 1,604 painted tiles depict a
domestic scene, with a huddle of ser-
vants making hot chocolate. Also of
great interest is the second floor, where
the Spanish baroque pieces are concen-
trated, including ceramics, textiles,
gold and silver work and jewellery
cases from the Tesoro del Delfín
(Treasure of the Grand Dauphin), the
rest of which is in the Prado.

Museo Nacional del Prado

*C/Ruiz de Alarcón 23, off Paseo del
Prado, Retiro (91 330 28 00, 91 330
29 00, 90 210 70 77, www.museodel
prado.es). Metro Atocha or Banco de
España*. **Open** 9am-8pm Tue-Sun.
Admission €8; €4 concessions; free
under-18s, EU students under 25. Free to
all 6-8pm Tue-Sat; 5-8pm Sun. *Paseo del
Arte ticket* €17.60. **Map** p128 B3 ⑥
The Prado is Madrid's best-known
attraction. In 2007, after long delays,
the new extension opened behind the
main building. The highly controver-
sial cube-shaped edifice designed by
Rafael Moneo houses the museum's
temporary galleries, as well as a huge
foyer containing the café/restaurant,
information points, book and gift shop.

The Prado embraces art from
the 12th to the 20th century, and contains the world's largest collection of
Spanish works. Its core is still the royal
holdings, however, so it reflects royal
tastes and political alliances from the
15th to the 17th centuries: court painters
Diego de Velázquez and Francisco de
Goya are well represented. Political ties

with France, Italy and the southern,
Catholic Netherlands also assure the
presence of works by Titian, Rubens
and Hieronymus Bosch.

It is impossible to do the Prado justice
in a single visit, and we don't suggest
you try. Pick up a floor plan when you
arrive to help you track down the don't-
misses. Rooms are being renumbered 1
to 100, and more reorganisation of works
is still taking place as part of the 2009-
2012 'second expansion' of the museum.

The ground floor contains Flemish
and Italian works from the 14th to the
16th centuries, including Breughel the
Elder's *Triumph of Death* and Bosch's
Garden of Earthly Delights (Room 56A,
which will become Room 3), as well as
Spanish art from the 12th to the 19th
centuries, including some of Goya's
major works, and in particular his mas-
terpiece *The Third of May* (Room 64,
which will become Room 89). The
ground floor central gallery also displays many works from the museum's
sculpture collection.

The highlight of the first floor is the
Velázquez rooms, in the Central Gallery.
Here you'll find the Prado's most
famous work, *Las Meninas* (Room 12,
which will become Room 50), often
described as the greatest painting in the
world, because of its complex interplay
of perspectives and realities. Elsewhere
on this floor are Italian paintings from
the 16th century and Spanish art from
the 16th to the 19th centuries, including
several works by El Greco, a room dedicated to Joaquín Sorolla (Room 60A,
which will become Room 99) and Goyas
from the period 1780 to 1800.

The second floor is devoted to
Spanish art from the 18th century, with
works by Paret, Meléndez and Goya,
and will soon also have new rooms for
European art from the 17th century,
with more paintings by Rubens,
among others.

Museo Naval

*Paseo del Prado 5 (91 532 87 89,
www.armada.mde.es). Metro Banco*

de España. **Open** 10am-2pm Tue-Sun. Closed Aug. **Admission** free. **Map** p128 B1 ❼

Madrid's naval museum contains examples of the booty accumulated by Columbus and other mariners during Spain's period of maritime expansion, and an array of navigational instruments, muskets, guns and naval war paintings. The most impressive room is dominated by a huge mural-map that traces the routes taken by Spain's intrepid explorers. This same room also holds the museum's most valuable possession: the first known map of the Americas by a European – a parchment paper drawing by royal cartographer Juan de la Cosa, believed to have been made for Ferdinand and Isabella in 1500. You'll need to show your passport or other form of ID to gain entry.

Palacio de Cibeles

Plaza de Cibeles (91 588 10 00). Metro Banco de España. **Map** p128 B1 ❽

This extraordinary construction, which is regularly compared to a sandcastle or wedding cake, was arguably the world's most spectacular post office until 2007, when it became the city council headquarters. Completed in 1918, it is the best example of the extravagant style favoured by Madrid's elite at its most expansive. The design was influenced by Viennese art nouveau, but it also features many traditional Spanish touches, with a grand entrance (complete with oversized revolving door), a Hollywood film-set staircase, soaring ceilings, stunning columns and grand marble floors. Sadly, however, the interior is now closed to the general public.

Palacio de Cristal

Parque del Retiro (91 574 66 14). Metro Retiro. **Open** Oct-Apr 10am-6pm Mon, Wed-Sat; 10am-4pm Sun. *May-Sept* 11am-8pm Mon, Wed-Sat; 11am-6pm Sun. **Admission** free. **Map** p129 D3 ❾

This 1880s glass and wrought-iron construction, an outpost of the Reina Sofía, is a lovely, luminous space for viewing art. Shows here often involve large-scale installations, sculpture or pieces conceived for the space.

Palacio de Velázquez

Parque del Retiro (91 573 62 45). Metro Retiro. **Open** Oct-Apr 10am-6pm Mon, Wed-Sat; 10am-4pm Sun. *May-Sept* 11am-8pm Mon, Wed-Sat; 11am-6pm Sun. **Admission** free. **Map** p129 D2 ❿

Built by Ricardo Velázquez for a mining exhibition in 1883, this pretty brick and tile building amid the trees of the Retiro is topped by large iron and glass vaults. Another Reina Sofía annexe, its galleries are wonderfully airy, and host very good temporary shows, including a recent one by Julian Schnabel.

Puerta de Alcalá

Plaza de la Independencia. Metro Retiro. **Map** p128 C1 ⓫

A short distance along C/Alcalá from Cibeles, in the middle of another traffic junction, stands one of the most impressive monuments built for King Charles III, a massive neo-classical gate designed by his favourite Italian architect, Francesco Sabatini, to provide a grand entrance to the city. It was built between 1769 and 1778, using granite and stone from Colmenar. Possible to miss in daytime traffic, it is unavoidably impressive at night.

Real Fábrica de Tapices

C/Fuenterrabía 2 (91 434 05 50, www.realfabricadetapices.com). Metro Menéndez Pelayo. **Open** Guided tours only 10am-2pm Mon-Fri (last tour approx 1.30pm). Closed Aug. **Admission** €4; €3 under-12s. **No credit cards. Map** p129 D5 ⓬

Goya created some of his freshest images as designs for Madrid's royal tapestry factory, founded in 1721. The hand-working skills and techniques used haven't changed, and are evident from the intricate, painstaking work carried out in its two sections – the

Museo Nacional del Prado p131

carpet room and the tapestry room. Goya designs are a mainstay of the work that's done here today. Guided tours are normally in Spanish, but if you call in advance an English-speaking guide can always be arranged.

Real Jardín Botánico

Plaza de Murillo 2 (91 420 30 17, www.rjb.csic.es). Metro Atocha. **Open** *Nov-Feb* 10am-6pm daily. *Mar, Oct* 10am-7pm daily. *Apr, Sept* 10am-8pm daily. *May-Aug* 10am-9pm daily. **Admission** €2.50; €1.25 student. Free under-10s. **No credit cards.** Map p128 B3 ⑬
Madrid's luscious botanical gardens were created for Charles III by Juan de Villanueva and the botanist Gómez Ortega in 1781. They are right alongside the Paseo del Prado, just south of the Prado museum, but inside this deep-green glade, with over 30,000 plants from around the world, it's easy to feel that city life has been put on hold. The building in the middle of the gardens is used as a gallery space.

San Jerónimo el Real

C/Moreto 4 (91 420 30 78). Metro Banco de España. **Open** *Oct-June* 10am-1.30pm, 5-8.30pm daily. *July-Sept* 10am-1pm, 6-8.30pm daily. Map p128 B2 ⑭
Founded in 1464 and rebuilt for Queen Isabella in 1503, this church was particularly favoured by the Spanish monarchs, and used for state ceremonies. Most of the original building was destroyed during the Napoleonic Wars, and the present church is largely a reconstruction that was undertaken between 1848 and 1883. The cloisters at the side of the church have been taken over for use as galleries by the Prado.

Eating & drinking

El Botánico

C/Ruiz de Alarcón 27 (91 420 23 42). Metro Banco de España. **Open** 8.30am-midnight daily. **Bar**. Map p128 B3 ⑮

Confusingly, this bar-restaurant actually sits on C/Espalter, just around the corner, and overlooking the botanical gardens. It's very quiet considering its proximity to the Prado, and has a peaceful, shaded terrace. It's a good spot for breakfast, and there are tapas later in the day.

Casa Portal

C/Doctor Castelo 26 (91 574 20 26, www.casa-portal.com). Metro Goya. **Open** 1.30-4.30pm, 8.30-11pm Mon-Sat. Closed Aug. €€. **Asturian**. Map p129 F1 ⑯
Casa Portal specialises in all things traditional from Asturias, hence the mountain of cheeses in the window and the cider being poured from a great height. This spot has been serving *fabada* (an Asturian bean stew with chorizo), tortilla, fish and shellfish for more than 50 years. Choose between the sawdust-strewn bar at the front and the dining room behind.

Estado Puro

Plaza Cánovas del Castillo 4 (91 330 24 00, www.tapasenestadopuro.com). Metro Banco de España or Sevilla. **Open** 11am-1pm Mon-Sat; 11am-5pm Sun. **Tapas**. Map p128 A2 ⑰
Chef Paco Roncero mans the kitchen here, which turns out classic tapas with a modern twist, as well as gazpacho, salads, sandwiches, meat and fish courses. The cool interior is the real attraction, however, evoking an upmarket diner, with a colourful 1950s-style mural. And with a terrace at the top of the Paseo del Prado, it's no surprise that this is a popular tourist lunch spot – despite the high prices.

Nightlife

Ananda

Estación de Atocha, Avda Ciudad de Barcelona s/n (91 524 11 44, www.ananda.es). Metro Atocha. **Open** midnight-7am Fri, Sat. **Admission** (incl 1 drink) €12. Map p128 C5 ⑱

This is the mother of all club terraces: the enormous 2,000sq m complex comes complete with two dancefloors (one indoors and one out), ten bars and plenty of cushion-strewn sofas and chairs, all of them done up in a bit of an Eastern theme. As this guide went to press, the club was closed for a refurbishment, expected to open again in 2011.

Arts & leisure

CaixaForum Madrid

Paseo del Prado 36 (91 330 73 00, http://obrasocial.lacaixa.es). Metro Atocha. **Open** 10am-8pm daily. **Admission** free. **Map** p128 B4 ⑲
See box p140.

Centro Cultural Casa de Vacas

Parque del Retiro (91 409 58 19). Metro Retiro. **Open** 11am-2pm, 5-9pm Mon-Fri; 11am-9pm Sat. Times may vary. **No credit cards**. **Admission** free. **Map** p129 D1 ⑳
This exhibition space in the Retiro, close to the boating lake, is run by the local council and offers shows on a variety of subjects, ranging from children's books to wildlife photography.

Centro Deportivo Municipal La Chopera

Calle Alfonso XII s/n, Parque del Retiro (91 420 11 54). Metro Atocha or Retiro. **Open** 8.30am-9.30pm Mon-Fri; 9am-9pm Sat, Sun. Closed Aug. **Admission** varies. **Map** p129 D3 ㉑
Shaded by the trees of the Retiro, La Chopera is a fine place to play tennis and 5-a-side football (*fútbol sala*).

Observatorio Astronómico Nacional

C/Alfonso XII 3 (91 527 01 07, www.oan.es). Metro Atocha. **Open** Guided tours 10am-1pm Fri. **No credit cards**. **Admission** free. **Map** p128 C5 ㉒
One of Charles III's scientific institutions, the Observatorio was completed after his death in 1790. Beautifully proportioned, it is Madrid's finest neo-classical building, designed by Juan de Villanueva. It still contains a working telescope, which can only be seen by prior request. One room is also open to the public, but only on Fridays and as part of a guided tour; tours should be requested by fax (91 527 19 35).

Paseo de la Castellana & Salamanca

While other cities have rivers cutting through them as navigational points of reference, Madrid has two great avenues: the Gran Vía and its continuation, C/Alcalá, running east–west, and the **Paseo de la Castellana** – which becomes the **Paseo de Recoletos** and the **Paseo del Prado** (see p126) as it runs north–south. Salamanca lies to the east of Paseo de la Castellana and Paseo de Recoletos.

Carlos María de Castro's 1860 plan for Madrid envisaged the expansion of the city north and east in a regular grid pattern, with restrictions on building height and public open spaces at regular intervals. Once the idea caught on, after the Restoration of 1874, the exodus of the wealthy proceeded apace, and the core of Salamanca was built up by 1900.

Streets such as Calles Jorge Juan, Ortega y Gasset, Goya and Juan Bravo yield top designers, art galleries and dealers in wine, silver or superior leather goods. Salamanca also has its own social scene, based around C/Juan Bravo, with shiny, smart bars and discos.

Museo al Aire Libre de la Castellana

Paseo de la Castellana 41. Metro Rubén Darío. **Map** p138 C1 ㉓

An unconventional museum, this 1970s space at the junction of the Castellana with C/Juan Bravo was the brainchild of engineers José Antonio Fernández Ordoñez and Julio Martínez Calzón. Designing a bridge across the avenue, they thought the space underneath would be a good art venue, and sculptor Eusebio Sempere convinced fellow artists to donate their work. All the major names in late 20th-century Spanish sculpture are represented – including Pablo Serrano, Miró, Chillida – and much of their work is spectacular, especially the dynamic stainless-steel *Mon Per a Infants* (A World for Children) by Andreu Alfaro, and the amazing cascade by Sempere that forms a centrepiece.

Museo Arqueológico Nacional

C/Serrano 13 (91 577 79 12, http://man.mcu.es). Metro Serrano. **Open** 9.30am-8pm Tue-Sat; 9.30am-3pm Sun. **Admission** Currently free to all while the museum is being renovated; call for details once these are completed. **No credit cards. Map** p138 C4 ㉔

The Museo Arqueológico Nacional shares the same building as the Biblioteca Nacional and Museo del Libro. It is currently undergoing long-term renovations (with no confirmed date for completion), but access is still permitted, although some areas may be closed to the public. It traces the evolution of human cultures from prehistoric times up to the 15th century.

Museo del Biblioteca Nacional

Biblioteca Nacional, Paseo de Recoletos 20 (91 580 77 59, www.bne.es). Metro Colón. **Open** 10am-9pm Tue-Sat; 10am-2pm Sun. **Admission** free. **Map** p138 B4 ㉕

Among the wealth of printed matter (the library holds over three million volumes) is every work published in Spain since 1716, Greek papyri, Arab, Hebrew and Greek manuscripts,

Nebrija's first Spanish grammar, bibles, and drawings by Goya, Velázquez, Rembrandt and many others. Given the precious and fragile nature of the texts, access was limited to scholars, but in 1996 the administration opened this museum, with interactive displays, to allow the public a glimpse of the library's riches.

Museo Casa de la Moneda

C/Dr Esquerdo 36 (91 566 65 44, www.fnmt.es). Metro O'Donnell. **Open** Sept-July 10am-5.30pm Tue-Fri; 10am-2pm Sat, Sun. Aug 10am-2pm Mon-Fri. **Admission** free.

This museum, dedicated to coins and currency, boasts a huge collection, dating from the 18th century, that is among the most important in the world. There are also seals, bank notes, engravings, rare books and medals, plus around 10,000 sketches and drawings from Spain, Italy and Flanders, ranging from the 16th to 18th century.

Museo de Ciencias Naturales

C/José Gutiérrez Abascal 2 (91 411 13 28, www.mncn.csic.es). Metro Gregorio Marañón. **Open** Sept-June 10am-6pm Tue-Fri; 10am-8pm Sat; 10am-2.30pm Sun. July, Aug 10am-6pm Tue-Fri; 10am-3pm Sat; 10am-2.30pm Sun. **Admission** €5; €3 concessions. Free over-65s and under-3s. **No credit cards.**

The Natural Science Museum occupies two spaces in a huge building overlooking a sloping garden on the Castellana. Much of the north wing is given over to temporary exhibitions, which tend to be hands-on, interactive and fun for kids. A large permanent exhibition of Mediterranean flora and fauna is also in this wing. The smaller space to the south contains a simpler, more old-fashioned presentation of fossils, dinosaurs and geological exhibits.

Museo Lázaro Galdiano

C/Serrano 122 (91 561 60 84, www.flg.es). Metro Gregorio Marañón.

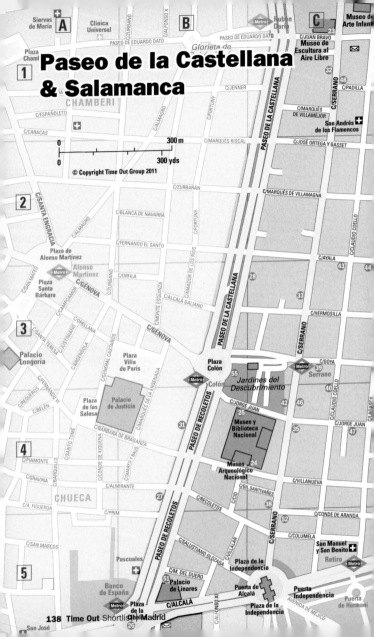

Paseo de la Castellana
& Salamanca

D
E
C/MALDONADO
Hospital de la Princesa
F

C/JUAN BRAVO
C/JUAN BRAVO
Metro
Núñez de Balboa
Los Doce Apóstoles
50
Sanatorio Nuestra Señora del Rosario
C/PADILLA
Nuestra Señora del Pilar
1

C/LAGASCA
C/VELÁZQUEZ
C/NÚÑEZ DE BALBOA
C/CASTELLÓ
53
C/GENERAL PARDIÑAS
C/GENERAL DÍAZ PORLIER

41
C/JOSÉ ORTEGA Y GASSET
Plaza del Marqués de Salamanca
C/JOSÉ ORTEGA Y GASSET
Lista
Metro
2

C/DON RAMÓN DE LA CRUZ
C/DON RAMÓN DE LA CRUZ

Santa María de Monte Carmelo
C/PRÍNCIPE DE VERGARA
C/AYALA
C/AYALA
C/GENERAL PARDIÑAS
C/GENERAL DÍAZ PORLIER
C/CONDE DE PEÑALVER

C/HERMOSILLA
30
C/HERMOSILLA
3

SALAMANCA
Nuestra Señora de Maravillas

Metro
Velázquez
C/GOYA
C/GOYA
Goya
Metro

C/VELÁZQUEZ
La Concepción
49
C/PRÍNCIPE DE VERGARA
C/ESPARTINAS
37
29
C/ALCALÁ
Corte Inglés
AVENIDA DE FELIPE II
54

C/GURTUBAY
C/NÚÑEZ DE BALBOA
C/CASTELLÓ
C/JORGE JUAN
C/LOPE DE RUEDA
C/JORGE JUAN
4

Metro
Príncipe de Vergara
C/VILLANUEVA
C/ANTONIO ACUÑA
C/DUQUE DE SESTO
36

C/ALCALÁ
C/AGUIRRE
AVENIDA DE MENÉNDEZ PELAYO
C/O'DONNELL

C/ALCALÁ
C/O'DONNELL
Puerta de Madrid

Plaza de El Salvador
Puerta América
5

Casa de Vacas
Plaza Galicia
PASEO DE BOLIVIA
PASEO DE COLOMBIA
C/DOCTOR CASTELO
C/LOPE DE RUEDA
C/MARIAZ
C/FERNÁN GONZÁLEZ

Plaza Maestro Villa

1 Sights & museums
1 Eating & drinking
1 Shopping
1 Nightlife
1 Arts & leisure

A new cultural forum

The Paseo del Prado has a cool new landmark.

Sure to become one of Madrid's icons, the **CaixaForum** (see p136) is the avant-garde cultural centre on the Paseo del Prado, designed by Herzog & de Meuron, with sponsorship from Catalan bank/social foundation 'La Caixa'. The centre is the result of a six-year conversion of the 1899 Mediodía Electrical Power Station, one of the few examples of industrial architecture in central Madrid.

The building is striking for its rusted metal appearance and its apparent defiance of the laws of gravity, with the front part of the structure appearing to float off the ground. Its adjacent 24-metre-high (79-foot) 'vertical garden', designed in conjunction with French botanist Patrick Blanc, complements the building's intense red, and is now one of Madrid's most photographed spots. Herzog has stated that the aim of the garden is to provide a connection with the botanical gardens opposite, and the leafy landscape of the Paseo del Prado.

The only material from the original power station that the architects were able to use was the building's brick shell, which needed to be fully restored and secured with cast iron. The extraneous parts of the building were removed with surgical precision – including the stone base, the removal of which opened up the new public square in front of the building, while simultaneously providing a sheltered space where summertime visitors can cool off.

Since opening in 2008, the CaixaForum has become one of Madrid's most-visited attractions – as much for its awe-inspiring aesthetics as the attractions held within. The centre runs a lively programme, with contemporary and traditional art exhibitions held alongside stimulating music and poerty events, as well as lectures, debates and workshops. Federico Fellini, Fotopres journalism, and the Fairtrade movement have been the focus of recent shows.

Open 10am-4.30pm Mon, Wed-Sun. Third floor closes at 2pm Mon, Wed-Fri. **Admission** €4; €2 concessions; free under-12s. Free to all Sun. **No credit cards**.

This unjustifiably little-known museum holds the extraordinarily eclectic collection of 15,000 paintings and *objets d'art*, covering 24 centuries, that was accumulated over 70 years by the financier and bibliophile José Lázaro Galdiano (1862-1947). Its holdings include paintings by Goya and Bosch, an important collection of work from the Dutch and English schools, and some wonderful Renaissance ornamental metalwork. The four-storey mansion and its gardens are a sight in themselves.

Plaza de Cibeles
Metro Banco de España.
Map p138 B5 26

Midway between the Puerta del Sol and the Retiro, this four-way intersection and its statue signify Madrid to Spaniards as much as the Eiffel Tower or the Empire State Building identify their particular cities. It is surrounded by some of the capital's most prominent buildings: the Palacio de Cibeles (see p132), the Banco de España (see p127), the Palacio Buenavista (now the Army headquarters) and the Palacio de Linares, which houses the Casa de América (see p146). The Ventura Rodríguez statue in the middle is of Cybele, the Roman goddess of fertility and symbol of natural abundance, on a chariot drawn by lions.

Eating & drinking

La Brasserie de Lista
C/Serrano 110 (91 411 08 67, www. labrasseriedelista.com). Metro Núñez de Balboa. **Open** noon-4pm Mon, Sun; noon-4pm, 9pm-midnight Tue-Sat. **€€. French**.

La Brasserie de Lista could be mistaken for one of the hundreds of similar establishments in Paris, all wood

panelling and parlour palms. On the menu: Caesar salad, onion soup with Emmental, sirloin steak with pepper sauce and hamburgers. The set menu is excellent, or there is a bar at the front where you can just enjoy some tapas.

Café Gijón
Paseo de Recoletos 21 (91 521 54 25, www.cafegijon.com). Metro Banco de España or Colón. **Open** 7am-1.30am Mon-Fri, Sun; 7am-2.30am Sat. **Café**. **Map** p138 B4 27

Still charming after all these years, this is Madrid's definitive literary café, open since 1888. It still holds poetry *tertulias* on Monday nights, and publishes a magazine filled with doodles and thoughts from visiting writers. A pianist tinkles the ivories to a packed terrace in summer, while in winter it's heaving inside.

Castellana 8
Paseo de la Castellana 8 (91 578 34 87, www.castellana8.es). Metro Colón. **Open** 11.30am-2.30am daily. **Bar**. **Map** p138 C3 28

A supremely stylish bar-restaurant-club, with black walls that are softened by clever uplighting, orange velvet cushions and a mellow soundtrack of jazz and blues. Brunch on Sundays is dished up with cocktails and live music, though not, sadly, on the terrace outside, which is limited to drinking only. The upmarket location and older clientele mean predictably higher prices.

Cervecería Santa Bárbara
C/Goya 70 (91 575 00 52, www. cerveceriasantabarbara.com). Metro Goya. **Open** 8am-midnight daily. **Tapas**. **Map** p139 F4 29

The prawns are the thing here, consumed in rosy platefuls by the uptown shoppers crowded round the horse-shoe-shaped bar. It is one of the city's meeting places, with a good selection of beers, and tables outside.

Estay

C/Hermosilla 46 (91 578 04 70,
www.estayrestaurante.com). Metro
Velázquez. **Open** 8am-2am Mon-
Sat. **Tapas**. **Map** p139 D3 ㉚

Estay's bright, air-conditioned interior,
usually filled with baying young moth-
ers heavily laden with shopping bags,
does not immediately suggest gastro-
nomic promise. Stick with the place,
however, and you'll enjoy scrumptious
and sophisticated tapas and cheap
wines by the glass.

José Luis

C/Serrano 89 (91 563 09 58, www.
joseluis.es). Metro Núñez de Balboa.
Open 9am-1am Mon-Sat; noon-1am
Sun. **Tapas**.

José Luis is one of Madrid's most
famous tapas bars, and is name-
checked in a song by the Catalan folk
singer Serrat. The food here is little
changed since the 1950s and of a high
standard; if your appetite is up to it,
try the *brascada* (sirloin with ham
and onions).

Nodo

C/Velázquez 150 (91 564 40 44,
www.restaurantenodo.es). Metro
República Argentina. **Open**
1-4pm, 9pm-midnight daily. **€€**.
Japanese/Mediterranean.

With minimalist decor and food to
match, Nodo keeps the famous and the
fashionable coming back for more.
Some say it's the best sushi in town.
Chef Albert Chicote's beef carpaccio
with foie gras and coriander coulis
typifies the menu, a successful blend
of Japanese and Mediterranean. The
sashimi and the tuna tataki with
garlic get high marks too; service
scores lower.

El Pavellón del Espejo

Paseo de Recoletos 31 (91 319
11 22, www.restauranteelespejo.com).
Metro Colón. **Open** 9am-1am Mon-
Thur; 9am-2am Fri-Sun. **Bar**.
Map p138 B4 ㉛

Not nearly as historic as the neighbouring Gijón, although it may look it:
when it opened in 1978, this place set
out to be the art nouveau bar Madrid
never had, with positively Parisian
1900s decor. Its terrace bar out on the
Paseo de Recoletas occupies a splendid glass pavilion reminiscent of a
giant Tiffany lamp. Fashionable and
comfortable, it has excellent tapas at
good prices.

Shopping

ABC Serrano

C/Serrano 61 & Paseo de la Castellana
34 (91 577 50 31, www.abcserrano.
com). Metro Rubén Darío. **Open** 10am-
9pm Mon-Sat; noon-8pm 1st Sun of
mth. **Map** p138 C1 ㉜

This upmarket mall has eight floors.
Four are dedicated to fashion, sports-
wear, jewellery, crafts and hi-fi. There
are three restaurants on the upper
floors, a café on the ground floor and a
lively summer *terraza* on the fourth.

Agatha Ruiz de la Prada

C/Serrano 27 (91 319 05 01, www.
agatharuizdelaprada.com). Metro
Serrano. **Open** Sept-June 10am-8.30pm
Mon-Sat. Aug 10am-2pm, 5-8pm Mon-
Sat. **Map** p138 C3 ㉝

Loud and colourful designs distinguish
this designer's work, many embla-
zoned with her trademark hearts and
flowers. The childrenswear range is
hugely popular, as is the homeware.

Amaya Arzuaga

C/Lagasca 50 (91 426 28 15, www.
amayaarzuaga.com). Metro Serrano.
Open Sept-June 10.30am-8.30pm
Mon-Sat. Aug 10.30am-2pm, 5-8.30pm
Mon-Fri; 10am-2pm Sat. **Map** p139
D3 ㉞

One of the few Spanish designers with
an international presence. The clothes
are not for everyday wear, but there are
some great outfits to be discovered,
with a hard-edged punky look. The
knitwear is of excellent quality.

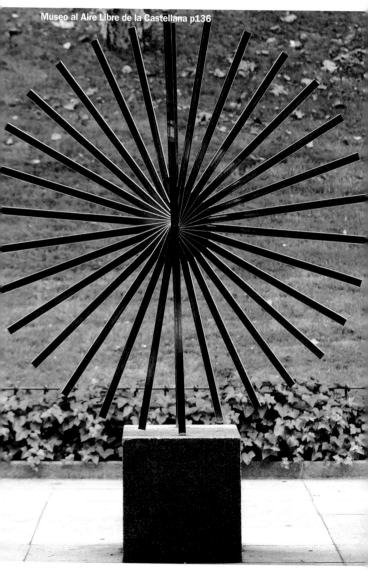

Museo al Aire Libre de la Castellana p136

Tours guide

A myriad ways to see the city.

If you'd like a guided overview of the city, or have a special interest in one particular element of it, then it might be worth checking out Madrid's varied tour companies.

If you'd like a straightforward bus city tour, then **Juliá Travel** (91 559 96 05, www.juliatravel. com), **Madrid Vision** (91 779 18 88, www.madridvision.es) and **Trapsatur** (91 541 63 21, www.trapsatur.com) are well-established companies.

For a two-wheeled way to see the city, consider a Segway tour. The oldest is **Madsegs** (659 824 499, www.madsegs.com) – for €65 (plus a €15 deposit) you'll get a three-hour tour, a helmet, refreshments and a photo CD.

For a more stylish tour vehicle, consider zipping about town in a little yellow **Go Car** (photo above; 91 559 45 35, www.go cartours.es/madrid; €35-€109), a computer-guided storytelling vehicle that allows you to undertake a personalised tour at your own pace.

If you'd rather go it on foot, however, your options are wide. The guides from **Carpetania Madrid** (91 531 40 18, www. carpetaniamadrid.com) are all art history specialists, offering expert guided tours of art museums and exhibitions for €9-€14 per person. The tourist board initiative **Descubre Madrid** (91 588 29 06, www.esmadrid.com/descubre madrid), meanwhile, has over 100 different itineraries (by foot and by bike), focusing on architecture, literature and history (€3.12-€7.75 per person). And **Letango** (91 369 47 52, www.letango.com) offers tailored tours with an emphasis on Spanish culture and history (prices vary).

For a more eccentric take on the city, check out the **Wellington Society** (609 143 203, www. wellsoc.org); Stephen Drake-Jones gives an entertaining slant on themes such as wine, bullfighting and Hemingway. Tours cost between €60 and €85 (plus a membership fee of €50).

Camper

C/Serrano 24 (91 578 25 60, www. camper.com). Metro Serrano. **Open** 9.30am-9pm Mon-Sat. **Map** p138 C4 🕉
Branches of the Mallorcan family firm continue to spring up all over the city. At this one, two large plinths display the entire men's and women's collection of funky shoes and sandals.

La Casa de los Chales

C/Duque de Sesto 54(91 574 25 73, http://lacasadeloschales.com). Metro Goya or O'Donnell. **Open** 8am-1.30pm, 5-9pm Mon- Sat. **Map** p139 F4 🕉
The 'House of Shawls' has a huge range of *mantones de Manila*, beautifully made fringed and embroidered shawls. Capes, handbags and feather boas complete the stock.

Concha García

C/Goya 38 (91 435 49 36, www. concha-garcia.com). Metro Goya. **Open** 10.30am-8.30pm Mon-Fri; 10.30am-2.30pm, 5-8.30pm Sat. **Map** p139 E3 🕉
Concha Garcia's two shops-cum-galleries are important showcases for contemporary and ethnic jewellery design, both national and international.

Farrutx

C/Serrano 7 (91 577 09 24, www.farrutx.com). Metro Serrano. **Open** Sept-June 10am-2pm, 5-8pm Mon-Fri; 10.30am-2pm, 5-8.30pm Sat. *July, Aug* 10.30am-2pm, 5.30-8.30pm Mon-Sat. **Map** p138 C4 🕉
Innovative and sharply elegant leather designs from this popular Mallorcan company, with bags and shoes too.

El Jardín de Serrano

C/Goya 6-8 (91 577 00 12, www.jardindeserrano.es). Metro Serrano. **Open** 9.30am-9.30pm Mon-Sat. **Map** p138 C3 🕉
This mall may be small but it's a gem, with designer boutiques, expensive shoe shops and a classy café.

Joaquín Berao

C/Claudio Coello 35 (91 577 28 28, www.joaquinberao.com). Metro Serrano. **Open** Sept-July 10am-2pm, 5-8.30pm Mon-Fri; 10.30am-2.30pm, 5-8.30pm Sat. *Aug* 10am-2pm, 5-8.30pm Mon-Fri; 10am-2pm Sat. **Map** p138 C4 🕘
Chunky, twisted and contorted, but also fluidly elegant, Joaquin Berao's solid silver bracelets, necklaces, earrings and chokers are increasingly the choice of those in the know.

Lavinia

C/José Ortega y Gasset 16 (91 426 06 04, www.lavinia.es). Metro Nuñez de Balboa. **Open** 10am-9pm Mon-Sat. **Map** p139 D2 🕘
Lavinia claims to be Europe's largest wine shop. In stark contrast to many of Madrid's dusty old *bodegas*, it's bright, airy and spacious, and staff are knowledgeable and helpful.

Loewe

C/Serrano 26 & 34 (91 577 60 56, www.loewe.com). Metro Serrano. **Open** 10am-8.30pm Mon-Sat. **Map** p138 C4 🕘
The world-famous, elite Spanish leather goods company, selling bags, shoes, cases and a small range of clothes. Prices are very high.

Mantequerías Bravo

C/Ayala 24 (91 576 02 93). Metro Serrano. **Open** 9.30am-2.30pm, 5.30-8.30pm Mon-Fri; 9.30am-2.30pm Sat. Closed Aug. **Map** p138 C3 🕘
A marvellous selection of foodstuffs, including meats, cheeses, wines, spirits, coffees and teas. Homesick Brits will be pleased with imports such as English mustard and cream crackers.

Mercado de la Paz

C/Ayala 28 (91 435 07 43, http:// mercadodelapaz.blogspot.com). Metro Serrano. **Map** p138 C3 🕘
A high-end market, with a dazzling range of products. Don't miss gourmet cheese stall La Boulette.

¡Oh, qué luna!

C/Ayala 32 (91 431 37 25, www.ohque luna.com). Metro Serrano. **Open** 10am-2pm, 5-8.30pm Mon-Fri; 11am- 2pm, 5-8.30pm Sat. **Map** p139 D3 ⓯
Glam, sexy lingerie, negligées and dressing gowns. It also does a line in bedlinen and swimwear.

Purificación García

C/Serrano 28 (91 435 80 13, www. purificaciongarcia.es). Metro Serrano. **Open** 10am-8.30pm Mon-Sat. **Map** p138 C4 ⓰
Purificación García is where Madrid's older but elegant woman heads when she wants something smart for the office. The clothes are very well priced for the quality of the fabrics.

Sybilla

Callejón de Jorge Juan 12 (63 274 97 76, www.sybilla.es). Metro Retiro or Serrano. **Open** 10.30am-8.30pm Mon-Sat. Closed 2wks Aug. **Map** p138 C4 ⓱
As well as her usual eye-catching outfits for actresses attending the Goyas (the Spanish equivalent of the Oscars), Sybilla also stocks a new range, Jocomomola, aimed at a younger crowd.

Las Tiendas de Serrano

C/Serrano 88 (no phone). Metro Rubén Darío. **Open** 10.30am-2.30pm, 5-8.30pm Mon-Sat. **Map** p138 C1 ⓳
A small shopping mall, dominated by shops selling upmarket designer fashion, party clothes and accessories.

Vinçon

C/Castelló 18 (91 578 05 20, www.vincon.com). Metro Velázquez. **Open** 10am-8.30pm Mon-Sat. **Map** p139 D4 ⓳
The Madrid outpost of the classic Barcelona design store occupies a former 1920s silver factory. It has everything for the cred-seeking homeowner – furniture, home and garden accessories and attractive gift ideas, often at surprisingly low prices.

Nightlife

Almonte

C/Juan Bravo 35 (91 563 54 70, www.almontesalarociera.com). Metro Diego de León. **Open** 9pm-5am daily. **Admission** minimum consumption 1 drink. **Map** p139 E1 ⓾
This 'flamenco disco' attracts a youthful crowd. The beautiful patrons flaunt it freestyle before *sevillanas* prompt a free-for-all. Try to work your way downstairs, where the most attention-grabbing dancing can be admired and – go on – attempted.

Ritmo & Compás

C/Conde de Vilches 22, Salamanca (91 355 28 00, www.ritmoycompas.com). Metro Cartagena or Diego de León. **Open** Bar 4pm-end of concert programme. **Admission** varies.
A music fanatic's paradise, Ritmo & Compás boasts 160 rehearsal rooms over two sites, recording studios, its own record label and courses and seminars. As a live venue it has a programme as diverse as the facilities, including pop-rock, reggae, northern soul, metal, blues, funk, techno and breakbeat. The stage and auditorium are well designed, allowing a good view from any angle.

Arts & leisure

Casa de América

Palacio de Linares, Paseo de Recoletos 2 (91 595 48 00, www.casamerica.es). Metro Banco de España. **Open** 11am-8pm Mon-Sat; 11am-3pm Sun. Guided tours 11am, noon, 1pm Sun. Closed Aug, except for cinema. **Admission** free. Guided tour €7; €4 concessions; free under-12s. **Map** p138 B5 ⓾
Housed in the 1872 Palacio de Linares, the Casa de América showcases Latin American art and has an important role in promoting cultural contacts between Spain and Latin America. There are film seasons, music, theatre

Plaza de Toros de las Ventas p148

and talks given by leading writers, film directors, playwrights and political figures. There are also print and video libraries, a bookshop and a terrace – the Terraza Jardin Brugal – with arts events in summer. Tours of the Palacio de Linares must be taken with a guide.

Chi Spa

C/Conde de Aranda 6, Salamanca (91 578 13 40, www.thechispa.com). Metro Retiro. **Open** 10am-9pm Mon-Fri; 10am-6pm Sat. **Map** p138 C5 ⑳
A sleek, sophisticated space that has separate areas for men and women offering specialised body and relaxation treatments, massages with essential oils and spices, hydrotherapy and aromatherapy.

Fundación Juan March

C/Castelló 77 (91 435 42 40, www.march.es). Metro Núñez de Balboa. **Open** *Mid Sept-June* 11am-8pm Mon-Sat; 10am-2pm Sun. *July, Aug* 11am-8pm Mon-Fri. **No credit cards** free. **Map** p139 E1 ⑬
This cultural foundation, set up by the wealthy financier Juan March in 1955, is one of the most important in Europe. Each year, a couple of major exhibitions are held here, and a decent selection of the foundation's 1,300 works of contemporary Spanish art is also on permanent display. The regular free concerts are also worth checking out.

Hammam Ayala

C/Ayala 126, Salamanca (91 187 52 20, www.hammamayala.com). Metro Goya, Lista or Manuel Becerra. **Open** 10am-8pm Tue, Thur; 1-10pm Wed, Fri, Sat; 1-8pm Sun. **Admission** *Basic ritual* €50. *Traditional ritual* €60. See box p55.

Palacio de Deportes de la Comunidad de Madrid

Avda Felipe II s/n, Salamanca (91 444 99 49, www.palaciodedeportes.com). Metro Goya. **Map** p139 F4 ⑭

This state-of-the-art 16,000-capacity sports palace is a multi-purpose venue that can host a wide range of indoor sports thanks to a modern system of retractable stands. As well as sports, you can catch spectacles such as *Disney on Ice* or any number of rock concerts: Springsteen, Depeche Mode and Coldplay have all performed here.

Plaza de Toros de Las Ventas

C/Alcalá 237 (91 356 22 00, museum 91 725 18 57, www.las-ventas.com). Metro Ventas. **Open** (Museum) *Nov-Feb* 9.30am-2.30pm Mon-Fri. *Mar-Oct* 9.30am-2.30pm Tue-Fri; 10am-1pm Sun. **Admission** (Museum) free.
It will soon be banned in Catalonia, but bullfighting in Madrid still draws the crowds. More than 22,000 spectators can catch a bullfight in this, Spain's largest arena, completed in 1929. It is in neo-Mudéjar style, with often playful use of ceramic tiling. Around it there is ample open space, so it's easy to get a good look at the exterior. It's not necessary to go to a *corrida* to see the ring from within either. Concerts are often held here, and alongside the ring there is the small Museo Taurino, which holds portraits of famous matadors, as well as *trajes de luces* (suits of lights).

Teatro Fernán Gómez, Centro de Arte

Plaza de Colón 4 (91 436 25 40, http://teatrofernangomez.esmadrid. com). Metro Colón. **Open** Exhibitions 10am-9pm Tue-Sat; 10am-7pm Sun. **Admission** *Exhibitions* free. *Shows* €14-€22. **Map** p138 B3 ⑮
The city council's only purpose-built cultural centre offers a mixed bag of theatre, puppets, opera and *zarzuelas* (traditional Spanish performances that alternate between spoken and sung scenes) in the summer, as well as art exhibitions, usually featuring important Hispanic artists.

Matadero Madrid p161

Beyond the Centre

North & west

Casa de Campo, Argüelles & Moncloa

Sights & museums

Casa de Campo

Once a royal hunting estate, the verdant, sprawling parkland of the Casa de Campo, to the west of the city, was only opened to the public under the Republic in 1931. Five years later, it became a key site for Franco's forces in the Civil War battle for Madrid, its high ground being used to shell the city centre and the university. Remains of trenches still exist.

Today, the Casa is home to the **Parque de Atracciones** funfair (see p151) and the **Zoo** (see p152), as well as swimming pools, tennis courts and a boating lake. Once you stray away from the criss-crossing roads much of the park is surprisingly wild.

A favourite way to visit is via the **Teleférico** cable car (see p152) from the **Parque del Oeste**, which runs over the trees almost to the middle of the Casa.

Couples seeking seclusion favour the Casa de Campo, and the area by the Teleférico has been a gay cruising spot, although police have been cracking down on this. In contrast, one new feature of the modern Casa is that Madrid's city authorities seem near set on turning the roads from Lago metro to the Zoo into a semi-official prostitution zone, with the aim of moving prostitution from the city centre. Consequently, by night, and often by day, there are female and transvestite prostitutes along these roads, displaying their assets pretty outrageously to cruising drivers.

Ermita de San Antonio de la Florida

Glorieta de San Antonio de la Florida 5 (91 542 07 22). Metro Príncipe Pío.

Ermita de San Antonio de la Florida p149

Open 9.30am-8pm Tue-Fri; 10am-
2pm Sat, Sun. **Admission** free.
This plain neo-classical chapel was completed by Felipe Fontana for Charles IV
in 1798. It is famous as the burial place
of Goya, and for the frescoes of the miracles of St Anthony, which he painted
here in 1798. Featuring a rare mix of ele-
ments, including Goya's simultaneously ethereal and sensual 'angels', they are
among his best and most complex
works. On the other side of the road into
the park is a near-identical second
chapel, built in the 1920s to allow the
original building to be left as a museum.
There are free guided tours of the
Ermita, in Spanish and English, at 11am
and noon on Saturdays.

Faro de Madrid

*Avda de los Reyes Católicos, Moncloa.
Metro Moncloa.* **Open** Currently
closed for restoration work. Expected to
reopen in September 2011. **Admission**
€1; 50¢ concessions.
This radio and communications tower,
at 92m (302ft), provides one of the best
views of the whole of the city and the
sierras in the distance. Diagrams along
the floor point out highlights of the city.
The best bit, though, is the stomach-
lurching ride up in the glass lift. Closed
for restoration since 2008, the tower is
due to reopen in autumn 2011.

Museo de América

*Avda de los Reyes Católicos 6, Moncloa
(91 543 94 37, http://museodeamerica.
mcu.es). Metro Moncloa.* **Open** 9.30am-
3pm Tue, Wed, Fri, Sat; 9.30am-3pm
Sun. **Admission** €3; €1.50 concessions.
Free to all Sun. No credit cards.
This museum comprises the finest collection of pre-Columbian American art
and artefacts in Europe – a combination
of articles brought back at the time of the
Conquest and during the centuries of
Spanish rule over Central and South
America, plus later acquisitions donat-
ed by Latin American governments. It's
a superb, intriguing collection, and temporary shows are usually interesting.

Museo Cerralbo

*C/Ventura Rodríguez 17, Argüelles
(91 547 36 46, http://.museocerralbo.
mcu.es). Metro Plaza de España.* **Open**
9.30am-3pm Tue-Sat; 10am-3pm Sun.
Admission €3; €1.50 concessions.
Free under-18s & over-65s. Free to
all Sun. No credit cards.
In a sumptuous late 19th-century mansion in Argüelles is the incredible private collection of artworks and artefacts
assembled by Enrique de Aguilera y
Gamboa, the 17th Marqués de Cerralbo.
A man of letters, politician and traveller
who collected pieces everywhere he
went, he bequeathed his collection to the
state with the stipulation that it should
be displayed exactly how he had
arranged it himself. Among the many
paintings is El Greco's *The Ecstasy of
St Francis of Assisi.*

Museo del Traje (Museum of Clothing)

*Avda Juan de Herrera 2 (91 550
47 00, http://museodeltraje.mcu.es).
Metro Moncloa.* **Open** Sept-June
9.30am-7pm Tue-Sat; 10am-3pm Sun.
July, Aug 9.30am-7pm Tue, Wed, Fri,
Sat; 9.30am-10.30pm Thur; 10am-
3pm Sun. **Admission** €3; €1.50
concessions. Free to all 2.30-7pm
Sat & all Sun. No credit cards.
This museum is a must for those inter-
ested in any aspect of clothing. The collections comprise some 21,000 garments
covering six centuries of Spanish fashion, though there are some much older
items, among them fragments of Coptic
cloth and Hispano-Muslim pieces. The
permanent exhibition shows up to 600
items at any one time. Facilities include
reading and rest rooms, a bookshop, a
café and a restaurant.

Parque de Atracciones

*Casa de Campo (90 234 50 09, 91 526
80 30, www.parquedeatracciones.es).
Metro Batán.* **Open** varies (see
website), but generally 11am-7pm
daily. **Admission** €10.60 over-3s;
€4 over-65s.

A funfair with something for everyone. The wildest ride is El Abismo, The Abyss, which is a 49-metre high roller that follows a 450m route of scary drops at 100kph. There is now a children's version too, so nobody has to miss the terror. Other new features include indoor paintball and a 4D cinema. There are long queues for some rides.

Teleférico de Madrid

Paseo del Pintor Rosales (91 541 74 50, www.teleferico.com). Metro Argüelles. **Open** *June-Aug* noon-1.45pm, 3-9pm Mon-Fri; noon-9.30pm Sat, Sun. Opening times for rest of year change on a weekly and monthly basis (see website). **Tickets** (return) €5.20; €4.60 concessions. Free under-3s.

An extraordinary 2.5km (1.5-mile) trip over the Casa de Campo and Parque del Oeste in a cable car. The views of the Palacio Real, Río Manzanares, city skyline and park are breathtaking. There are even interesting close-ups of the park's seedier goings-on. In the winter, the cars rarely operate on weekdays.

Templo de Debod

Montaña del Príncipe Pío (91 366 74 15). Metro Plaza de España or Ventura Rodríguez. **Open** *Apr-Sept* 10am-2pm, 6-8pm Tue-Fri; 10am-2pm Sat, Sun. *Oct-Mar* 9.45am-1.45pm, 4.15-6.15pm Tue-Fri; 10am-2pm Sat, Sun. **Admission** free.

This Egyptian structure, which sits on the outskirts of the Parque del Oeste, dates back 2,200 years and is dedicated to the gods Amun and Isis. It was sent, block by block, by the Egyptian government in 1968 in thanks for Spain's help in preserving monuments threatened by the Aswan Dam.

Zoo Aquarium Madrid

Casa de Campo (91 512 37 70, www.zoomadrid.com). Metro Batán. **Open** 11am-dusk daily. **Admission** €18.80 over-8s; €15.25 3-7s & over-65s; free under-3s.

This attractively landscaped zoo is located slap bang in the heart of the Casa de Campo. The animals look as happy as can be expected of beasts held in captivity, although the big cats could really do with a bit more leg-room. At the Tierra de Gorilas ('Land of Gorillas') a sheet of reassuringly thick glass separates you from the massive, glowering silverbacks that prowl about. Children will enjoy walking through the shark tank and dolphinarium. There is also a petting zoo and a train ride.

Eating & drinking

A'Casiña

Avda del Ángel, Casa de Campo (91 526 34 25, www.acasina.com). Metro Lago. **Open** 1.30-4pm, 8.30pm-midnight Mon-Sat; 1.30-4.30pm Sun. **€€. Galician.**

A'Casiña is one of several restaurants specialising in regional cuisine – in this case Galician – in the Casa de Campo. The restaurant is a reconstruction of a *pazo*, a Galician manor house, and really comes into its own in summer, with tables outside in the garden. Expensive but top-quality fish, shellfish and beef are the highlights, along with favourites from the region, such as *caldo gallego*, a broth made with pork, potatoes and cabbage. There is also a tapas bar, for a cheaper seafood experience.

Bruin

Paseo del Pintor Rosales 48, Argüelles (91 541 59 21). Metro Argüelles. **Open** 11am-11pm Tue-Thur, Sun; 11am-2am Fri, Sat. **€. No credit cards. Ice-cream.**

A wonderfully old-fashioned ice-cream parlour, with a terrace overlooking the Parque del Oeste. In contrast to its 1950s feel, some of its 40 own-made flavours are decidedly modern: try olive oil, tomato, idiazábal cheese, tomato or sherry. Diabetics get a look-in, too, with the sugar-free varieties.

Casa Mingo
Paseo de la Florida 34, Casa de Campo (91 547 79 18, www.casamingo.es). Metro Príncipe Pío. **Open** 11am-midnight daily. **€. No credit cards.**
Asturian.

A vast and noisy Asturian cider house, open since 1888, and a great opportunity to rub elbows with *madrileños* enjoying themselves at one of the long wooden tables. The restaurant does only three things: roast chicken, salad and cider. Turn up before the city gets hungry (around 1.30pm) if you want a terrace seat, or take out a chicken and a bottle of cider and head for the River Manzanares for a picnic.

Nightlife

DU:OM
Sala Heineken, C/Princesa 1, Argüelles (91 547 57 11, www. salarena.com). Metro Plaza de España.

A dual-personality club night, held at a well-known concert venue (see right), with diametrically opposed sounds on each floor. Downstairs Iván Pica and Hugo Serra mix a selection of electro house tracks with whooshing high-level sweeps and pounding 4/4 beats that keep the crowd dancing all night long. Upstairs it's an anything-goes policy with Spanish pop (or *pachanga*) thrown together with commercial hip hop, cheesy dance tracks and eurotrance.

El Johnny
Colegio Mayor Universitario San Juan Evangelista, C/Gregorio del Amo 4, Moncloa (91 534 24 00, http:// cmusanjuan.com). Metro Metropolitano.

This auditorium, located in a student residence, is actually much more prestigious than you might think. Contrary to its appearance, it's one of the city's most discerning jazz clubs – hundreds of great names have passed through the doors here in the 30-plus years of its existence. Look out for the annual spring jazz festival and the Flamenco por Tarantos festival in April.

Madrid Arena
Casa de Campo, Avda de Portugal s/n (91 722 04 00, www.madridarena.org). Metro Alto de Extremadura or Lago.

A behemoth of a venue, refurbished just a few years ago, and well laid out, with good facilities and great acoustics. There are plenty of macro-raves here too – it's not all just about the guitars.

Sala Heineken
C/Princesa 1, Argüelles (91 547 57 11, www.salarena.com). Metro Plaza de España.

The venue formerly known as Arena (but not to be confused with Madrid Arena, for which, see above), Sala Heineken plays host to several club nights, but is also a fairly hot live music venue. The layout is not especially conducive to everyone getting a good view of the action, but it's an intimate venue, with recent visitors including the likes of !!!, Peaches and the Kaiser Chiefs.

Arts & leisure

Golem
C/Martín de los Heros 14, Argüelles (information 91 559 38 36, box office 90 222 16 22, www.golem.es). Metro Plaza de España. **No credit cards.**

This legendary four-screen cinema, until recently known as the Alphaville, was the first of Madrid's arthouses and played a crucial role in the Movida during the 1980s. The screens and sound systems are showing their age and tiering is inadequate, but the basement café is still a fashionable meeting place with a bohemian atmosphere.

Piscinas Casa de Campo (Open-air municipal pools)
Avda del Ángel s/n, Casa de Campo (91 463 00 50). Metro Lago. **No credit cards.**

Landlocked Madrid is stiflingly hot in the summer months, so at weekends half the city seems to turn up at this beautiful, leafy complex with three open-air pools set in green meadows (expect queues on midsummer weekends). Topless bathing is tolerated, and there's an informal gay area.

Renoir Plaza de España

C/Martín de los Heros 12, Argüelles (information 91 541 41 00, box office 90 222 91 22, www.cinesrenoir.com). Metro Plaza de España.
The flagship cinema of the enterprising Renoir chain. Screens are on the small side and the queuing system in the cramped foyer is haphazard, but good sound systems and a keen crowd of film fans ensure enjoyable viewing.

Sala Berlanga

C/Andrés Mellado 53, Argüelles (91 349 97 73, www.arteria.com). Metro Argüelles, Islas Filipinas or Intercambiador de Moncloa.
The old California cinema, refurbished to a tune of €2 million by SGAE, reopened as Sala Berlanga in June 2010 – much to the delight of local cinephiles. Named after Spanish film director Luis García Berlanga, the 250-seat VO (original version) cinema is one of the city's most technologically advanced. It runs special seasons and festivals, with a strong focus on documentary, shorts and underground films.

Chamberí
Sights & museums

Museo Sorolla

Paseo del General Martínez Campos 37 (91 310 15 84, http://museosorolla. mcu.es). Metro Gregorio Marañón or Iglesia. **Open** 9.30am-8pm Tue, Sat; 10am-3pm Sun. **Admission** €3; €1.50 concessions. Free to all Sun.
No credit cards.
Often considered a neo-Impressionist, Valencia-born Joaquín Sorolla was really an exponent of 'luminism', the celebration of light. He was renowned for his iridescent, sun-drenched paintings, including portraits and family

scenes at the beach and in gardens. Sorolla's leisured themes and greetings-card-esque aesthetic are easy to dismiss, but most find his luminous world at least a little seductive. This delightful little museum, housed in the mansion built for the artist in 1910 to spend his latter years, has been recently restored and boasts 250 works. The garden, Moorish-inspired but with an Italianate pergola, is a delightful, peaceful oasis of calm.

Sala del Canal de Isabel II

C/Santa Engracia 125 (91 545 10 00, www.cyii.es). Metro Ríos Rosas. **Open** 11am-2pm, 5-8.30pm Tue-Sat; 11am-2pm Sun. **Admission** free.
This water tower, built in elaborate neo-Mudéjar style in 1907-11 is considered a gem of Madrid's industrial architecture. It is now home to a stylish exhibition space that specialises in photography, ranging in quality from good to world-class. Two kilometres north of here, just off the Plaza de Castilla, is the Fundación Canal (www.fundacioncanal.com), another arts and education centre run by the Canal de Isabel II.

Eating & drinking

Chamberí's **Plaza de Olavide** is something of a neighbourhood hub, and a great place to enjoy tapas alfresco. It buzzes with relaxed conversation in the summer months.

Bar Tomate

C/Fernando El Santo 26 (91 702 38 70, http://www.grupotragaluz.com/ rest-tomate.php). Metro Colón. **Open** 8.30am-midnight Mon-Wed, Sun; 8.30am-2.30am Thur-Sat. Closed Sundays Aug. **Main courses** €8-€10. **€€. Mediterranean.**
Open all day, this establishment is great for breakfast, a snack, lunch or dinner. It specialises in light and tasty Mediterranean cuisine, such as gorgonzola croquettes, anchovies and red

Museo Sorolla

piquillo peppers on toast, asparagus tempura and individual tortillas. There are good deals available at breakfast time.

Bodegas la la Ardosa

C/Santa Engracia 70 (91 446 58 94). Metro Iglesia. **Open** 9.30am-3pm, 6-11.30pm daily. Closed mid July to end Aug. **€**. **No credit cards**. **Tapas**.
A tiny bar with a lovely old tiled exterior (confusingly marked No.58) and walls lined with bottles of wine. There are especially good *patatas bravas* and fried pigs' ears, as well as sardines, an array of wonderful shellfish and good beer. Not to be confused with the Malasaña bar of the same name.

La Favorita

C/Covarrubias 25 (91 448 38 10, www.restaurante-lafavorita.com). Metro Alonso Martínez or Bilbao. **Open** 1.30-4pm, 9pm-midnight Mon-Fri; 9pm-midnight Sat. **€€€**. **Castilian/ Navarran**.
Opera fanatic Javier Otero converted this charming 1920s mansion into a restaurant and filled it with singing waiters – conservatoire students or artists just starting out on their careers. It's a surprisingly fun way to dine. And the food, made using fresh ingredients from Navarra, also hits a high note. Reservations are essential.

Santceloni

Hotel Hesperia Madrid, Paseo de la Castellana 57 (91 210 88 40, www.restaurantesantceloni.com). Metro Gregorio Marañón. **Open** 2-4pm, 9-11pm Mon-Fri; 9-11pm Sat. Closed Aug. **€€€€**. **Nueva cocina**.
Named after the village where the famed Barcelona restaurateur Santi Santamaria was born, and run by his protégé Oscar Velasco, the Santceloni was given its first Michelin star after less than a year. Santamaria's success is due to the use of only the best local ingredients. The menu changes frequently but might include crab in sherry with creamed onion and celery, or one of Santamaria's trademark dishes: ravioli of sliced raw prawn with a filling of ceps. There's also a tasting menu.

Sergi Arola Gastro

C/Zurbano 31 (91 310 2169, www.sergiarola.es). Metro Rubén Darío. **Open** 2-3.30pm, 9-11.30pm Mon-Fri; 9-11.30pm Sat. Closed 3 wks Aug, 10 days Dec. **€€€€**. **Nueva cocina**.
This is the flagship restaurant of Sergi Arola, one of Spain's top chefs, and has two Michelin stars. There is no menu as such, just a fixed range of courses that changes according to seasonal availability of ingredients. The art deco dining room makes a change from the bland beigeness of his previous premises at the Hotel Miguel Angel. Sergi's wife, Sara, runs the front of house with sommelier Daniel Poveda and barman Diego Cabrera, who mixes fierce cocktails in the downstairs lounge.

Sudestada

C/Ponzano 85 (91 533 41 54). Metro Ríos Rosas or Cuatro Caminos. **Open** 1-4pm, 9.30pm-midnight Mon-Sat. Main courses €8-€20. Set menu €30. **€€**. **Asian**.
Run by young Argentines with a passion for Asian food, Sudestada is the new Madrid branch of a Buenos Aires favourite. In its short life it has already received a well-respected Spanish restaurant award, and is packed out every night. Given the authentic spiciness of its curries – from all over Southeast Asia – this gives the lie to the idea that Spanish diners prefer their food bland. Less *picante* options include Vietnamese rolls and dim sum from Singapore.

Taberna de los Madriles

C/José Abascal 26 (91 593 06 26, www.losmadriles.com). Metro Alonso Cano. **Open** 11am-midnight Mon-Sat. **€**. **No credit cards**. **Tapas**.
The speciality of this diminutive bar is the pincho Los Madriles, with red pep-

per and anchovies. Also worth trying are the tuna and prawn pinchos, the fried potatoes and the *callos* (broths). Decorated with hundreds of black and white photos of its regulars as kids, this old-style bar can get a bit cramped, but has tables outside in summer.

Nightlife

Changó

C/Covarrubias 42 (91 446 00 36). Metro Alonso Martínez or Bilbao.
One of Madrid's clubs converted from old theatres, Changó plays host to two top nights. First up is Nature, a long-running Thursday night dedicated to breaks, electro and techno. Second is Chill, attracting a supposedly more sophisticated crowd with its deep house. Third is L'Inferno, which moved to Changó in 2010, and has become one of the city's most popular club nights for dance music lovers.

Clamores

C/Alburquerque 14 (91 445 79 38, www.salaclamores.com). Metro Bilbao.
This emblematic jazz club opened in 1979. Stocking what is apparently the widest range of cavas and champagnes in Madrid, it has a very varied pro-gramme these days, with tango, pop, rock, bossa, samba and folk all on the bill as well as the jazz that made its name. The live acts sprawl into late-night jam sessions on Friday and Saturday nights. There are no live performances on Monday or Sunday nights.

Galileo Galilei

C/Galileo 100 (91 534 75 57, www. sala galileogalilei.com). Metro Islas Filipinas or Quevedo.
Whatever kind of music you like, you'll likely find it here. There's Latin jazz, flamenco, salsa, singer-songwriters and myriad types of fusion. There are also occasional comedy nights. It's a former cinema, and as such is very spa-cious, though the mock-Hellenic decor can be a bit over the top.

Arts & leisure

Parque del Canal de Isabel II

Entrance on Avda de las Islas Filipinas (91 533 17 91, www.cyii.es). Metro Canal or Ríos Rosas.
Open since 2007, this lovely outdoor sports complex/park consists of a 1.5-kilometre running track and pedestrian pathway, a golf course, two football pitches and eight *pádel* courts. It is beautifully landscaped with lavender, rose bushes, cypress trees, water fountains, benches and shaded areas, and there's a great vibe on summer evenings, when the park buzzes with runners, old folk on their evening strolls, families and more serious sporty types.

Teatros del Canal

C/Cea Bermúdez 1 (91 308 99 50, www.teatrosdelcanal.org). Metro Canal.
Consisting of two theatres – the Sala Roja (Red Room) and the Sala Verde (Green Room) – the Teatros del Canal performing arts centre opened in the barrio of Chamberí a couple of years ago, to much local excitement. The flashy avant-garde building designed by Spanish architect Juan Navarro Baldeweg utilises advanced audio-visual technology and has impressive interiors. The centre also houses the Centro Danza Canal (CDC) dance school, and the Víctor Ullate-Ballet-Comunidad de Madrid dance company. Guided tours of the building are available for €4 (€3 concessions).

Verdi

C/Bravo Murillo 28 (information 91 447 39 30, www.cines-verdi.com/ madrid). Metro Canal or Quevedo.
No credit cards.
This relative newcomer to the ranks of VO (*versión original*) cinemas has five screens showing a lively mix of arthouse, Spanish, independent and mainstream foreign films.

Sights & museums

Museo Tiflológico

C/La Coruña 18 (91 589 42 19, http://museo.once.es). Metro Estrecho. **Open** 10am-2pm, 5-8pm Tue-Fri; 10am-2pm Sat. Closed Aug. **Admission** free. Owned and run by ONCE, the organisation for blind and partially sighted people, this special museum presents exhibitions of work by visually-impaired artists (the name comes from the Greek 'tiflos', sightless). Work here is intended to be touched, and is generally sculptural, three-dimensional, rich in texture and highly tactile.

La Residencia de Estudiantes

C/Pinar 21-23 (91 563 64 11, www. residencia. csic.es). Metro Gregorio Marañón. **Open** (during exhibitions, phone to check) 10am-8pm Mon-Sat; 10am-3pm Sun. **Admission** free.
From its foundation in 1910 until the war in 1936, the Residencia de Estudiantes was the most vibrant cultural centre in Madrid, and a powerful innovative force in the whole country. Though it was a students' residence – García Lorca, Buñuel and Dalí all stayed there in the early days – 'La Resi' also organised visits to Madrid by leading artists and scientists of the day. The Civil War and subsequent regime severely stifled intellectual freedom and the Residencia languished until the late 1980s, when it was resurrected as a private foundation. It hosts talks by international figures, conferences and exhibitions, recitals, films and concerts.

Eating & drinking

Asador Donostiarra

C/Infanta Mercedes 79, Tetuán (91 579 08 71, www.asadordonostiarra. com). Metro Tetuán. **Open** 1-4pm, 9pm-midnight Mon-Sat; 1-4pm Sun. €€€. **Steakhouse**.

If you love meat and you love Real Madrid, you may want to splurge on a night out at the once-preferred *asador* (steakhouse) of David Beckham and the rest of the team, located near the Bernabéu stadium. The celeb crowd is as legendary as the *solomillo*, and they often give away signed photos and other goodies from the team.

El Comité

Plaza de San Amaro 8, Chamartín (91 571 87 11). Metro Santiago Bernabéu. **Open** 1.30-4.30pm, 9pm-1am Mon-Fri; 9pm-1am Sat. Closed 1wk Aug. €€€. **French**.
Yes, it's out of the way and has the feel of an elite club, but this somehow enhances the appeal. A romantic French restaurant offering exceptionally good food at a price, El Comité also offers the chance to see Madrid's discreetly elegant top people at play. Great starters include Harry's Bar carpaccio and a tempura of langoustines; a main-course highlight is the steak tartare, and the snails *bourguignonne* are legendary. A classic.

Fast Good

C/Padre Damián 23, Chamartín (91 343 06 55, www.fast-good.com). Metro Cuzco. **Open** 12.30-11.30pm daily. €€. **Nueva cocina/Fast food**.
A fast food joint devised by culinary wizard Ferran Adrià has to be worth trying. In a colour-crazy, super-designed deli you can pick out innovative salads like the foie with green beans or panini with brie and spinach. The crowning glory, however, is the Fast Good hamburger – a superlative specimen, and now there's an organic version too. Everything is made fresh and light – even the fries are cooked in olive oil.

Nightlife

69 Pétalos

C/Alberto Alcocer 32 (no phone). Metro Colombia or Cuzco. **No credit cards**.

Open in its current form since 2007, 69 Pétalos, not far from the Bernabéu stadium, is a popular spot for twentysomethings, who come for the mix of pop, funk, latin jazz, house and indie nights (featuring Depeche Mode et al). Pop-art style decor, stage performers and an interesting mix of people creates a buzzing vibe from around 2am.

Macumba

Estación de Chamartín (91 733 35 05, 902 49 99 94, www.comunidad spaceofsound.com). Metro Chamartín. **No credit cards.**

Friday night here is Danzoo; Saturdays see Sunflowers for an Ibizan vibe and lots of go-go dancers; but Macumba's real crowd-puller is Space of Sound on Sunday nights. It's the city's biggest all-day party. The crowd is weirdly territorial, with one area that's mainly gay, another that's predominantly straight and even a group of transsexuals claiming an area by one of the bars. The sound system here is unmatched and, along with the resident DJs, the promoters bring in the likes of Deep Dish and Steve Lawler.

Segundo Jazz

C/Comandante Zorita 8, Cuatro Caminos, Tetúan (91 554 94 37, www.segundojazz.es). Metro Cuatro Caminos or Nuevos Ministerios.

Founded many years ago by the owner of the legendary Whisky Jazz Club, this is Madrid's longest standing jazz joint. Nowadays, as well as jazz, the programme takes in Brazilian groups, singer-songwriters and '60s cover bands banging out Beatles songs. A great atmosphere and friendly staff make it an essential stop, but don't get there too early: concerts start at midnight.

Arts & leisure

Auditorio Nacional de Música

C/Príncipe de Vergara 146, Prosperidad (information 91 337 01 40, tickets 91 337 03 07, www.auditorionacional. mcu.es). Metro Cruz del Rayo or Prosperidad.

This impressive concert hall has capacity in its main auditorium for over 2,000, and a smaller chamber hall, La Sala de Cámara. As well as the OCNE, the Auditorio hosts the Comunidad de Madrid's orchestra, ORCAM, and is the provisional home of the Joven Orquesta Nacional de España. The best concerts are those by invited international orchestras. Top seasons are the Grandes Intérpretes, the Liceo de Cámara (Fundación Caja Madrid), Ibermúsica, Ciclo de Cámara y Polifonía and the contemporary Música de Hoy programme. Look out too for organ recitals. Tickets for the Auditorio usually go on sale about a fortnight before the performance; they're generally cheaper for Sunday morning concerts.

Estadio Santiago Bernabéu

Paseo de la Castellana 144, Chamartín (91 398 43 00, www.realmadrid.com). Metro Santiago Bernabéu.

The era of the 'Galácticos' is surely fading. Yes, Real Madrid's present and future look decidedly iffy. Fans are looking to a new generation of players to bring back glory, something they expect from a club that has won more domestic and European honours than any other. Tickets for games at Real Madrid's stadium can only be bought over the phone on 902 32 43 24, but getting hold of one can be extremely difficult as 90% of tickets are taken up by the club's members. For information on stadium tours, call 90 230 17 09.

Fundación Canal

C/Mateo Inurria 2, Chamartín (91 545 15 06, www.fundacioncanal.com). Metro Plaza de Castilla.

Set up by Madrid's water company, the Canal Isabel II, in recent years this foundation has become active in all areas of the arts, programming various types of occasionally excellent exhibitions and

Real Palacio de El Pardo

BARBARA V y M

concerts year-round. Music programming has included seasons of chamber music performed by musicians from the Orquesta de la Comunidad de Madrid.

The northern suburbs
Sights & museums

El Pardo
Bus 601 from Moncloa.
Around ten miles (15 kilometres) to the north-west of the city lies a vast expanse of verdant and well-looked after parkland. This area contains the main residence of the Spanish royal family, the Palacio de la Zarzuela. But the reason most people will venture up here is to visit the house where General Franco lived and worked for the 35 years up to his death in 1975: the Real Palacio de El Pardo (see below), situated in the peaceful 18th-century town of El Pardo. The hills and woodlands are also worth a visit, being remarkably unspoilt thanks to those long protected years of dictatorial and regal status, and they contain an amazingly rich array of wildlife.

Real Palacio de El Pardo
C/Manuel Alonso (91 376 15 00, www.patrimonionacional.es). Bus 601 from Moncloa. **Open** Apr-Sept 10.30am-5.45pm Mon-Sat; 9.30am-1.30pm Sun. Oct-Mar 10.30am-4.45pm Mon-Sat; 10am-1.30pm Sat. **Admission** €4; €2.70 concessions. Wed free to EU citizens.
No credit cards.
In 1405, Henry III constructed a hunting lodge here, but the first monarch to take a really serious interest in El Pardo's excellent deer and game hunting estate was Charles I of Spain (Charles V of the Holy Roman Empire), who built a sizeable palace here. His successor, Philip II, added many important works of art but most of these were lost in a fire in 1604, and after various architectural changes the building was finally reconstructed on Charles III's orders by 18th-century architect Francesco Sabatini.

In addition to its main role today as a diplomatic rendezvous, the palace is partially open to the public and there are tours of its ornate and gaudy interior with its ornamental frescoes, gilt mouldings and some fine tapestries, many of which were woven in the Real Fábrica de Tapices to Goya designs. There's an ornate theatre, where censorious film fan Franco used to view films with his cronies before deciding on their suitability for the great unwashed, but in truth the only rooms of real fascination are the Generalisimo's bedroom, dressing room and '70s bathroom – decorated to his own specifications.
Outside you can wander in the palace's attractive gardens or explore or picnic in the magnificent surrounding parkland known as Monte de Pardo – even though much of this is still closed to the public.

South & east

South of the centre
Sights & museums

Matadero Madrid
Paseo de la Chopera 14 (91 517 73 09, www.mataderomadrid.com). Metro Legazpi. **Open** 6-10pm Tue-Fri; 11am-10pm Sat, Sun. **Admission** varies.
No credit cards.
A century-old neo-Mudéjar building that was once the city's municipal slaughterhouse is now showing its sensitive side in Matadero Madrid, the city's new innovative and multidiscipliniery arts centre. The vast, ambitious space consists of ten different buildings, and the Madrid City Council hopes it will be a key sociocultural symbol for the city.

Museo del Ferrocarril
Paseo de las Delicias 61 (91 506 83 33, www.museodelferrocarril.org). Metro Delicias. **Open** 10am-3pm Tue-Sun. Closed Aug. **Admission** €5; €3.50 concessions. Free to all Sat.
No credit cards.

Housed in the elegant but disused Delicias station, with ironwork by Gustave Eiffel, Madrid's railway museum has an evocative collection of models, old locomotives, railway equipment and memorabilia.

Planetario de Madrid

Avenida del Planetario 16, Parque Tierno Galván, Legazpi, South of centre (91 467 38 98, 91 467 34 61, www.planetmad.es). Metro Arganzuela-Planetario. Shows vary; phone to check. Closed 1st 2wks Jan. **Admission** €3.55; €1.55 2-14s, over-65s. **No credit cards.**

Close to the IMAX (see right), the Planetarium has seasonal exhibitions on the solar system as well as 45-minute shows. The narration is only in Spanish.

Nightlife

Fabrik

Avda de la Industria 82, Ctra Fuenlabrada-Moralejos de Enmedio (902 93 03 22, www.grupo-kapital. com//fabrik). Metro Fuenlabrada then bus 496, 497.

Fabrik is a converted warehouse kitted out with a dazzling array of disco surprises: a 60kW sound system; a huge outdoor terrace complete with a fake river and two covered dancefloors; and, in the main arena, a vertical and horizontal megatron to shoot freezing nitrogen into the crowd. The monthly Sunday session Goa is the highlight (see www.tripfamily.com for information). It's a bit of a schlep to get here, but well worth the taxi fare.

Arts & leisure

Atlético de Madrid

Estadio Vicente Calderón, Paseo Virgen del Puerto 67, South of centre (91 366 47 07, www.clubatleticodemadrid.com/ shop 91 366 82 37). Metro Pirámides.

Now back in the first division, 'El Atleti' won the UEFA Europa League in 2010. The loyal *rojiblanco* faithful create a vibrant atmosphere in the 57,000-capacity Calderón stadium and, though the football itself can often leave more than a little to be desired, it is not uncommon for tickets to sell out entirely. When available, tickets can now be bought via the website, or by telephone: 902 53 05 00. In 2006, a museum was added near Gate 23 (91 365 09 31, 11am-7pm Tue-Sun, admission €4-€8).

IMAX Madrid

C/Meneses s/n, Parque Tierno Galván, Legazpi, South of centre (91 467 48 00, www.imaxmadrid.com). Metro Méndez Álvaro. **Admission** €7.10-€12.20.

The hourly wildlife and scientific shows are only in Spanish, but the 3D and Omnimax presentations are awesome enough to be enjoyed by all children.

Eastern suburbs

Sights & museums

Faunia

Avda de las Comunidades 28, Eastern suburbs (91 301 62 10, www.faunia. es). Metro Valdebernardo. **Open** Opening times are subject to weekly variations; check the website or call before a visit. **Admission** €25.50 over-8s; €19.50 3-7s & over-65s; free under-3s.

Part zoo, part theme park, Faunia recreates the world's different ecosystems in a series of domes. Best of the bunch is the Amazon jungle house, which echoes with the screech of exotic birds; an intense tropical storm is simulated every half hour. And in summer, there's Penguin World, an impressive reconstruction of a polar zone.

Nightlife

Corral de la Pacheca

C/Juan Ramón Jiménez 26, North of centre (91 353 01 00, www.corralde lapacheca.com). Metro Cuzco.

This grand centre of flamenco sits on the site of a 17th-century theatre and boasts a history of star performers and even starrier punters.

Essentials

503

Hotel Mercure Santo Domingo

Hotels

For a compact city, Madrid has an unusually large number of hotels. This can only be a good thing for visitors, with intense competition meaning higher standards of accommodation and service, even in the lower-priced places. In fact, the difference between budget and mid-range hotels is becoming increasingly marginal, with the newer *hostales* now offering en suite bathrooms in most rooms. Fans of boutique hotels, meanwhile, will be pleased to hear that the concept has finally made it to Madrid.

Star ratings are somewhat arbitrary in Spain, and the difference between four- and five-star hotels can be hard to spot. Mid-range hotels have traditionally not been the city's strong point, but this is changing thanks to chains such as **Room Mate** and **High Tech Hotels**.

Sol & Gran Vía

Hostal Triana
1st floor, C/Salud 13 (91 532 68 12, www.hostal triana.com). Metro Gran Vía. €.
A popular and efficiently run business, this traditional, good-value 40-room *hostal* has been open for more than four decades, and attracts guests of all ages. Rooms are sparklingly clean with modern en suite bathrooms. It's worth booking early.

Hotel Arosa
C/Salud 21 (91 532 16 00, www.best westernarosa.com). Metro Gran Vía. €€.
This friendly, well-equipped and good-value 134-room hotel is situated right in the heart of the action. The spacious, air-conditioned rooms all come with modern wooden furnishings and bright marble bathrooms, and some of the more expensive doubles have a private

seating area looking out on to the busy Gran Vía. The public areas include a kitschy fake leopard-skin reception, and a stylish restaurant and bar.

Hotel Carlos V

C/Maestro Victoria 5 (91 531 41 00, www.bestwesternhotelcarlosv.com). Metro Sol. €€.
The corporate feel is avoided in this Best Western hotel with homely touches, from the motley but charming crew running reception and the *trompe l'oeil* lift door, to the tapestries in the corridors and the botanical prints in the elegant breakfast room. The rooms on the top floor are the nicest, and some have their own large, Astroturfed terraces.

Hotel de las Letras

Gran Vía 11 (91 523 79 80, www.hotel delasletras.com). Metro Gran Vía. €€.
The Hotel de las Letras plumps for bold paintwork in red, orange and purples, with literary quotations strewn across its walls. It does this with remarkable aplomb, thanks to stylish furniture and well-designed rooms. Bathrooms are huge, and even standard rooms come with balconies. Downstairs is a comfortable spa and gym, along with a small library with free internet access. A gem.

Hotel Emperador

Gran Vía 53 (91 547 28 00, www.emperadorhotel.com). Metro Santo Domingo. €€€.
It's little surprise that this hotel gets so booked up – it's perfectly situated for visiting the city's major sights and has a wonderful rooftop swimming pool (also open to non-residents for a fee). Rooms are conservatively decorated; the renovated bathrooms are a huge improvement on the old brown 1970s-style suites.

Hotel Mercure Santo Domingo

C/San Bernardo 1 (91 547 98 00, www.hotelsantodomingo.es). Metro Santo Domingo. €€.

SHORTLIST

Best new hotels
- chic&basic Mayerling (p167)
- Hostal Gala (p167)
- Hotel Selenza Madrid (p174)
- Radisson Blu, Madrid Prado (p174)

Best for style fiends
- Hostal Gala (p167)
- Hotel Abalu (p173)
- Hotel de las Letras (p165)
- Hotel Mercure Santo Domingo (p165)
- Hotel Selenza Madrid (p174)
- Room Mate Oscar (p173)

For old Madrid grandeur
- Hostal Sud-Americana (p171)
- Hotel Orfila (p176)
- Hotel Palacio San Martín (p169)
- Hotel Santo Mauro (p176)
- Westin Palace (p171)

Best views
- Hotel Palacio San Martín (p169)
- ME Madrid (p171)
- Radisson Blu, Madrid Prado (p174)

For taking a dip
- Hotel Emperador (p165)
- Hotel Mercure Santo Domingo (p165)
- Hotel Wellington (p174)

Best dining
- Hotel Hesperia Madrid (p176)
- Hotel Selenza Madrid (p174)
- Villa Magna (p176)

Best family-run *hostales*
- Hostal Armesto (p169)
- Hostal Casanova (p169)
- Hostal Horizonte (p169)
- Hostal Martín (p171)

Designer Apartments in Madrid
Starting at €100/day

www.spain-select.com

SPAINSELECT

chic&basic Mayerling

Courteous staff welcome guests to this slick Mercure hotel, which features a small(ish) but appealing rooftop pool and 80 individually decorated rooms – which will jump to 200 rooms once the hotel is merged with the Best Western Santo Domingo in the near future (the two buildings will be linked via passageways). Huge walk-in showers are a real indulgence.

Tryp Ambassador

Cuesta de Santo Domingo 5-7 (91 541 67 00, www.trypambassador.solmelia. com). Metro Santo Domingo. €€€.
Located in a former palace, the Ambassador manages to retain a vaguely baronial air despite being part of a chain. Suits of armour stand guard in the corridors, while plush upholstery adorns the public spaces and the large, light-filled atrium. Breakfast is expensive (€17) but abundant and good.

chic&basic Mayerling

C/Conde de Romanones 6 (91 420 15 80, www.chicandbasic.com). Metro Tirso de Molina. €€.

See box p168.
Other locations *C/Atocha 113, Huertas & Santa Ana (91 369 28 95). Chic&basic Colors, C/Huertas 14, Huertas & Santa Ana (91 429 69 35).*

Hostal Gala

C/Costanilla de los Ángeles 15 (91 541 96 92, www.hostalgala.com). Metro Santo Domingo. €€.
See box p168.

Hostal Oriente

C/Arenal 23 (91 548 03 14, www.hostaloriente.es). Metro Ópera. €.
Right on the doorstep of the opera house, and just a short walk from Sol, the comfortable Oriente is in an excellent location. The 19 rooms all have compact bathrooms, TVs and air-conditioning, and the friendly staff are a further draw.

Hostal Riesco

Third floor, C/Correo 2 (91 522 26 92, www.hostalriesco.es). Metro Sol. €.
The Riesco is a *hostal* that feels more like a hotel, what with its dark wood lobby, stucco ceilings and chintzy curtains. All rooms come with en suite bathrooms, and several have balconies bedecked with flowers. The location is

Cheap and chic

Where to find style on a budget.

Hostal Gala

Madrid's range of well-priced but stylish hotels has steadily increased over the past few years, so that those looking for hip aesthetics no longer have to fork out to find them, while those on a budget shouldn't need to settle for bland decor and peeling paint.

One of the first companies to spot a gap in the market for stylish but cheap accommodation was Room Mate, which now has four hotels in Madrid. **Room Mate Oscar** (see p173) is one of the most popular, due to its location in one of Chueca's main squares and its huge roof terrace – complete with bar and pool (unsurprisingly, a prime hangout for the gay scene). The hotel oozes affordable chic, from the ergonomic white plastic chairs to the chequered grey and white bathrooms.

Quick to follow on Room Mates' stylish heels was the chic&basic chain. **Chic&basic Mayerling** (see p167) – the second Madrid hotel from the mini-chain – opened in 2009 in a former textiles warehouse. It offers 22 simple but stylish lodgings in M, L and XL, with an abundance of white,

plus glass-walled bathrooms with power showers. Complimentary breakfast, tea- and coffee-making facilities and a great sun terrace with loungers are further draws.

The good-value High Tech 'Petit Palace' chain of hotels, meanwhile, is perfect for techno fiends on a budget. Now with 22 hotels in the city, the compact but sleekly designed rooms have flatscreen TVs and free ADSL connection; more expensive rooms come with a PC and an exercise bike, while superior rooms have showers with solariums, saunas and radios. Many of the hotels are centrally located, including the **Petit Palace Arenal** (see right).

One of the newest mid-range hotels is also one of Madrid's most stylish, and independently owned to boot. **Hostal Gala** (see p167) is a well-located boutique *hostal* on a quiet but central street, run by a friendly couple. The 22 rooms are comfortable, with wooden floors, air-con, retro-modern wallpaper and spacious bathrooms with power showers. Some rooms have balconies, while the superior double has a lounge area.

hard to beat – it's rare to find such good-value accommodation so close to Sol and the Plaza Mayor.

Hotel Palacio San Martín

Plaza de San Martín 5 (91 701 50 00, www.intur.com). Metro Ópera or Sol. €€.

The Hotel Palacio San Martín is housed in a 19th-century former palace, but it was only established as a hotel in 2001. It has maintained much of the glory of its previous palatial career, with period façade, high stucco ceilings and an attractive central courtyard. A lovely rooftop-terrace restaurant looks out over the surrounding area.

Petit Palace Arenal

C/Arenal 16 (91 564 43 55, www.hthoteles.com). Metro Sol. €€.
See box left.
Other locations throughout the city.

Barrio de las Letras

Hostal Alaska

4th floor, C/Espoz y Mina 7 (91 521 18 45, www.hostalalaska.com). Metro Sol. €.

Exceptionally large rooms for this price range, decorated with splashes of bright blue, give this comfortable, colourful *hostal* a bit of a beachside feel.

The atmosphere is homely, and guests have use of a fridge and washing machine. The five doubles and one single all come with bathrooms, and many have balconies.

Hostal Armesto

1st floor, C/San Agustín 6 (91 429 90 31, www.hostalarmesto.com). Metro Antón Martín. €.

This great-value six-room *hostal* in the centre of Huertas is run by a friendly husband-and-wife team. Rooms are spotless and all have their own small bathroom; some boast views over the garden of the San Agustín palace next door. A good choice for art lovers on a budget, being well situated for the art museum triumvirate.

Hostal Casanova

1st floor, C/Lope de Vega 8 (91 429 56 91). Metro Antón Martín. €.

Run by a friendly family and in a quiet street off pedestrianised C/Huertas, this *hostal* is especially good value for those travelling in threes. Rooms are basic but bright, some with bathrooms, and all with air-conditioning.

Hostal Horizonte

2nd floor, C/Atocha 28 (91 369 09 96, www.hostalhorizonte.com). Metro Antón Martín. €.

Hotel Emperador p165

Friendly Rentals
Quality Apartments, Smart Price

MADRID

BARCELONA
PARIS
ROME
LONDON
NEW YORK
BERLIN

and many more…

Have a look at our great selection of apartments in Madrid.
Friendly Rentals offers more than 2000 holiday and corporate apartments in top
destinations – Barcelona, Rome, New York, London, Madrid, Paris, Berlin
and many more…
We offer high quality apartments, all located in the best areas.

www.friendlyrentals.com

Friendly Rentals Madrid
San Marcos 3, Bajo 1
28004 Madrid, Spain
Tel: +34 91 521 28 76

Friendly Rentals Head Office
Pasaje Sert, 4 bajos
Barcelona 08003 Spain
Tel: +34 93 268 80 51

Tel: 0800 520 0373 UK Free
Email: info@friendlyrentals.com

BARCELONA MADRID ROME LONDON VALENCIA LISBON NEW YORK PARIS SAN SEBASTIAN MILAN BERLIN
FLORENCE BUENOS AIRES ALGARVE GRANADA SITGES MALLORCA SEVILLE COSTA BRAVA CADIZ

One of the oldest *pensiones* in Madrid, the Horizonte has stayed in the same friendly family throughout its 65-year history. The manager is the young and helpful Julio César, a font of knowledge about the history and cultural life of the city. Rooms are clean and comfy, and the welcoming atmosphere unbeatable.

Hostal Martín

1st floor, C/Atocha 43 (91 429 95 79, www.hostalmartin.com). Metro Antón Martín. €.
This first-floor *hostal* has a pleasantly rough-and-tumble family feel. The 20 high-ceilinged, air-conditioned rooms all come with an en suite bathroom. The helpful couple who run it speak various languages and can book you into other hotels if you're moving on to other parts of the country. The hearty breakfast includes fresh fruit and good coffee.

Hostal Sud-Americana

Paseo del Prado 12 (91 429 25 64, http://hostalsudamericana.com). Metro Banco de España. €.
This place has a real feel of Old Madrid. White walls, high ceilings and dark wooden furniture give the rooms a centuries-old atmosphere, and some have lovely views over the Paseo del Prado. One bathroom is shared between eight rooms, but all have their own washbasin. It's very difficult to find this sort of old-world elegance elsewhere at such a cheap price.

Hotel Lope de Vega

C/Lope de Vega 40 (91 360 00 11, www.hotellopedevega.com). Metro Antón Martín. €€.
A stone's throw from the Prado, this anonymous-looking hotel's rooms are done up in standard-issue mid-range decor, but are a good size, comfortable and many have large balconies. Posted outside each one is information about playwright Lope de Vega, and the corridors are lined with pictures of his productions. Its nearby sister hotel, the Hotel del Prado, has a wine theme.

Hotel Mora

Paseo del Prado 32 (91 420 15 69, www.hotelmora.com). Metro Atocha. €.
If you like marble, you'll love the Mora's foyer, with its caramel-coloured columns and chandeliers. The rooms are functional but comfortable, and some have views over the tree-lined Paseo del Prado. Not surprisingly, given the location and price, it can be hard to get a room, so try to book early.

Hotel Urban

Carrera de San Jeronimo 34 (91 787 77 70, www.derbyhotels.com). Metro Sevilla or Sol. €€€.
The Derby Hotels (which also owns the nearby Hotel Villa Real) is owned by archaeologist Jordi Clos, and ancient figurines and artworks are found throughout – a perfect counterpoint to the hip glass and steel atrium and sexily designed rooms. Pluses include friendly staff and a rooftop plunge pool.

ME Madrid

Plaza Santa Ana 14 (91 701 60 00, www.memadrid.com). Metro Sevilla or Sol. €€€.
Although plans to turn this into Europe's first Hard Rock hotel didn't quite come off, the Melia chain appropriated the lovely old Hotel Reina Victoria to showcase its 'ME' brand. Despite being on the small side, rooms are very comfortable, with luxury bed linen, posh toiletries and lots to keep gadget-fiends happy. The rooftop bar has amazing views of the city.

Westin Palace

Plaza de las Cortes 7 (91 360 80 00, www.westinpalacemadrid.com). Metro Banco de España. €€€.
One of the most famous hotels in Madrid, the Palace combines old-world elegance with cutting-edge facilities. The lounge areas and atrium have an air of sumptuousness, and the hotel's bars and restaurants are popular with visiting celebs and politicians from the parliament buildings across the road.

Hotel de las Letras p165

Lavapiés

Hostal Apolo

C/Juanelo 24 (91 360 08 00, www. hostalapolomadrid.com). Metro Tirso de Molina. €.

This is the best of the few hotel options in the lively and multicultural Lavapiés area. The new owner is eager to please and proud of his establishment. Rooms are rather functional but clean and good value, and all have en suite bathrooms.

Chueca

Barbieri International Hostel

2nd floor, C/Barbieri 15, Chueca (91 531 02 58, www.barbierihostel.com). Metro Chueca or Gran Vía. €.

Right in the middle of Chueca, this hotel is popular with budget travellers of all nationalities. The double rooms and dorms for three or seven people are basic but clean, and there are kitchen facilities, a TV room with DVD player and a book exchange service. Staff are very friendly, the atmosphere relaxed and there's no curfew.

Hostal Benamar

2nd floor, C/San Mateo 20 (91 308 00 92, www.hostalbenamar.es). Metro Alonso Martínez or Tribunal. €.

Well situated between Chueca and Alonso Martínez, this *hostal* can be divided into two different parts. The friendly owners promote the recently renovated section, which has marble floors, modern en suite bathrooms and computers in every room. The other section is older but clean, with shared bathrooms and cheaper rates.

Hostal Santa Bárbara

3rd floor, Plaza de Santa Bárbara 4 (91 446 93 08, www.hostalsanta barbaramadrid.com). Metro Alonso Martínez. €.

This well-connected *hostal* provides friendly service in a secure building. The rooms are basic but clean and

every one has walk-in shower facilities. The friendly Italian owner and the staff all speak good English.

Room Mate Oscar

Plaza Vázquez de Mella 12 (91 701 11 73, www.room-matehotels.com). Metro Chueca or Gran Vía. €€.

See box p168.

Other locations Room Mate Alicia, C/Prado 2, Santa Ana (91 389 60 95); Room Mate Laura, Travesía de Trujillos 3, Sol & Gran Vía (91 701 16 70); Room Mate Mario, C/Campomanes 4 (91 548 85 48).

Malasaña & Conde Duque

Hostal Sil & Serranos

C/Fuencarral 95 (91 448 89 72, www.silserranos.com). Metro Bilbao. €.

Clean and smartly decorated, these *hostales* are well located for night-time revelling. Although interior rooms are darker, the noise is minimal and the price slightly lower. All rooms have air-conditioning, small bathrooms and TV, and the properties are run by a fun couple.

Hotel Abalu

C/Pez 19 (91 531 47 44, www.hotel abalu.com). Metro Noviciado. €.

The Abalu is near the Gran Vía and metro, but its extravagant interior pulls in as many visitors as its location. The rooms range from restrained to gloriously over the top; the staff are friendly although sometimes hard to pin down.

Hotel Alexandra

C/San Bernardo 29-31 (91 542 04 00, www.halexandra.com). Metro Noviciado. €.

A few minutes' walk from the Gran Vía and the metro, the Alexandra is well located for sightseeing. All rooms are clean and pretty quiet, but you can request an interior room to avoid the traffic noise. Although the hotel is slightly anonymous in its style, the staff are friendly and the area and prices just that little bit less touristy than if you cross the Gran Via towards Sol.

The Retiro & Salamanca

AC Palacio del Retiro

Alfonso XII 14 (91 523 74 60, www.ac-hotels.com). Metro Banco de España or Retiro. €€€€.
With their palette of greys and browns, the rooms can seem a little dour after the frothy extravagances of the belle époque building in which they are housed. The hotel is beautifully located near the park and Prado, however, and amenities are good – rooms feature plasma-screen TVs and CD players – as is breakfast (as one would expect for €29).

Hostal-Residencia Don Diego

C/Velázquez 45 (91 435 07 60, www.hostaldondiego.com). Metro Velázquez. €€.
The Hostal-Residencia Don Diego lies above a row of upmarket private apartments on one of Madrid's most exclusive streets. Rooms are plain but clean and good value, and, because of the location, the *hostal* is popular with the business crowd and those attending trade shows at the IFEMA.

Hotel Alcalá

C/Alcalá 66 (91 435 10 60, www.nh-hoteles.com). Metro Príncipe de Vergara. €€.
Even though the chain status of this hotel gives it uniformity and a certain anonymity, the Hotel Alcalá provides visitors with modern accommodation, supplemented by good facilities and thoroughly professional staff. Its location and style make it a popular choice.

Hotel Ritz

Plaza de la Lealtad 5 (91 701 67 67, www.ritzmadrid.com). Metro Banco de España. €€€€.

When Madrid's Ritz opened, in 1910, the handful of bathrooms, one telephone per floor and lift were considered the height of luxury. Today, the 167 rooms maintain some of the original belle époque style, though the swirly carpets and occasionally shabby fittings are incongruous in such a setting. Guests must abide by a strict dress code in the restaurant.

Hotel Selenza Madrid

C/Claudio Coello 67 (91 781 01 73, www.selenzahotelmadrid.com). Metro Serrano. €€€.
This hotel achieves the perfect blend of modern and classic. It's housed in a 19th-century Salamanca building, and has smart black-and-white chequered tiles and upholstered chairs in the public areas, impressive staircases and mod cons throughout. Rooms are comfortable, with huge beds, muted tones and slick bathrooms. The Michelin-starred restaurant is another plus.

Hotel Wellington

C/Velázquez 8 (91 575 44 00, www.hotel-wellington.com). Metro Retiro. €€€.
More than half a century after it opened, the Wellington remains an extremely graceful place in which to stay, with chandeliers, marble and murals, and groups of guests in formal eveningwear milling around the lobby. The hotel is just a stone's throw from the city's most expensive shopping area, Salamanca, and has a summer pool with terrace – an ideal location for relaxing after all that retail therapy.

Radisson Blu, Madrid Prado

C/Moratín 52, Plaza de Platería Martínez (91 524 26 26, www.radissonblu.com/pradohotel-madrid). Metro Antón Martín. €€.
In prime tourist territory, just steps from the Prado and the CaixaForum, the Radisson Blu is a useful new addition to the city's hotel offerings, with a

slick interior, modern artwork and comfortable rooms equipped with all mod cons and great views.

Argüelles

Hotel Husa Princesa

C/Princesa 40 (91 542 21 00, www.hotelhusaprincesa.com). Metro Ventura Rodríguez. €€€.
Beyond the Plaza de España and the hustle and bustle of Gran Vía lies the Husa Princesa, decorated with large reproductions of Goya and Velázquez classics in each room. The hotel's gym and large sports complex are impressive, incorporating an indoor pool, saunas, steam baths and 150 exercise machines, plus a beauty treatment area.

Hotel Tirol

C/Marqués de Urquijo 4 (91 548 19 00, www.t3tirol.com). Metro Argüelles. €€.

Room Mate Oscar p173

Situated within easy reach of the Parque del Oeste, the Tirol is the most child-friendly hotel in the city, featuring family rooms with separate spaces for kids, a children's play area and discounts for family stays. The hotel is now part of the T3 chain.

Villa Magna
Paseo de la Castellana 22 (91 587 12 34, www.villamagna.es). Metro Rubén Darío. €€€€.
This Park Hyatt hotel more than lives up to its reputation. The enormous lobby, full of jewellery displays and international businessmen, leads to two excellent restaurants and a wonderful champagne bar. The 150 rooms and suites, looking out over the busy Paseo de la Castellana or the exclusive C/Serrano, have good facilities and, like the rest of the hotel, are spacious and elegantly decorated. There's also a top-notch gym.

Chamberí

Gran Hotel Conde Duque
Plaza Conde del Valle Suchil 5 (91 447 70 00, www.hotelcondeduque.es). Metro San Bernardo. €€€.
A quiet, out-of-the-way hotel with front rooms facing a pretty, leafy plaza. Rooms are tastefully kitted out with yellow and green upholstery, while the belle-époque salon downstairs serves afternoon tea. Beds are king-size and one room, 315, has a waterbed. Previous guests have included Celia Cruz and Marcel Marceau, and Pedro Almodóvar has been spotted in the bar.

Hotel Hesperia Madrid
Paseo de la Castellana 57 (91 210 88 00, www.hesperia-madrid.com). Metro Gregorio Marañón. €€€€.
Hesperia Madrid is what you'd call 'contemporary luxury'. The dimly lit entrance gives way to white and cream surroundings; in contrast, guest rooms feature dark wood and strong tones.

Interior rooms have larger bathrooms, though guests wanting a jacuzzi and terrace will have to move up to the Executive and Presidential levels. The Catalan restaurant, Santceloni (see p156), has two Michelin stars.

Hotel Orfila
C/Orfila 6 (91 702 77 70, www.hotelorfila.com). Metro Alonso Martínez or Colón. €€€€.
This small mansion in a tranquil residential area has been transformed into an elegant five-star hotel. Built in the 1880s as a private home, the Orfila also contained a theatre and a literary salon in the 1920s. Thankfully, the hotel has held on to its 19th-century decor. Bedrooms are wonderfully quiet, and the restaurant looks on to a lovely garden patio.

Hotel Santo Mauro
C/Zurbano 36 (91 319 69 00, www.hotelcsantomauro.com). Metro Rubén Darío. €€€€.
This exquisite hotel is discreetly hidden away in the streets that separate the Castellana from busy C/Santa Engracia. The elegant and peaceful entrance prepares guests for the experience to come. The 51 rooms, housed in two parts of what was the residence of the Duke of Santo Mauro, are luxuriously decorated, and boast king-size beds and floor-to-ceiling picture windows hung with opulent silk drapes.

InterContinental Madrid
Paseo de la Castellana 49 (91 700 73 00, www.madrid.intercontinental.com). Metro Gregorio Marañón. €€€.
The InterContinental is a long-standing Madrid favourite. The elegant decor in the lobby extends to the rooms, most of which overlook the Paseo de la Castellana. The hotel appeals to a wide-ranging clientele, being well located for the business districts but also offering special packages for fans visiting the Bernabéu football stadium.

A home from home

Apartment rentals are gaining popularity in Madrid.

Spain Select

An increasing number of properties in Madrid – most equipped with fully-fitted kitchens, balconies or terraces, and all mod cons – are now available for tourists to rent on a daily, weekly or monthly basis as an alternative to hotels. If you're in town for a week or more, this can be a more economical way to lodge in the city than staying in hotels; even with the luxurious apartments, the fees are sometimes the same as many mid-range hotels. They're also a godsend for those who like to actually get a sense of what it's like to live in the city they're visiting – or who simply want a sense of independence or privacy. What's more, you'll save money on food if you cook for yourself on some nights.

Apartment-rental agencies save you the hassle of contractual negotiations that you'd encounter if you were to rent an apartment independently, and include free Wi-Fi, a cleaning service and 24-hour assistance. For short-term rentals all over town, the best agency to try is **Spain Select** (www.spain-select.com, 91 523 74 51), which offers a host of hand-picked, high-quality and centrally located properties. Most properties sleep between two and six people. If you want to stay in the heart of the action, in luxurious surroundings, then opt for the Plaza Mayor apartment (€1,190-€1,260 per week, based on two people sharing) housed in an 18th-century building, and with a balcony overlooking the square. An equally attractive apartment in the characterful Plaza de la Paja, in the heart of the city's tapas scene, costs between €875 and €945 for two people. There are hundreds more options all over town, with a good number in the traditional barrio of Salamanca.

Another agency with plenty of apartments on its books is **Friendly Rentals** (www.friendly rentals.com, 34 93 268 80 51). Less focused on luxury and personal service than Spain Select, it's nevertheless a good option for those looking for a nicely decorated home from home in a central Madrid location.

ESSENTIALS

Getting Around

Arriving & leaving

By air

Barajas Airport

Madrid's huge Barajas Airport is 13km (8 miles) north-east of the city on the A2 motorway. Thanks to the Richard Rogers-designed terminal T4, the airport is used by around 50 million passengers per year. All other traffic is distributed between three existing terminals. There is a tourist office and rail reservations desk in T1 and two tourist offices in T4. For airport information, call 91 321 10 00, 91 393 60 00 or the premium rate number 90 240 47 04, or check www.aena.es.

Airport Express

91 406 88 10.
The city council's new express airport bus runs a daily 24-hr service (every 15 mins in the day and every 35 mins at night). The easily identifiable yellow buses – which run between T1, T2, T4 and, in town, O'Donnell, Cibeles and Atocha – take around 40 mins and the journey costs just €2.

Aerocity

91 747 75 70, www.aerocity.com.
Provides shuttle services between the airport and city-centre hotels. Handy for small groups and cheaper than taking several taxis. Prices vary between €17 and €38, depending on group size. The company has two airport reservation desks.

Metro from the airport

The metro is, alongside the Airport Express (see above) the cheapest way to get to central Madrid, costing only €2. Bear in mind that the Aeropuerto metro station is between T2 and T3, which means that if you arrive at T1, you have a 10-15min walk to get there. From the airport it's five to seven stops on metro line 8 (pink) and 12mins to Nuevos Ministerios. From here it's around another 15mins to travel into the centre of Madrid. You can save money by buying a Metrobús ticket at the airport station.

Taxis from the airport

Taxi fares to central Madrid should be around €20-€25, including a €5 airport supplement. There are further supplements after 10pm and on Sundays (for both, 18¢ per km). There are lots of taxis at Barajas, but ignore any drivers who approach you inside the building, just use the ones at the ranks outside the terminal.

Train from the airport

The new RENFE cercanías line from the airport was still being built when this guide went to print. Once completed, in 2011, it will take you from T4 to Sol in ten minutes.

By bus

Almost all international and long-distance coach services to Madrid terminate at the **Estación Sur de Autobuses**, C/Méndez Álvaro, to the south of central Madrid (information 91 468 42 00 or www.estacionautobusesmadrid.com). It's next to metro (line 6) and cercanía (local train lines C5, C7 and C10) stations, both also called Méndez Álvaro. Bus 148 also runs from there to the city centre (Plaza del Callao and Plaza de España). Taxi fares from the bus station carry a €2.50 supplement.

By train

Spanish national railways (**RENFE**) has two main stations in Madrid. Trains from France, Catalonia and northern Spain arrive at **Chamartín**, on the north side of the city, some distance from the centre. High-speed AVE trains from Andalucía, Barcelona and Valencia, express services from Lisbon and trains from southern and eastern Spain arrive at **Atocha**, at the southern end of the Paseo del Prado. Atocha is also the main hub of RENFE's local rail lines (cercanías) (see p180).

Metro line 10 is the fastest from Chamartín to the city centre, and Atocha RENFE (the train station; not the same metro as Atocha) is four metro stops from Sol on line 1. A taxi fare to the centre from Chamartín should be around €13, including a €2.50 station supplement. There are extra supplements at night and on Sundays (18¢ per km). The same need for caution with cabs at the airport (see left) applies to drivers touting for fares at main rail stations.

RENFE Information

90 232 03 20 or 90 224 02 02, www.renfe.es. **Open** *Information* 24hrs daily. *Reservations* 5am-10.30pm daily.

Estación de Atocha

Glorieta del Emperador Carlos V (Renfe information 914 68 83 32). Metro Atocha Renfe, Salamanca & the Retiro. **Map** p128 B5.

Estación de Chamartín

C/Agustín de Foxá, Chamartín. Metro Chamartín.

Public transport

To really get to know Madrid, it's best to explore on foot. Most of the main attractions are within walking distance of each other and for

orientation purposes think of Puerta del Sol as the centre. However, public transport is cheap and efficient – both bus and metro will get you where you want to go within half an hour, although it's best to avoid the buses during rush hour.

Fares

Compared to fare structures in many other capital cities, Madrid's is simple – €1 for a single journey on the bus or metro (excluding Metro Sur, which is €1.75, and Barajas Airport, which is €2) within the capital, no matter how long the journey. On most metro trips you can change any number of times as long as you don't leave a station.

However, it's easier and more economical to buy a ticket for ten journeys (*billete de diez/Metrobús*), which can be used on the bus and metro, available at all metro stations and some *estancos* and *kioskos*, but not on the bus. You can share the ticket between two or more people and keep it for as long as you like (or until the prices go up). The current price of a Metrobús is €6.40.

On the metro, you simply insert the ticket into the machine at the gate that leads through to the platform; remember to collect it afterwards. There is no checking or collection of tickets at station exits. On buses, the Metrobús should be inserted arrow downwards into the blue and yellow machine just behind the driver.

Metro

The metro (www.metromadrid.es) is the quickest and simplest means of travelling to most parts of the city. Each of its 13 lines is identified by a number and a colour on maps and at stations.

The metro is open 6am-2am daily. Tickets are available at all stations

ESSENTIALS

from coin-operated machines and staffed ticket booths. Trains run every 3-5 minutes during weekdays, and about every 10-15mins after 11pm and on Sundays. The metro can get packed in rush hours (7.30-9.30am, 1-2.30pm, 7.30-9pm).

Buses

Buses are run by **Empresa Municipal de Transportes** (EMT; information 91 406 88 00, www.emtmadrid. es). See above for information about fares and tickets.

Most run from about 6am-11.30pm daily, with buses every 10-15mins (more often on more popular routes). Night buses then take over. You board buses at the front, and get off via the middle or rear doors. The fare is the same for each journey (€1), however far you go.

Night buses
Between midnight and around 5am in the morning there are 24 night routes in operation – N1 to N24 – called Búho (Owl) buses. All begin from Plaza de Cibeles and run out to the suburbs, and are numbered in a clockwise sequence. Although the Metro closes at nights, at the weekends special buses, called Metro Búho, cover the routes of the 11 central metro lines (L1-L11). The buses alight at the bus stop nearest to each metro station.

Cercanías/local trains

The highly efficient cercanías local network of railways has been expanding in recent years to link the suburbs with the centre more directly. It consists of 12 lines converging on Atocha, several of which connect with metro lines along their routes. The new Sol station opened in 2009 – and this will in the future link up with Gran Vía metro station and T4 at Barajas airport, meaning that both the suburbs and airport can be reached directly from central Madrid.

Cercanías trains are also useful for trips to Guadarrama, Aranjuez and El Escorial. Cercanías lines run from 5-6am to 11pm-midnight daily, with trains on most lines about every 10-30mins. Fares vary with distance, but the lines are included in the monthly season ticket.

Taxis

Madrid taxis are white, with a diagonal red stripe on the front doors. They are rarely hard to find, except late at night at the weekend or on days when it's raining heavily. When a taxi is free there is a 'Libre' (free) sign behind the windscreen, and a green light on the roof. If there is also a sign with the name of a district in red, it means the driver is on his way home, and is not obliged to take you anywhere that isn't near that particular route. There are taxi ranks, marked by a blue sign with a white T, throughout the centre of Madrid. Within the city, it's fine to flag cabs down in the street. To avoid being swindled by a non-official taxi, make sure the driver has their licence number visible on the front and a meter, and ask for the approximate fare beforehand.

Official fare rates are shown inside each cab (in English and Spanish), on the right-hand sun visor and/or the rear windows. The minimum fare is €1.85, which is what the meter should show when you first set off. The minimum fare is the same at all times, but the additional charge increases at a higher rate at night (11pm-6am) and on Sundays and public holidays, and there are extra supplements for trips starting from the bus and train stations (€2.50); to and from the trade fair complex (€2.50), and to and from the airport

(€5). Drivers are not officially required to carry more than €12 in change; some accept credit cards.

To get a receipt, ask for '*un recibo, por favor*'.

Cycling

Cycling in Madrid is only for the experienced in view of the heavy traffic and lack of cycle lanes (there are a few in parks and by the river). However, bike lanes are gradually improving, and bikes are a great idea for trips to the larger parks (Retiro, Casa de Campo) and the Madrid Sierras. Bikes can be taken free of charge on some cercanías lines and on the metro at weekends. There are an increasing number of associations in Madrid dedicated to cycling, such as **Pedalibre** (www. pedalibre.org) and **Ciclos Otero** (www.oterociclos.es).

Driving

Driving in the city is rarely a quick way of getting anywhere thanks to traffic jams, and finding a parking space is another headache.

Car & motorbike hire

Most companies have a minimum age limit (usually 21) and require you to have had a licence for over a year. You will also need a credit card (as opposed to a debit card), or leave a big cash deposit (sometimes up to €500). Check if IVA (VAT), at 16 per cent, and unlimited mileage are included. All companies require you to take out a *seguro franquicia* – a fixed amount you have to pay in the event of an accident or any damage caused to the vehicle, and which is put on your credit card when you take the car (usually around half the hire cost – it is only charged if you return the vehicle damaged).

Parking

The city police (Policía Municipal) give out tickets readily (many locals never pay them). Be careful not to park in front of doorways with the sign '*vado permanente*', indicating an entry with 24-hour right of access. The **ORA** (Operación Regulación Aparcamiento) system now applies to the whole city centre.

ORA

Non-residents must pay to park in zones painted in blue or green from 9am to 8pm Mon-Fri and 9am to 3pm Sat (9am-3pm Mon-Sat in August). Pay-and-display machines are located on pavements. Maximum validity of tickets is two hours in blue zones and one hour in green, after which a new card must be used, and the car parked in a new spot. Cars parked in the ORA zone without a card can be towed away. In the blue areas, tickets cost up to €2.55 for two hours and in the green areas, €1.80 for one hour. All streets in this zone that have no additional restrictions posted are ORA parking areas.

Car parks

There are some 50 municipal car parks around Madrid, indicated by a white 'P'-on-blue sign. There are central car parks at Plaza de las Cortes, Plaza Santa Ana, C/Sevilla, Plaza Jacinto Benavente, Plaza Mayor, Plaza Descalzas, C/Tudescos and Plaza de España. .

Towing away

If your car seems to have been towed away, call 91 787 72 90 and quote your number plate to be told which pound it has gone to. You can also locate your car by entering your registration plate number at www.madridmovilidad.es/madrid_ movilidad/bases.aspx. Bring ID and all car papers when you pick it up.

ESSENTIALS

Resources A-Z

Accidents & Emergencies

Madrid has a general number, **112**, to call for the emergency services. However, you can be kept on hold for a long time; it's usually quicker to call direct.

Ambulancia/Ambulance
061/092/91 335 45 45.
Bomberos/Fire service Madrid capital 080. Whole comunidad 085.
**Policía Municipal/
City Police** 092/91 588 50 00.
**Policía Nacional/
National Police** 091.
Guardia Civil General 062/
900 101 062.

In a medical emergency, call **061** for an ambulance, or go to the casualty department (*urgencias*) of any of the city's major hospitals. All are open 24 hours daily; Clínico or Gregorio Marañón (for both, see below) are most central. If you have no EHIC or insurance, you can be seen at any casualty department (pay on the spot and get reimbursed back home by presenting the invoices and medical reports). In a non-emergency, pharmacists are very well informed.

Hospitals

Hospital Clínico San Carlos
C/Profesor Martín Lagos, Moncloa (91 330 30 00, www.hcsc.es). Metro Moncloa.
**Hospital General Gregorio
Marañón** *C/Doctor Esquerdo 44-46, Salamanca (91 586 80 00, www.hggm.es). Metro O'Donnell.*

Dentists

Dentistry is not covered by EU reciprocal agreements, so private rates apply.

Clínica Dental Cisne *C/Magallanes 18, Chamberí (91 446 32 21, 24hr emergencies mobile 661 857 170, www.clinicadentalcisne.com). Metro Quevedo.* **Open** Call for opening hours. **Credit** AmEx, DC, MC, V.
Map p102 C1.

Pharmacies

Pharmacies (*farmacias*) are signalled by large, green, usually flashing, crosses. Those within the official system of the College of Pharmacies are normally open 9.30am-2pm, 5-8pm Mon-Sat. At other times a duty rota operates. Every pharmacy has a list of the College's *farmacias de guardia* (duty pharmacies) for that day posted outside the door, with the nearest ones highlighted (many now show them using a computerised, push-button panel). Duty pharmacies are also listed in local newspapers, and information is available on 010 and 098 phonelines and www.cofm.es. At night, duty pharmacies may look closed; knock on the shutters to be served.

Customs

If tax has been paid in the country of origin then EU residents do not have to declare goods imported into Spain from other EU countries for personal use. However, customs officers can question whether large amounts of any item are for your own use, and random checks are made for drugs.

Quantities accepted as being for personal use include:
• up to 800 cigarettes, 400 small cigars, 200 cigars or 1kg of loose tobacco
• 10 litres of spirits, 20 litres of fortified wine or alcoholic drinks with under 22% of alcohol, 90 litres of wine (under 22%) or 110 litres of beer.

Limits for non-EU residents and goods brought from outside the EU:
• 200 cigarettes or 100 small cigars or 50 cigars or 250g (8.82oz) of tobacco
• 1 litre of spirits (or 2 litres of any other alcoholic drink with under 22% alcohol
• 50g (1.76oz) of perfume
• 500g coffee, 100g tea
There are no restrictions on electrical goods, within reasonable limits, and visitors are also allowed to carry up to €6,000 in cash.

Disabled travellers

Madrid is not a city that disabled people, especially wheelchair users, will find easy to get around. However, the situation is improving as new buildings are constructed with accessibility in mind and old ones are gradually adapted. Access to public transport is patchy.

There is an excellent guide, *Guía de Accesibilidad de Madrid*, which is published by the Ayuntamiento (city council) in collaboration with the disabled association **FAMMA**. This booklet is available from the FAMMA office at C/Galileo 69 (91 593 35 50, www.famma.org), and can also be accessed via the city council website (www.madrid.es).

Electricity

The standard current in Spain is now 220V, but a few old buildings in Madrid still have 125V circuits, so it's a good idea to check before using electrical equipment in older hotels. Plugs are all of the two-round-pin type. The 220V current works fine with British 240V products, with a plug adaptor. With US 110V appliances you will need a current transformer.

Embassies

For a full list look in the local phone book under *embajadas*. Lots of embassies have moved to the Torre Espacio on Paseo de la Castellana in the past few years.

British Embassy *Torre Espacio, Paseo de la Castellana 259D, Northern suburbs (91 714 63 00/visas 807 457 577/ passports 807 450 051, http://ukinspain.fco.gov.uk).* Metro *Begoña.* **Open** 9am-5.30pm Mon-Fri. *Visa/passport lines* 9am-6pm Mon-Fri. For information on British passports, call 807 429 026 (9.30am-5.30pm).

Health

EU nationals are entitled to free basic medical attention if they have the **European Health Insurance Card (EHIC)**, which replaced the old E111 form in January 2006. Travellers from the British Isles should apply for one online at www.dh.gov.uk (providing name, date of birth, and NHS or NI number) at least ten days before leaving home.

Internet

Madrid has lots of cybercafés, particularly around Puerta del Sol. In summer 2010, it was also announced that Plaza Santo Domingo, Plaza Mayor and also the city's buses are now free Wi-Fi zones.

Lost property
Airport & rail stations

If you lose something before check-in at Barajas Airport, report the loss to the **Aviación Civil** office (AENA) in the relevant terminal, or call the lost property office in T1 (91 393 61 19, 8am-9pm) or T4 (91 746 64 39, 7am-11pm). If you think you've mislaid anything on the RENFE rail network, look for the **Atención al Viajero** desk or **Jefe de Estación** office at the main station nearest to where your

ESSENTIALS

property went astray. The **Centros de Viajes** in the Chamartín and Atocha train stations are the official lost property centres for the municipal train network. Call 902 24 02 02 for both and ask for the Centro de Viaje or information on *objetos perdidos*.

EMT (city buses)

C/Cerro de la Plata 4, Salamanca (91 406 88 43, www.emtmadrid.es). Metro Pacífico. **Open** 8am-2pm Mon-Fri. *Phone lines* 8am-9pm Mon-Fri.
The lost-property office for items that have been lost on Madrid's city or airport buses.

Oficina de Objetos Perdidos

Paseo del Molino 7 & 9, South of centre (91 527 95 90). Metro Legazpi. **Open** *Oct-May* 9am-2pm Mon-Fri. *July-Sept* 9am-1.30pm Mon-Fri.
This office mainly receives articles found on the metro or in taxis, but if you're lucky, something lost in the street may turn up here.

Money

Spain is part of the euro zone. One euro is made up of 100 céntimos. One thing to remember is that the British/ US practice on decimal points and commas is reversed (so 1.000 euros means one thousand euros, while 1,00 euro is one euro). There are banknotes for €5, €10, €20, €50, €100, €200 and €500, in different colours and designs. Then there are three copper coins (five, two and one céntimo), three gold-coloured coins (50, 20 and 10 céntimos) and large coins for one euro (silver centre, gold rim) and two euros (gold centre, silver rim).

There are many small bureaux de change in Madrid (*cambio*), particularly on Gran Vía and Puerta del Sol.

Opening times

Eating, drinking and shopping all happen late in Madrid. The siesta has faded to a myth, but *madrileños* do operate to a distinctive schedule. Most shops open from 10am to 2pm, and 5-5.30pm to 8-8.30pm, Monday to Saturday, although many stay closed on Saturday afternoons. Food markets open earlier, around 8am. In July and especially in August most shops and services (such as the Post Office and administrations) close in the afternoon. August is also the time when most shops, bars and restaurants close for their annual holidays (from two weeks up to the whole month). Major stores and malls are open from 10am to 9pm without a break, Monday to Saturday. Big supermarkets (Al Campo, Carrefour) open from 10am to 10pm Mon-Sat and the first Sunday of each month.

Madrileños still eat, drink, go out and stay out later than their neighbours in virtually every other European country. Most restaurants are open 1.30-2pm to 4pm, and 9pm to midnight, and many close on Sunday nights and Mondays, and for at least part of August. Many businesses finish at 3pm in the summer. Many museums close on Mondays.

Police

Reporting a crime

If you are robbed or attacked, you should report the incident as soon as possible at the nearest Policía Nacional station (*comisaría*), where you will be asked to make an official statement (*denuncia*). It is very unlikely that anything you have lost will ever be recovered, but you will need the *denuncia* in order to make an insurance claim.

Comisaría del Centro *C/Leganitos
19, Sol & Gran Vía (information 060,
station 91 548 79 85, operator 902 10
21 12). Metro Santo Domingo or Plaza
de España.* **Map** *p51 B2.*
Chamberí *C/Rafael Calvo 33 (91 322
32 78). Metro Iglesia. Map p324 K6.*
Huertas/Retiro *C/Huertas 76-78 (91
322 10 17). Metro Antón Martín.*
Salamanca *C/Príncipe de Asturias 8
(91 444 81 20). Metro Manuel Becerra.*

Postal services

If you just need normal-rate stamps
(*sellos*), it's easier to buy them in an
estanco (see below).
**Oficina Príncipal de Correos en
Madrid** *Paseo del Prado 1, Retiro (91
523 06 94, www.correos.es). Metro
Banco de España.* **Open** *8.30am-
9.30pm Mon-Fri; 8.30am-2pm Sat.*
Map *p128 B1.*
The central post office relocated
from the Palacio de Cibeles, to
this building nearby in 2008.

Estancos

The main role of the tobacco shop
or *estanco* (look for a brown and
yellow sign with the word
'tabacos') is, of course, to supply
tobacco-related products. But they
also sell stamps, phonecards and
Metrobús and monthly abono
tickets. Some have photocopiers/
fax facilities.

Safety

As in most major cities, street crime
is a problem in Madrid and tourists
are often targeted. Pickpocketing
and bag-snatching are much more
likely than violent crime. Places to
be especially on your guard are the
Puerta del Sol, Gran Vía, Plaza
Mayor, Plaza Santa Ana and, above
all, the metro, the Rastro and Retiro
park. The Lavapiés district also
has a reputation for street crime.

Smoking

From 2 January 2011, a tough anti-
smoking law came into effect in
Spain. Madrid's famously smoky
bars and restaurants are now strict
no-smoking zones, and smokers are
no longer allowed to light up near
hospitals or in school playgrounds.
The metro is also no-smoking.
   There have been reports that,
since the ban, smokers have been
using the excuse of going out for a
cigarette to avoid paying for drinks
in bars, so it may become more
usual to pay for drinks upfront.

Tax

There are different rates of sales
tax (IVA): for hotels and restaurants,
the rate is eight per cent; in shops,
it's generally 18 per cent. IVA is
normally included in listed prices –
if not, the expression '*mas IVA*' (plus
tax) must be stated after the price.
In shops displaying a 'Tax-Free
Shopping' sticker, non-EU residents
can reclaim tax on large purchases.

Telephones

Dialling & codes

It is necessary to dial provincial
area codes with all phone numbers
in Spain, even when you are
calling from within the same area.
Hence, all normal phone numbers
in the Madrid area are preceded by
91, and you must dial this whether
you're calling within Madrid,
from elsewhere in Spain or from
abroad. Numbers beginning 900
are freephone lines; 901, 902 or
906 numbers are special-rate
services and can be very pricey,
especially if dialled from a mobile
phone. Spanish mobile phone
numbers have six digits and
begin with a 6.

ESSENTIALS

International & long-distance calls

To call abroad, dial 00 followed by the country code, then the area code (omitting the first zero in UK numbers) and number. To call Madrid from abroad, dial the international code (00 in the UK, 001 from the USA), then 34 for Spain.

It's often worth using a call centre (*locutorio*) for international calls. There are many around Lavapiés, Huertas and Malasaña, or visit www.ociolatino.com.

Time

Spain is an hour ahead of UK time, six hours ahead of US EST and nine hours ahead of PST. Daylight saving time runs concurrently with the UK.

Tipping

There are no rules or percentages for tipping and in general Spaniards tip very little. It is usual to leave five or ten per cent for a restaurant waiter, rarely more than €4, and people often leave a few *céntimos* of small change in a bar. It's also usual to tip hotel porters, toilet and cinema attendants. In taxis the norm is around five per cent, although you can give more for longer journeys, or if a driver has been especially helpful.

Tourist information

As well as the *centros de turismo* listed below, the city also runs a phone information line for locals, 010, that can be useful to visitors.

During July and August, pairs of young information guides, in bright yellow and blue uniforms, are sent to roam the central area ready to answer enquiries in a courageous variety of languages. They also staff information stands at Puerta del Sol, Plaza del Callao, Plaza Mayor, by the Palacio Real and by the Prado.

Centro de Turismo de Madrid *Plaza Mayor 27, Los Austrias (91 588 16 36). Metro Sol.* **Open** 9.30am-8.30pm daily. **Map** p66 C2.

Centro de Turismo Colón *Plaza de Colón, Salamanca (91 588 16 36). Metro Colón.* **Open** 9.30am-8.30pm daily. **Map** p138 B3.

Oficinas de Turismo de la Comunidad de Madrid *C/Duque de Medinaceli 2, Huertas (91 429 49 51, 902 10 00 07). Metro Banco de España.* **Open** 8am-8pm Mon-Sat; 9am-2pm Sun. **Map** p67 E2.

Visas & immigration

Spain is one of the EU countries that is party to the Schengen Agreement (which includes all of the EU except the UK, Ireland or the countries that joined in May 2004). These countries share immigration procedures and have reduced border controls between each other. To enter Spain nationals from countries that are party to the agreement need only show their national ID card, but British, Irish, those from the new EU countries and all non-EU citizens must have full passports.

Additional visas are not needed by US, Canadian, Australian, New Zealand or Israeli citizens for stays of up to three months. Citizens of South Africa and some other countries do need a visa to enter Spain. They can be obtained from Spanish consulates in other European countries as well as in your home country.

Water

Madrid's tap water is good and safe to drink. If you want tap rather than bottled water in a restaurant specify that you want *agua del grifo*.

Vocabulary

Many young people now use the familiar form for you (*tú*) most of the time; for foreigners, though, it's advisable to use the more polite *usted* with people you do not know, and certainly with anyone over the age of 50. In the phrases listed here all verbs are given in the *usted* form.

Basics

hello *hola*; good morning, good day *buenos días*; good afternoon, good evening *buenas tardes*; good night *buenas noches*; goodbye/see you later *adiós/hasta luego*; please *por favor*; thank you (very much) (*muchas*) *gracias*; you're welcome *de nada*; do you speak English? *¿habla inglés?* I don't speak Spanish *no hablo español*; I don't understand *no entiendo*; speak more slowly, please *hable más despacio, por favor*; wait a moment *espere un momento*; Sir/Mr *señor (sr)*; Madam/Mrs *señora (sra)*; Miss *señorita (srta)*; excuse me/sorry *perdón*; excuse me, please *oiga* where is… *¿dónde está…?* why? *¿porqué?* when? *¿cuándo?* who? *¿quién?* what? *¿qué?* where? *¿dónde?* how? *¿cómo?* is/are there any…? *¿hay…?* very *muy*; and *y*; or *o*; with *con*; without *sin*; open *abierto*; closed *cerrado*; what time does it open/close? *¿a qué hora abre/cierra?* pull *tirar*; push *empujar*; I would like… *quiero…*; how many would you like? *¿cuántos quiere?* I like *me gusta*; I don't like *no me gusta*; good *bueno/a*; bad *malo/a*; well/badly *bien/mal*; small *pequeño/a*; big *gran, grande*; expensive *caro/a*; cheap *barato/a*; more/less *más/menos*; how much is it? *¿cuánto es?* price *precio*

Getting around

a ticket *un billete*; return *de ida y vuelta*; excuse me, do you know the way to…? *¿oiga, señor/señora, sabe como llegar a…?* left *izquierda*; right *derecha*; here *aquí*; straight on *recto*; near *cerca*; far *lejos*

Time

morning *la mañana*; midday *mediodía*; afternoon/evening *la tarde*; night *la noche*; now *ahora*; later *más tarde*; yesterday *ayer*; today *hoy*; tomorrow *mañana*; tomorrow morning *mañana por la mañana*; early *temprano*; late *tarde*; delay *retraso*; at what time…? *¿a qué hora…?* in an hour *en una hora*; at 2 *a las dos*; at 1.30 *a la una y media*

Numbers

0 *cero*; 1 *un, uno, una*; 2 *dos*; 3 *tres*; 4 *cuatro*; 5 *cinco*; 6 *seis*; 7 *siete*; 8 *ocho*; 9 *nueve*; 10 *diez*; 11 *once*; 12 *doce*; 13 *trece*; 14 *catorce*; 15 *quince*; 16 *dieciséis*; 17 *diecisiete*; 18 *dieciocho*; 19 *diecinueve*; 20 *veinte*; 21 *veintiuno*; 30 *treinta*; 40 *cuarenta*; 50 *cincuenta*; 60 *sesenta*; 70 *setenta*; 80 *ochenta*; 90 *noventa*; 100 *cien*; 1,000 *mil*

Days & months

Monday *lunes*; Tuesday *martes*; Wednesday *miércoles*; Thursday *jueves*; Friday *viernes*; Saturday *sábado*; Sunday *domingo*; January *enero*; February *febrero*; March *marzo*; April *abril*; May *mayo*; June *junio*; July *julio*; August *agosto*; September *septiembre*; October *octubre*; November *noviembre*; December *diciembre*

Menu Glossary

Restaurant basics

Primer plato (entrante) first course; **segundo plato** second or main course; **postre** dessert; **plato combinado** quick, one-course meal, with several ingredients served on the same plate; **aceite y vinagre** oil and vinegar; **agua** water (**con gas/sin gas** fizzy/still); **pan** bread; **vino** wine (**tinto** red, **blanco** white, **rosado** rosé); **cerveza** beer; **la cuenta** the bill; **servicio incluído** service included; **propina** tip.

Tapas basics

Bocadillo sandwich in a roll; **cazuelita** small hot casserole; **montados** canapé-style mixed tapas, often a slice of bread with a topping; **pincho/pinchito** small titbit on a toothpick/bite-sized tapa; **pulga/pulguita** small filled roll; **ración** a portion (small plateful); **tabla** platter; **tosta** slice of toast with topping; **una de...** one portion of...; **por unidad** per item.

Cooking styles & techniques

Adobado marinated; **al ajillo** with olive oil and garlic; **al chilindrón** (usually chicken or lamb) cooked in a spicy sauce; **a la marinera** (fish or shellfish) cooked with garlic, onions and white wine; **a la parilla** charcoal-grilled; **al pil-pil** (Basque) flash-fried in sizzling oil and garlic; **a la plancha** grilled directly on a hot metal plate; **al vapor** steamed; **asado (al horno de leña)** roast (in a wood oven); **crudo** raw; **en salsa** in a sauce or gravy;

escabechado, **en escabeche** marinated in vinegar with bay leaves and garlic; **estofado** braised; **frito** fried; **guisado** stewed; **hervido** boiled; **(en) pepitoria** casserole dish, usually of chicken or game, with egg, wine and almonds; **relleno** stuffed.

Sopas y potajes (soups & stews)

Caldo (gallego) broth of pork and greens; **cocido** traditional stew of Madrid; **fabada** rich Asturian stew of beans, chorizo and morcilla; **gazpacho** cold soup with tomatoes, pepper and cucumber; **purrusalda** (Basque) soup of salt cod, leeks and potatoes; **sopa de ajo** garlic soup; **sopa castellana** garlic soup with poached egg and chickpeas; **sopa de fideos** noodle soup.

Huevos (eggs)

Huevos fritos fried eggs; **revuelto** scrambled eggs; **tortilla asturiana** omelette with tomato, tuna and onion; **tortilla francesa** plain omelette; **tortilla de patatas** Spanish potato omelette.

Pescado y mariscos (fish & shellfish)

Almejas clams; **atún, bonito** tuna; **bacalao** salt cod; **bogavante** lobster; **caballa** mackerel; **calamares** squid; **camarones** small shrimps; **cangrejo, buey de mar** crab; **dorada** bream; **gambas** prawns; **langostinos** langoustines; **lubina** sea bass; **mejillones** mussels; **mero** grouper; **merluza** hake; **ostras** oysters; **pescaditos**

whitebait; **pulpo** octopus; **rape** monkfish; **salmonete** red mullet; **sardinas** sardines; **trucha** trout; **vieiras** scallops.

Carne y embutidos (meat & charcuterie)

Bistec steak; **buey, vacuno** (cuts solomillo, entrecot) beef; **butifarra** Catalan sausage; **callos** tripe; **caza** game; **cerdo** pork; **chuletas, chuletones, chuletillas** chops; **cochinillo** roast suckling pig; **conejo** rabbit; **cordero** lamb; **costillas** ribs; **estofado de ternera** beef stew; **hígado** liver; **jamón ibérico** cured ham from Iberian pigs; **jamón serrano** cured ham; **liebre** hare; **lomo (de cerdo)** loin of pork; **morcilla** black blood sausage; **riñones** kidneys; **salchichas** frying sausages; **sesos** brains; **ternera** veal (more accurately young beef).

Aves (poultry)

Codornices quails; **faisán** pheasant; **pato** duck; **pavo** turkey; **perdiz** partridge; **gallina, pollo** chicken;

Arroz y legumbres (rice & pulses)

Alubias white beans; **arroz a banda** rice cooked in shellfish stock; **arroz negro** rice cooked in squid ink; **fideuà** similar to paella, but with noodles; **fríjoles** kidney beans; **garbanzos** chickpeas; **judiones** haricot beans; **lentejas** lentils.

Verduras (vegetables)

Acelgas Swiss chard; **alcachofas** artichokes; **berenjena** aubergine/ eggplant; **calabacines** courgettes/ zucchini; **cebolla** onion;

champiñones mushrooms; **col** cabbage; **ensalada mixta** basic salad of lettuce, tomato and onion; **ensalada verde** green salad, without tomato; **espárragos** asparagus; **espinacas** spinach; **grelos** turnip leaves; **guisantes** peas; **habas** broad beans; **judías verdes** green beans; **lechuga** lettuce; **menestra** braised mixed vegetables; **patatas fritas** chips; **pepino** cucumber; **pimientos** sweet peppers; **pimientos de piquillo** slightly hot red peppers; **pisto** mix of cooked veg, similar to ratatouille; **setas** oyster mushrooms; **tomate** tomato; **zanahoria** carrot.

Fruta (fruit)

Arándanos summer berries; **cerezas** cherries; **ciruelas** plums; **fresas** strawberries; **higos** figs; **macedonia** fruit salad; **manzana** apple; **melocotón** peach; **melón** melon; **moras** blackberries; **naranja** orange; **pera** pear; **piña** pineapple; **plátano** banana; **sandía** watermelon; **uvas** grapes.

Postres (desserts)

Arroz con leche rice pudding; **bizcocho** sponge cake; **brazo de gitano** swiss roll; **flan** crème caramel; **helado** ice-cream; **leche frita** custard fried in breadcrumbs; **membrillo** quince jelly; **tarta** cake; **tarta de Santiago** almond cake; **torrijas** sweet bread fritters.

Quesos (cheeses)

Burgos, villalón, requesón cottage-like cheeses, often eaten as dessert; **cabrales** blue Asturian goat's cheese; **idiazábal** Basque sheep's milk cheese; **mahón** cow's milk cheese from Menorca; **manchego** hard sheep's-milk cheese; **torta del casar** sheep's milk cheese from Extremadura.

ESSENTIALS

Index

ESSENTIALS